Circuits of Culture

VISIBLE EVIDENCE

Michael Renov, Faye Ginsburg, and Jane Gaines, Series Editors

(for additional series titles, see page 248)

VISIBLE EVIDENCE SERIES, VOLUME 20

Circuits of Culture

Media, Politics, and Indigenous Identity in the Andes

Jeff D. Himpele

University of Minnesota Press

Minneapolis

London

Portions of the Introduction were previously published in "Arrival Scenes: Complicity and Media Ethnography in the Bolivian Public Sphere," in *Media Worlds: Anthropology on New Terrain,* edited by Faye D. Ginsburg, Lila Abu-Lughod, and Brian Larkin (Berkeley: University of California Press, 2002), 301–16; copyright 2002 by the Regents of the University of California; reprinted with permission of the University of California Press. Portions of chapter 1 previously appeared in "Film Distribution as Media: Mapping Difference in the Bolivian Cinemascape," *Visual Anthropology Review* 12, no. 1 (1996): 47–66; copyright 1996 by the American Anthropological Association; reprinted with permission of the University of California Press. Portions of the Conclusion were previously published in "Packaging Indigenous Media: An Interview with Ivan Sanjinés and Jesús Tapia," *American Anthropologist* 106, no. 2 (2004): 354–63; copyright 2004 by the American Anthropological Association; reprinted with permission of the University of California Press.

Unless otherwise credited, photographs in this book were taken by the author.

Published by the University of Minnesota Press
111 Third Avenue South, Suite 290
Minneapolis, MN 55401-2520
http://www.upress.umn.edu

Library of Congress Cataloging-in-Publication Data

Himpele, Jeffrey D., 1965–
    Circuits of culture : media, politics, and indigenous identity in the Andes / Jeff D. Himpele.
        p.   cm. — (Visible evidence ; v. 20)
    Includes bibliographical references and index.
    ISBN: 978-0-8166-3918-2 (hc : alk. paper)
    ISBN-10: 0-8166-3918-3 (hc : alk. paper)
    ISBN: 978-0-8166-3919-9 (pb : alk. paper)
    ISBN-10: 0-8166-3919-1 (pb : alk. paper)
    1. Motion pictures—Social aspects—Andes Region.   2. Television broadcasting—Social aspects—Andes Region.   I. Title.
    PN1993.5.A47H56 2007
    302.23'4098—dc22

                                                                        2007024573

Printed in the United States of America on acid-free paper

The University of Minnesota is an equal-opportunity educator and employer.

12 11 10 09 08   10 9 8 7 6 5 4 3 2 1

For my son Brian
and in memory of my mother,
Mary Himpele

Contents

Acknowledgments

Though their understandings and practices of circulation inspire this book, many of the people who assisted me or with whom I spent time in La Paz only appear "behind the scenes" of the following pages. I am very grateful to Pedro Susz K., director of the Cinemateca Bolivia, for his support of this project, his engaging conversations, and for sharing with me his personal collection of photographs from early Bolivian films. At the Cinemateca, I thank Elizabeth Carrasco, archivist, for her generous help in locating materials, and Ana and Javier for their assistance with my research. I am grateful for interviews and visits with filmmakers who brought Bolivia's film history to life for me: Jorge Ruiz and his son, Guillermo Ruiz; Antonio Eguino, Paulo Agazzi, and Alfredo Ovando; Eduardo López and Francisco Cajías at Conacine; Jac Avila; and the late Beatriz Palacios of Grupo Ukamau. I appreciate the assistance of the staff at RTP Channel 4 in La Paz, where *The Open Tribunal of the People* was taped. I especially want to thank cameraman Bernabe for sharing his work and stories with me, and Marta for taking me behind the scenes at the Social Wing.

During indigenous video tours and festivals in the United States, I received assistance from the Film and Video Department at the National Museum of the American Indian in New York, specifically Elizabeth Weatherford, Amalia Cordova, Gabriela Zamorano, and Carol Kalafatic. Finally, I extend my gratitude to the members of Cefrec and Caib, Ivan Sanjinés, Marcelina Cárdenas, Jesús Tapia, Humberto Claros, Patricio Luna, and María Morales for sharing their work, views, and travels with me.

The research for this book has involved movement across various social spaces in La Paz, but I was able to call the Alvarado family in San Pedro my home and family. They have done more than I can say or repay to support me and this project, especially Nelly Alvarado, who assisted me in translating documents and meeting people and shared her companionship. With their *cariño,* the entire family regarded my work and me as their own.

The book is deeply rooted in my own background in television and video production, from which I sought to use its techniques to inform anthropology and, conversely, to direct my research and theory back into documentary filmmaking. Thus, that journey began before my academic training while I was working in video production with Larry Costa and Tom DeAngelis in New Jersey. In 1989, while I was an undergraduate at the University of Chicago, I received my first real opportunity to try out the connections I wanted to make between anthropology and filmmaking from Alan Kolata, who invited me to do video work at his archaeology project in Tiwanaku and introduced me to the Andes and Bolivia. The faculty and colleagues of the anthropology department of Princeton University offered years of intellectual rigor and support for my work in Bolivia while I was working and then teaching there. Members of that department provided valuable comments on much earlier versions of this work, and they have left their collective indelible imprint. Among them, James Boon contributed an inspiring vision of the plurality of culture and of the cinema. Seminars and conversations with John Kelly have been invaluable for thinking about the commodity form and capitalism. Kay Warren shared her own ongoing work with me, and our conversations on indigenous movements have guided my analysis of issues in indigenous politics. Kay's generosity and enthusiasm enabled me to bring together filmmaking and anthropology in my research. As department manager, Carol Zanca offered professional support and moreover important friendship that enabled my work on this project over many years. At Princeton I received funding for early parts of this research and writing from a Mellon Foundation Field Research Grant; a MacArthur Foundation Research Grant on Peace and Conflict; and travel grants from the Center of International Studies, the Council on Regional Studies, and the Program in Latin American Studies.

Funding for later research in Bolivia on *The Open Tribunal of the People* was awarded by California State University, Fullerton, in the form of General Faculty Research Awards and a Junior Faculty Research Award. In sorting through hours of tapes and transcripts and research data at Fullerton, I benefited from the assistance of Javier Calvera, Bethany Wengerd, and Lori Jennex.

This book was completed at the anthropology department of New York University, an ideal environment for working on culture, politics, and media. Discussions with all colleagues in the department, which began well before I arrived, have been invaluable. As chair, Fred Myers supported an environment that productively advanced my own thinking; our conversations and his own work inspired important avenues for thinking about the representation and circulation of culture. Thomas Abercrombie's work on the practices of Indianness in Bolivia and our discussions about the contemporary political scene there helped to unlock the multilayered and cultural dynamics of Andean Bolivia. The Graduate Program in Culture and Media, directed by Faye Ginsburg, could not be a better setting to realize the connections between documentary filmmaking and media ethnography that I have sought. Furthermore, Faye's work in connecting culture and media and her careful reading and enthusiasm for this book have been important fuel for it. I am also grateful to the participants in seminars at New York University, where I have had the opportunity to test ideas in this book and receive valuable feedback—my Capitalism seminars in 2002, 2004, and 2005, and Faye Ginsburg's seminars on media ethnography in 2002 and 2004. A Goddard Junior Faculty Fellowship in 2004 allowed crucial time to advance the writing of this project.

Earlier versions of several chapters in this book were read to the anthropology departments at Bard College, the University of Chicago, Cornell University, Cal State University, Fullerton, New York University, and Rutgers University as well as for the Indigenous Cosmologies working group at the Center for Religion and Media at New York University, where audiences were an important source of feedback. Conversations and projects with other colleagues have been especially meaningful in thinking about media, culture, and Bolivia. My appreciation goes to Robert Albro, Quetzil Castañeda, Colleen Cohen, Carol Greenhouse, Aisha Khan, Brian Larkin, Meg McLagan, Fran Mascia-Lees, John Traphagan, Terence Turner, and Deborah Yashar. I am grateful for close readings of this manuscript by Deborah Poole, whose thoughtful comments and precise criticism helped to fine-tune this analysis. At the University of Minnesota Press, Jason Weidemann has been a patient and careful editor and I am grateful for the work of Adam Brunner, Laura Westlund, Nancy Sauro, Lynn Walterick, and Carolyn Weaver.

Finally, while doing the research and writing for this book I have been surrounded by friends and family who always created an arena of great humor and support. My thanks go to Stephen Scott and Elaine, my best friends, and to my brothers and sisters, Laurie, Don, Cindy, and Bill. Time spent working with my father years ago was the first context in which I understood that circulation was a lived space; his and my mother's love has been a vital force propelling this work. This book is dedicated to the memory of my mother and to my son Brian, who continues to inspire me and always brings joy to my life.

Preface

▶

From Indigenism to Indigeneity

In a spectacular ritual ceremony atop the monumental pre-Inca archaeological site at Tiwanaku, on the high plains near Lake Titicaca, Bolivia's
president-elect Evo Morales was lauded by the region's highest indigenous
priests and tens of thousands of indigenous spectators as "Supreme Leader
of the Aymara." Morales, wearing an Aymara pendant, poncho, and native headwear and carrying the ornate baton traditionally held by indigenous authorities, participated in ritual offerings to the spirit world and
proclaimed his commitment to serve all of Bolivia's people on the eve of
his official inauguration in La Paz (see Figure 1 in the Introduction). This
unprecedented event celebrated Bolivia's first self-identified indigenous
president in revolutionary terms as a momentous decolonizing reversal in
a region that has remained dominantly indigenous since the Spanish invasion of the Andes almost five hundred years earlier. Known as a leader of
the mobilized *cocaleros,* or coca farmers, who was raised in the Aymara
high plains, Morales was elected with a clear majority of his country's
popular vote a month earlier in December 2005. The grassroots social
movements that Evo Morales assembled in his MAS party (Movement
Toward Socialism) merged indigenous movements for real political participation with the claims of nonindigenous poor with whom they shared
the experiences of twenty years of failed neoliberal reforms as a broad
national problem. These coalitions represented the mobilized front of a
heterogeneous new Bolivian "popular public" oriented around images
of Andean indigeneity (Albro and Himpele n.d; Canessa 2006; Postero
2005). For these new popular movements seeking to set the agenda of the
Bolivian national project, the preinaugural event at Tiwanaku represented

a compelling moment of triumph. If the multitudes surrounding Morales in Tiwanaku staged the historical prophecy of the return of Indian body politic, "un gran cuerpo de acción colectiva," then the striking figure of Morales atop ancient Tiwanaku's monumental Akapana pyramid, already thirteen thousand feet above sea level and surrounded by the high Andean peaks as a backdrop, signaled that performances of indigeneity had moved into peak positions in Bolivia's contemporary political scene.

Morales's appearance at Tiwanaku was not the first time a Bolivian president visited a cultural landmark upon his inauguration. Days after taking office in 1989, Jaime Paz Zamora began a tradition of landing by helicopter near the city of Cochabamba at the shrine of the Virgin of Urkupiña during its August festival. The Virgin's festival and its ritual climb up the Calvario hill, considered "backward," "superstitious," and "Indian" until the 1950s, is now the country's largest, attended by thousands of pilgrims from around the country and across social classes, including presidents, who thank her for success and ask for prosperity (Lagos 1993). The festival happens amid centuries of coexisting indigenous and Catholic cosmologies in the Andes, yet the presence of Aymara ritual specialists, or *yatiris,* dramatically indexes a powerful undercurrent of indigenous ritual knowledge and practices that disrupts a reading of the event as "syncretic" (Albro 1998b). The arrivals of Paz Zamora and his successors can be seen as an attempt to manage this situation with a national frame defined by cultural mixture. Thus, his visit was a benchmark in an attempt to nationalize the Virgin of Urkupiña, transforming her into a powerful "folkloric" icon as the "Patroness of National Integration." Presidential visits to Urkupiña became meaningful as part of a nationalist project that brought indigenous cultures into the orbit of a popular nation-state throughout the twentieth century. Conspicuous scenes of native Andean peoples have been attached to the national project in photography, film, dance, and music, originated and disseminated from the rising nonindigenous mestizo (mixed European and indigenous) middle class of politicians, artists, intellectuals, and writers (Abercrombie 2003; de la Cadena 2000; Poole 1997). Inspired by *indigenism,* a widespread current of thought that valorized the great indigenous societies and cultures of the past such as the Tiwanaku, these *indigenistas* sought reforms to create a new popular national society that incorporated the considerably large populations of Quechuas and Aymaras who were identified as *pueblos originarios* and considered to be the descendants of pre-Conquest Andean nations and empires. Their efforts to ally with and improve the lives of poor Indians in rural high plains and valleys by toppling the minority *criollo* European-descended oligarchy culminated in the Bolivian national revolution in 1952. After the revolutionary government abolished the feudal servitude that bound many *originarios* to rural haciendas and opened up suffrage and land to indigenous peasants and villages, Quechuas and Aymaras and smaller indigenous groups were no longer known as Indians but as "peasants" who were to be assimilated into urban modernity as defined by the new Westernized mestizo political elites. Since these policies prefigured the disappearance of Indians as a condition for national progress, and because suffrage was based on literacy, the contemporaneous Aymara and Quechua communities at the time of the revolution were excluded from full political participation, but their images were regarded as folkloric national icons of the country's heritage.

Overturning these indigenist relations of representation and their underlying linear temporality, the 2005 election of Evo Morales promised an agenda for full participatory citizenship for all Bolivians, as articulated by potent images of a return to indigenous self-determination. Morales's appearance at Tiwanaku, rather than Urkupiña, brought the national project to a cultural site widely regarded as representing indigenous autochthony, notwithstanding other attempts to nationalize it, for example, in archaeology (see Ponce Sanginés 1981 [1922]). The dramatic scenes at Tiwanaku on the eve of the presidential inauguration in early 2006 were staged to overturn, if not *indigenize,* the romantic imagery of indigenist nationalism with a spectacle of *indigeneity*—political actors who have placed the national project into the orbit of indigenous symbols, cosmology, historical consciousness, and political values.

The provocative images of indigeneity that pervade the current Bolivian political scene have appeared at a particular historical moment and are enmeshed in a worldwide network of relationships, a "contemporary global conjuncture," in which cultural difference has emerged as a mobilizing concept (Turner n.d.). After 1989, significant ethnic movements surged in parts of Africa, Asia, and Eastern Europe where representational and liberal democracies in varied forms were constituted. Following more than a decade of authoritarian rule across much of South America, the transitions to democracy in the early 1980s led to neoliberal policies that turned from populist strategies of national massification (Martín-Barbero 1993) to cultural pluralism, or "neoliberal multiculturalism" (Hale 2005), as a technique for activating and managing civil society through cultural difference. While labor movements were losing strategic potency and the circulation of transnational media escalated, cultural plurality and identities became the prominent loci of the new social movements across Latin America (Alvarez, Dagnino, and Escobar 1998; Martín-Barbero 1993; Warren and Jackson 2002). In this mediated context of self-conscious attention and valorization of cultural difference, indigeneity emerged as an assemblage of conscious discourses and strategies embedded in a global environment of nonindigenous activists, human rights discourses, NGOs, and organizations worldwide such as the UN's Permanent Forum on Indigenous Issues (formed during the International Decade of the World's Indigenous People, 1995–2004) and transcontinental indigenous alliances. Alongside Bolivia, in Ecuador, Colombia, and Guatemala, indigenous mobilizations pushed their agendas for human rights, land reforms, education, and economic policies onto their national political stages; indigenous actors have entered into electoral politics where they are making claims specific to their status as native citizens (Yashar 2005) as well as on behalf of their nations. As part of the oppositional challenges led by movements with an indigenous face, like the Zapatistas in Mexico, social movements and elected regimes in Latin America also have formed antiglobalization front lines, confronting neoliberal restructuring policies, contracts with transnational corporations, the social policies of the World Bank, and the Washington consensus. In a series of popular uprisings that have driven out two presidents and forced out transnational corporations in the past several years, Bolivia has seen the most dramatic challenges to globalization and the political establishment at once, advanced by indigenous peoples who are representing Bolivia's cultural plurality with their own indigeneity. Whatever their accompanying networks and specific goals, performances of indigeneity enact cultural self-representation as a demonstration of self-determination, the capacity for assembling a variety of ambient cultural and political resources (Canessa 2002; Ginsburg 1997; Oakdale 2004; Turner 2002b; Warren 1998).

It is worth considering briefly the anthropological connection between culture and representation as essential ingredients of movements for self-determination. Culture and representation, in all their complex dynamics and particular historical forces and forms, are distinct qualities of human societies and indispensable dimensions of our social life and knowledge. In evolutionary terms, culture as much as biology is a crucial ingredient with which modern human groups make themselves and their particular modes of material life, consciously and unconsciously. Further, symbolic culture is the medium in which groups constitute and represent themselves and their differences to themselves and to others. Activists who have taken up anthropology's defining category of culture in these terms assert the vital stakes in representing their identities and their struggles to defend and empower specific modes of collective cultural life. As the anthropologist Terence Turner has argued, we have expanded and modified our keystone category of culture to encompass and comprehend the contemporary forms as well as the world-historical conditions in which groups make culture the source of their claims and in which they self-consciously produce and represent "culture" (1993, 423–24). Representational media, such as video or film, therefore need to be seen as cultural forms, or as what Faye Ginsburg calls "culture/media" (1994), because they are used to serve the specific *cultural* goals and practices of the groups who use them, including the vital stakes that are attached to "culture" itself. Projects for self-determination that take up representational media use them as the means for political ends; moreover, these media are their own ends as well, since they demonstrate the human capacity for culture, agency, and self-representation at once.

In the current political landscape in Bolivia, where social movements have been foregrounding cultural indigeneity as the source for collective rights as well as popular national sovereignty, centers for indigenous video making have recently appeared to enact these same connections between culture, media, politics, and well-being, producing remarkable documentaries and fictions that are intended to represent their identities and uphold indigenous cosmologies as vital to their communities. In so doing, indigenous filmmakers are overturning the earlier indigenist and recent multiculturalist political structures for representing Indianness in which their own capacity for self-representation had not been fully realized. Their celebrated fictional works re-create community legends while incorporating styles from popular media for community audiences and propelling them to festivals and venues worldwide. In these projects for cultural self-determination, they are *indigenizing* the circuits of popular culture and politics by intervening and assembling their own works from the circulatory systems of media.

Circuits of Culture charts the emergence of indigenous video as a crucial moment of transformation toward a new episode of indigenous representation in the Bolivian national imagination, which can be seen in terms of its circulatory systems and practices. The range of cultural media in Bolivia is of course very broad and diverse; urban and rural cultural and social life are dominated by music, parades, festivals, and dance fraternities. Yet this book focuses on key sites in the representational media of film, television, and video as indexes of the wider historical processes that have shaped the present. Furthermore, like the other "live" or corporeal forms of cultural media just mentioned, these representational media are also decidedly mobile. That is, their intrinsically moving images both index and constitute the historical world in motion. They also mobilize a worldwide array of disparate resources that are assembled, packaged, and recirculated as a "film," a "video," or "TV episode." Emphasizing this mobility, this book asks how these representational media have been used as tools for steering the historical worlds they index. What are the specific social practices, trajectories, and infrastructures that propel these media through social worlds? If practices of assembly and circulation are related to self-determination, how do film distributors, filmmakers, and their publics negotiate the uneven worldwide circuits of media? *Circuits of Culture* views these "cinematic media" and their circulatory systems as precipitates of the historical processes and motion that are intrinsic to cultural life, political forms, and social *movements*.

When the transition to the Morales administration began after the election in December 2005, the interim government "brought the state to a halt," as the newspaper *La Razón* reported (December 22, 2005). As Bolivians waited to see what the MAS regime would be able to accomplish, Vice-President Alvaro García Linera projected Bolivia's future as an "Andean-Amazonian capitalist" state, controlling a greater share of the hydrocarbon wealth extracted by transnational companies in order to build national industries that would transfer profits to communities that are "properly" Andean and Amazonian. This formation would integrate multiple regimes of circulation, with their respective cultural forms of exchange, to redistribute wealth, resources, and authority along existing cultural lines. More broadly, the proposal is to indigenize the capitalist state by imagining and representing the nation-state as, and enmeshed within, world-wide circulatory matrices.

▶

Cultures of Circulation

In this book, I investigate how the circulatory systems of media have mediated the formulations of indigenism and indigeneity that have driven the Bolivian nation-state. Beginning with La Paz as a prominent arena of representational media and indigenization in Bolivia, I trace how key social transformations have been enmeshed in the circuits of Bolivian media worlds and social imagination. Here, I draw from archival materials, films, and interviews with filmmakers to chart how romantic and folkloric images of indigenous peoples were incorporated into populist national projects by non-Indian mestizos and inserted into the circuits of popular culture and politics that dominated in Bolivia for most of twentieth century. When I was doing ethnographic research in the 1990s, a popular television program, *The Open Tribunal of the People*, was featuring urban indigenous peoples as active historical protagonists rather than as nostalgic signs of national heritage. Connected to their own televisual appearances and the nonindigenous TV host Carlos Palenque, urban indigenous middle classes were also emerging as a political presence in their own right, using the media to disseminate their agendas for populist national politics. Just after the beginning of the twenty-first century, indigenous video makers began touring the United States with their works, which were praised by various film festival audiences as well as Bolivian communities near Washington, D.C. By traveling and disseminating indigenous cultural identities and their ways of knowing in video form, video makers performed powerful scenes of *indigeneity*—defining themselves as contemporary indigenous subjects who are active cultural producers engaged with the institutions and technologies of modernity.

This book draws from my ethnographic and historical research in La Paz that began in 1992; this long-term ethnographic project has allowed me to observe how the remarkable process of indigenization has emerged and is shaped by the daily lives of the city's residents. In fact, when I began my research in La Paz, people were at first unsure about my project; filmmakers and neighbors alike were curious about why an anthropologist would be studying them in the city and not in the countryside, "out there with the Indians," the Aymaras and the Quechuas in the rural high plains and valleys. At the same time, city-born Bolivians expressed to me their understanding that people in the United States imagined that all Bolivians were either narcotraffickers or "Indians, running around the jungle wearing nothing but leaves and feathers." My research among the "popular classes" of the city, however, revealed that a boundary between Indians and non-Indians was not easily drawn; in fact, indigenous identity was something achieved in practice as it moved in and out of view. In the city, Indianness appeared in a variety of social events from household gatherings to public festivals as it was enacted and claimed, but sometimes rejected, as an aspect of peoples' identities (Himpele 1996a). The city's central boulevard, the Paseo de Prado, is a public arena for exhibiting Bolivians' relation to Indianness. In "folklore" parades, Westernized elites and middle classes rehearse and perform in dance fraternities using costumes in which they can inhabit Indianness and convert it into their own national memories (Abercrombie 1991). In the same parades, well-off urban Aymaras in the Morenada dance groups ostentatiously flaunt signs of their rural past and self-consciously exaggerate Indianness as a sign of their prosperity, as Aymaras, in the modern city. As the most prestigious dancers in parades I saw, the urban Aymaras were both producing and enacting their influence as a new indigenous popular public that was markedly urban. As my research began, these pageants were indigenizing popular culture and subverting the boundaries between culture, sociality, and politics; similarly, popular politics was taking on a new slant toward indigenous cosmology, religion, and ethnic autonomy (Delgado-P 1994; Pacheco Balanza 1992, 60). La Paz itself became a fascinating place to study "indigenous culture."

As competing elements of identity production, urban popular culture in La Paz proliferated alongside the intensified circulation of transnational media of film, video, and television moving through Bolivia and across Latin America (Himpele 1996b). Yet at precisely the time when disciplines in the social sciences were seeking to theorize the world-historical conditions of transnationalism and globalization in the early 1990s, I was struck by how little ethnographic attention was given in the scholarly literature to the specific practices of cultural circulation and systems of media distribution. Building on the work of scholars who were studying the shifting meanings and values of a range of cultural forms—films, television, commodities, and art—as they traveled across distinct transnational contexts, I sought to theorize the mobility of cultural forms and practices in terms of their particular systems of circulation in space and over time.

The emphasis on circulation that I advance in this book has been fundamentally shaped by my conversations and interviews with filmmakers, audiences, and distributors. Its significance is further grounded in the practices of circulation and imagination that characterize social life in La Paz and the neighborhood of San Pedro where I resided. During the period in the 1990s in which I carried out fieldwork, La Paz witnessed a social crisis precipitated by the neoliberal reforms that had begun in 1985, which at first were solutions to a period of unimaginable hyperinflation. I saw unemployed itinerant vendors walking the busy street markets that were expanding along the streets and sidewalks of the surrounding neighborhoods. For Aymara entrepreneurs in these markets, business and life revolved around the movement of commodities in the streets and markets; a common job in these sectors was driving a taxi or bus, and many women and families own small trucking businesses. Among the city's popular classes that are dedicated to the street markets, exchange networks take priority over industrial production (Buechler 1978; Buechler and Buechler 1996; Harris 1989; Medina 1992; Seligman 2004) and class, prestige, and well-being are marked and achieved through redistribution (Albó and Preiswerk 1986). Massive protest marches were typically aimed at the transportation infrastructure and clogged the city's circulatory system, stopping traffic and bringing the city to a halt. As a response to new political tensions and economic conditions, there was also an ongoing expansion of patron-client exchange networks that use the moral language of fictive kinship *(compadrazgo)* to mobilize labor between the countryside and the city (Crandon-Malamud 1993). Similarly, there was also a dramatic increase in participation in neighborhood and citywide festivals and parades. In the Gran Poder parade, organized around the neighborhood patron saint of the city's well-to-do Aymara commercial neighborhood, tens of thousands of dancers descend the city's canyon streets and parade down the central Prado, indigenizing the center of the city itself. These pageants and social events are fueled by the exchanges of *compadrazgo* during ostentatious displays of mobile wealth and lively competition between Aymara and mestizo middle classes (Himpele 2003). In domestic events, such as baptisms and weddings, various forms of sponsorship and exchange obligations, which are often generalized as an Andean form of exchange known as *ayni,* sustain the circulation of wealth and resources that enable significant life processes to be collective events. As an ethnography, this book is embedded in these social networks and circulatory matrices that cut across the canyon walls of the city.

In perhaps the most significant and vital influence on this book's perspective, people among whom I lived and spent time in La Paz sought their own well-being through the display and the propitiatory regulation of vital circulatory flows. The cultural importance of circulation became apparent in performing a practice called the *ch'alla,* which involves spilling drops of beer or alcohol onto the floor "for the Pachamama." The Pachamama is conventionally translated as Earth Mother, because she is symbolized by the ground itself, although her presence is not limited to the terrain; more broadly, she is a female cosmological force that mediates social and natural reproduction and *cariño* (caring) and may also be referred to as "the spirit." Offerings to the Pachamama are practiced while casually drinking; more ceremoniously, beer or alcohol is sprinkled onto new acquisitions, for example, or outside a doorway before traveling. In the annual *martes de ch'alla* celebration (Tuesday of the *ch'alla*) held at homes and places of business, families gather to make blessings of pure alcohol or beer, spilled or even shaken and sprayed onto the ground and sprinkled on or toward key sites of group significance, which are decorated with firecrackers, confetti, and streamers to call attention to them. At multiple levels of magnitude, the *ch'alla* is an attempt to participate in a cosmological process of circulation in which what is redistributed and nourished in the human world and what is faithfully offered to the parallel and capricious spirit world will be reflected and reciprocated back to the human world. Typically, wishes are invoked in whispers to the spirits and recipients during the *ch'alla* as a manner of articulating and spatializing the sites of cosmological circulation. In this form of mediation, the offer of libations to the spirits traverses, organizes, and engages the humble human world with greater and unpredictable cosmological forces. As with the circulation of money and blood, displaying, propitiating, and continuously mediating the flows through key sites is vital for unity, well-being, and even life itself.

Overview

Completed as Evo Morales's administration got underway, this book analyzes the cinematic mediation of Indianness as a decisive representational strategy that has taken on shifting political values, meanings, and forms in different historical moments in Bolivian media. Bolivia is an apt site for examining this issue since a vast majority in La Paz claims Indianness as an element of its identity at some time and in some way. I combine a textual approach seeking social meanings of media with an analysis of the material environments of social production and imagination where media circulate. In part I, I analyze La Paz as a media capital and as a unique arena for the indigenization of urban social worlds. I explore how film distributors coordinate the circulation of films through La Paz in narrative pathways that mark and rank cultural difference at theaters along the city's steep topography. In the slippage and friction between publics, media, and the matrices of circulation in which they are all enmeshed, I will show, moviegoing publics come into being and are defined according to where they appear in the theater circuit. Yet in the tension between the forces of stabilization and those of circulation, there is no guarantee that these publics will stay still. I also show how worldwide film distribution through La Paz reveals significant disjunctures between and within national communities imagined to be connected and moving simultaneously through historical time. In part II, I consider both the materiality and the structural conditions of cinema that filmmakers have had to negotiate as a problem of circulation, emphasizing the ways their films used the inherent mobility of cinema to convey the historical worlds they have sought to represent or bring about. The chapters in part III discuss the ways in which the popular television program *The Open Tribunal of the People* exploited the scale of dissemination of mass media to produce testimonial scenes of the social problems among the city's indigenous and poor classes that helped to build the metropolitan region's key populist political movement oriented with an Andean frame of identification.[1] The conclusion examines the contemporary indigenous video movement that has emerged in conjunction with the transformations in popular and national politics in which indigeneity has attained crucial political value. By traveling the circulatory matrices of film and televisual motion picture media in the capital city of La Paz, *Circuits of Culture* explores the indigenization of media and popular publics in urban Andean Bolivia.

Introduction:
Arenas of Circulation
and Ethnographic Circuits

▶

The Devil Meets *The Lion King*

With my 35mm camera in hand, I descended the steep city streets to the
center of La Paz and positioned myself among the crowd lining both
sides of the avenue across from the Cinema Monje Campero. On this last
Saturday of July in 1994, thousands of university students from all over
Bolivia, organized in dance fraternities according to their academic majors, were parading through the city performing indigenous and mixed
European-indigenous (mestizo) dances in the University Folklore Parade.
In this annual event, the students seek to rescue and celebrate their own
indigenous heritage by parading iconic dress and choreographed dances.
While several groups were dressed in less expensive handmade rural indigenous costumes rarely seen in the city, most of the participants were
dressed in rented costumes of a standard set of Bolivian folkloric characters: devils, the *cholas morenas,* Inca princesses, African slaves, and the
popular leaping lasso-wielding slave drivers *(caporales)*. By three o'clock,
young spectators from the crowd entered the street and danced behind
the caporales. The night before, enterprising Aymara women and men
had staked out space along the parade route in order to set up benches
and sell seats the next day. During the event, their children were walking
around selling sandwiches, beer, and snacks to the crowd of spectators on
the parade route along the Paseo del Prado. This four-lane boulevard that
defines the center of the city is divided by a garden promenade with wide
sidewalks, fountains, and sculpted shrubbery. Standing along the Prado
in La Paz, the country's most prominent public space that runs along the
bottom of the urbanized bowl-shaped canyon as if it were center stage in

a performance arena, I held up my camera as a series of dancing devils began to enter the frame.

For years the *Diablada,* the devil's dance, has received gasps and admiration from crowds from across the city's social classes as elaborately costumed Devils and their female counterparts, the blonde and blue-eyed China Supay, taunt the audience and skip down the street, turning back and then forward again, three abreast, holding each other's outstretched hands and accompanied by familiar theme music. Rather than a performance of the malevolence associated with Christianity, the devil dance characterizes ambiguity. This mythic devil, which is neither good nor bad, fights against the Christian saints but must also be propitiated by them because he has control over the autochthonous powers in the dark world underground.[1] As daylight shone on the Devils, dancers and spectators conjured up powerful images of Indianness in dances dramatizing the conversion of anticolonial indigenous forces into a pageant of postcolonial national citizenship (Abercrombie 1991). National identity, in the cultural terms of *mestizaje,* is made from this unified mixture of European-inspired modernity and Indianness.

Only two months earlier during the fervor of Bolivia's participation in the World Cup in Chicago, many people in La Paz were boasting that the Diablada had been performed in Chicago to represent Bolivia. By the time of this parade, however, they were expressing outrage on the airwaves, newspapers, and in the streets that the Diablada was being performed in neighboring Chile, for the Chileans also were claiming the dance as part of their national heritage. One Bolivian radio commentator asserted the worst part: "We are left powerless. These national dances are our poems, our paintings. The state has no cultural policies to support them, and so our culture is mishandled." Whatever the original meanings of the dancing devils, they were claimed as prized vehicles of national heritage, traveling urban and international cultural circuits as popularized images of Bolivianized Indianness.

From my position on the Prado, the Devils in front of me were just feet away and in the foreground of another spectacle taking place across the street at Bolivia's busiest movie theater, the Cinema Monje Campero. Above the entrance the billboard announced "Today! Great Debut," boasting the debut of Disney's blockbuster *The Lion King*. Though the film had been showing there for six weeks, the theater would extend the spectacle of its debut for two months. When it was first publicized in La Paz, *The Lion King* made the headlines because it was going to arrive merely one week after its U.S. premiere, bringing the city into near synchrony with the worldwide movie debut and moving audiences ahead in the traffic of global filmed commodities. When the film opened, CNN-International reported that it had already earned $200 million since first opening just one week earlier in the United States and that it had become the most successful Disney film, including its related merchandise sales, which had shot up 20 percent. Along the crowds watching the parade, itinerant vendors were selling thin cardboard "Lion King" sunshades that had been sent to the local distributor with other promotional materials from Buena Vista, Disney's film distributor. As with the tensions over the original home of the Diablada, there was also debate in the United States over the national origin of Disney's story, if from the United States or Japan. The day after the parade, the ticket seller at the Monje Campero told me that business had gone down 70 percent the day before, indicating that although audiences in La Paz may have been enthusiastically embracing *The Lion King,* the movie was eclipsed by the attention diverted to Devils dancing down the Prado by the spectators who, in my lens, had their backs turned to the movie theater while facing the national folklore parading down this public stage.

From my vantage point, I contemplated the friction in this scene in the heart of Bolivia's most prominent public space in which *The Lion King*'s bold billboard loomed above the Devils in the Prado. It could serve as an instance of the discourse of cultural imperialism, a dualist view in which Hollywood and Disney are external agents of a global corporate mass media invasion (Boyd-Barrett 1977, 1982; Tomlinson 1991). In this account, the dense traffic of corporate media from capital-rich countries flows in one direction toward poorer countries that are put into "cultural dependency" for their own media programming, thereby threatening national traditions and culture. In this view of the parade, the spectators with their backs turned appeared to be resisting the foreign conquest by defending their collective national identities represented by the spectacular Devils.

Yet isn't resistance more complicated than opposition? Can it also be viewed as a sign of seduction? After all, just as I was doing, the spectators on my side of the street were facing both *The Lion King* and the Devils, as seen in the lower foreground of my frame, suggesting an attraction to both streams of media. Additionally, many spectators along the parade route were using those Lion King sun visors from Disney. What is more, the Diablada had traveled to Chicago and Chile as a controversial icon of national culture and a manifestation of the mixture of European and indigenous cultures. If this picture demonstrates that this city's popular culture necessarily extends beyond the national territory, then the same also holds for *The Lion King.* As the debate surrounding the origins of the *Lion King* story indicates, both Disney and the Hollywood film industry also contain their own international moments, what Toby Miller et al. (2005) call "the new international division of cultural labor." In this scene La Paz is a "media capital," where the multidirectional traffic of cultural media meet (Curtin 2003). Challenging the view of the meeting of *The Lion King* and the Devil as the binary confrontation of discrete foreign and unitary domestic cultures, or global and local, the spectators' loyalties to these multiple media streams re-render the sharp and static image of an invasion into a perceptible blur. Ethnographically clarifying such a scene requires a mode of seeing that allows one to "see bifocally" (Peters 1997) the simultaneity of the near and the distant, yet each in its own turn.

Each time I clicked the camera shutter, I suspended the moment in the intersection of transnational mass media and folkloric national culture that were streaming past each other as strips of serial images traveling through the city: *The Lion King* was arriving vertically, first coming in by plane from Hollywood and then streaming past the lamp in the film projector and displayed on the screen in the cinema; the Devils, said to be emerging from a cultural underground, were dancing horizontally across my field of view past the cinema. By adjusting the lens aperture, the focus, and shutter speed I could visually explore the dynamics of the motion and distance between the Devils and *The Lion King* occupying the foreground and background respectively. A shallow depth of field prevented them both from coming into clear focus at once, blurring the outlines between them. To compensate, I could change the focus to sharpen either the foreground or the background, making each the figure and ground of the other by simulating the movement of my own position forward and backward. As I alternated between foreground and background this way, I visibly redirected clarity from one to the other. As the cinema in the background came into focus, its hazy alter, the dancing Devils in the foreground, seemed to call for attention; when the Devils came into focus, the cinema in the background sought a clearer presence. Furthermore, this shifting spatial difference between me and each of these moving image strips produced a perceptible motion blur. As I moved my camera along with the Devils as they danced past me, *The Lion King* blurred in the background (see Figure 1); when I held focus on the cinema, the movement of the Devils effected a blur. By matching the motion of one character, the camera revealed the motion of the other. In effect, then, the superimposition of *The Lion King* and the Devils onto a single two-dimensional plane in the camera and then in print revealed the motion of two simultaneous cultural processes passing in front of the lens; moreover, the superimposition signaled that the elements of popular culture were being mediated through divergent circuits in social space.

Figure 1. Costumed Devils dance La Diablada down Paseo del Prado and past
Cinema Monje Campero, where *The Lion King* continues its debut.

Rather than a clear-cut invasion, the blurred motion and superimposed pathways of *The Lion King* and the Devils registered in the photos supply visible evidence of what Jesus Martín-Barbero calls the *mediations* that direct transnational media along the multiple social contexts and cultural spaces of the city. More specifically, he writes, "That is to say, to the institutions, the organizations and the subjects, to the diverse social temporalities and the multiplicity of cultural matrices from which media technologies constitute themselves. . . . It concerns the specificity of cultural processes as the articulators of communicative practices with social movements" (1988, 454; see also 1993, 187). Emphasizing the sites of media consumption where new meanings are produced and localized (1993, 196; 1988, 449), Martín-Barbero argues that transnational mediation has activated culture and communications as key sites of modern sociality, opening up urban popular classes to new hybridized sets of loyalties and affiliations that extend beyond the unifying frame of the nation. Until the late 1960s, he writes, populist national projects in Latin America had sought to form a homogeneous national citizenry through cultural mixture and synthesis (e.g., *mestizaje*) by tying national development to modern communications. Urban Latin America experienced its national cinemas and television as instruments for the "massification" of the preexisting expressions of popular culture, transforming "the mass into the people and the people into the nation" (1993, 164). Succeeding these state-led schemes for massification and modernization in countries like Brazil, Mexico, Venezuela, and Argentina, the contemporary "mediations" of transnational media have come to saturate everyday life and are defining features of Latin American cities, where communications media originating beyond the national frame are principal elements with which popular classes fabricate plural cultural identities and political affiliations.

Are we able to see a moment in a similar history of mediation between Bolivian popular culture and transnational cinema in the photos of *The Lion King* and the Devils? The history of popular culture and media in Bolivia actually offers some striking contrasts with Martín-Barbero's periodization, which largely draws from industrialized cinema in Mexico and is often taken to stand for Latin America. Consider that the meeting of *The Lion King* and the Devils in my photos represents the mediation of two forms of mass media in Bolivia. Of course these parades and the commercial cinema are both translocal, as I have already described, yet to be sure they are not equally prominent beyond Bolivia. In La Paz, however, a year-round series of similar urban folklore parades represents an extensive network of commodity production, self-representation, social production, and social status among the city's popular classes. Just as Martín-Barbero described earlier uses of industrial mass media in Mexico, where regional cultural differences would be assimilated and circulated (i.e., popularized) as "folklore" expressive of the nation's unique culture(s) (1993, 155), the same holds for these contemporary folkloric events in La Paz that also express regional and cultural differences. Yet it is these numerous folkloric spectacles of popular culture that represent the salient technology of national identity around which people also organize their social lives, along with their loyalties, affiliations, and differences. As one Aymara woman, Eugenia, told me after dancing in the Gran Poder parade one year, "We Bolivians are very *folklorista*." The production of costumes and rehearsals for these events is pervasive and involves activities virtually year-round, though not for everyone. As another Aymara woman who is Pentecostal commented to me, "It is the devil that makes those people dance and drink." Looking up and down the parade route past the Cinema Monje Campero at the tens of thousands of people in different dance groups, each dancing in synchrony, it is not difficult to view these parades as mass media.

These folkloric spectacles in Bolivia challenge the uniformity with which the industrialized mass media can be argued to be the most salient space of collective imagination and modernization across Latin America (e.g., García Canclini 2001; Martín-Barbero 2000; Sinclair 1996). Put differently, the distinctive predominance of folkloric media and spectacles in Bolivia expands the range of designations for mass media in Latin America, as well as for cultural politics, as David Guss has also shown in his study of Venezuela as "the festive state" (2000). While popular film and television were used as a mass media for creating modern national citizens in Mexico, Argentina, and Chile (Martín-Barbero 1993, 166), countries whose films have circulated in Bolivia, filmmaking in Bolivia has been episodic at best, and color commercial television channels went on the air more recently, around 1985 (Rivadeneira 1988). Martín-Barbero's account of transnational mediation is only one instance of the intersecting circuits of "culture" that can mediate the imagination of collectivities in Latin American popular culture and politics (Alvarez et al. 1998; García Canclini 1995; Masiello 2001; Radcliffe and Westwood 1996; Rowe and Schelling 1991; Williams 2002; Yúdice, Franco, and Flores 1992).

Remarkably, at the same time that a marked intensification of the flow of global films, television, and consumer commodities followed market liberalization policies after 1985, folklore parades and festivals also proliferated and increased in size as key arenas of national imagination as well as cultural subversion (Abercrombie 1991, 2003; Albó 1991a; Albro 1997; Crandon-Malamud 1993; Goldstein 2004; Himpele 2003; Rogers 1998). Indigenous dress and folkloric events represent not so much the staging of the authentic indigenous origins of the nation, the "motionless point of departure from which modernity is measured" (Martín-Barbero 1988, 459) as in earlier indigenism, but they have become mobile vehicles in which Bolivians across the social classes of La Paz are enacting national modernity and performing differences. If the Diablada is a mestizo enactment of the conversion of the colonized Indian into the modern national, then the Morenada, which is danced by well-to-do Aymaras and has become the most prestigious dance in parades, carries out the indigenization of the national (see Himpele 2003). These festival parades and the Prado itself have become prominent venues for this "indigenization" of the city and the national heritage through cultural performances. By the early 1990s, Bolivian scholars were theorizing the city and the reorientation in popular culture and politics toward such indigeneity (Albó 1991a; Albó 1991b; Pacheco Balanza 1992; Rivero and Encinas 1991). Most recent performances of indigeneity have shaped the turbulent social movements that brought about the 2005 popular election of Evo Morales, the country's first self-identified indigenous Aymara, as an expression of the majority of the almost nine million people in Bolivia who recognize their indigenous backgrounds. While indigenous issues have become an axis of national politics in Latin America, few indigenous movements represent such a widespread popular movement or claim the national project as does the Bolivian. Here, as the popular national project is taken up in indigenous politics, indigeneity entails mobilizing images that are decisively reshaping politics and the modern national profile, and this movement can now be seen in the development of centers for indigenous video making.

By now, perhaps it is evident that the scene on the Prado captured in my photographs lacked certain serial images that were displaced from view—films made in Bolivia. In fact, the absence of Bolivian films on the stage of the Prado is telling of alternative media histories that have been left "off the map" (Ginsburg et al. 2002a, 14) in film histories that privilege the pathways of circulation and the magnitude of industrial media production. While the particularly Bolivian circumstances that I have begun to describe here reveal the unevenness in filmmaking and film histories across the region, from its outset in the early twentieth century Bolivia's cinema history has been shaped in transnational circuits running through La Paz. On this point, then, I take issue with Martín-Barbero's periodization of mediation in Mexico and other industrialized Latin American countries, which asserts the relative historical novelty of transnational mediation. Recently, film scholars have shown that the cinema appeared across Latin America from transnational networks, even when filmmaking has been attached to national projects (López 2000a; Noriega 2000; Page 2005). This book locates Bolivia "on the map" of the transnational pathways of what I call "cinematic media," the audiovisual media of film, television, and video that are defined by the intrinsic movement of images and examines projects aimed at constituting, contesting, and representing the Bolivian nation-state and its publics.[2] By bringing Bolivian filmmaking into the picture and setting it against the backdrop of translocal processes running through the scenes like the meeting of *The Lion King* and the Devil, this book traces key configurations in the Bolivian national imaginary and its emergent formulations of indigeneity.

▶ ───

Mediating Indigeneity

The histories of cinematic media in Bolivia have been intertwined with two historical processes in La Paz: the popularization of indigenism and the indigenization of the popular. Produced and disseminated by nonindigenous culturally mixed mestizos heading populist national projects in the early twentieth century, *indigenista* movements inserted moving images of Indianness into urban and worldwide circuits of national folklore and popular culture. As sign-vehicles of Bolivia's national heritage, indigenous images were brought into the orbit of the mestizo national project, whose paternalist goal was to create a homogenous middle class popular nation of non-Indian Bolivians. The recent indigenization of the Bolivian national profile has coincided with a reverse process—the indigenization of the popular. Replacing the project of *mestizaje* with a new frame surrounding indigenous plurality as the articulatory image for the national project (Albro 2005), indigeneity consciously redistributes the static iconic images rendered earlier by indigenism. Entering the circuits of popular politics, indigenous subjects have been reshaping political discourse into projects that at once serve indigenous communities, their cosmologies, and the popular national project. Indigeneity has accumulated decisive political value in Bolivia and among social movements and nongovernmental organizations worldwide, mobilizing coalitions of social activists around formulations of contemporary indigenous subjects engaged with global forces, defending the nation, and enacting self-representation. As the metropolitan area of the capital city of La Paz continues to be depicted as increasingly Aymara and Quechua, these movements are indigenizing the highland urban and political arenas in which the nation-state is mediated.

To situate this ethnography in the media capital of La Paz, part I of this book analyzes how urban publics have been constituted within the circulatory systems of cinema that are entrenched in the social landscape. Specifically, I start with how distributors and audiences draw from circulating social discourses about the city's populace as they map out and move through the infrastructure of film traffic. I theorize the narrative dynamics of film traffic as it specifies and gathers publics at sites along a circuit of venues, defining the status of urban publics by their staggered access to films circulating through the city's theaters. I then turn to the material development of this circulatory infrastructure. During the periods of rapid urbanization and immigration from the rural countryside in the twentieth century, cinemas constructed up and down the city canyon provided a roadmap that plotted the expanding "popular classes" as former peasant Indians (cholos) and their city-born families in higher elevations of the city, above the Westernized middle and wealthy professional classes who enjoyed earlier access to the built spaces of modernity.

Part II shifts to the construction and meanings of the "national cinema" as it has been assembled from elements in translocal processes. Tracing the circulation of filmmakers, films, technologies, and techniques of filmmaking that have passed through La Paz, I analyze how films have been used as vehicles to channel the imagery of indigenism through the circuits of popular culture and politics.[3] In documentary and fiction films, filmmakers tied to the mestizo national project surrounding the 1952 Social Revolution excavated the national heritage from the ruins of antiquity, celebrated its indigenous culture as folklore, and revealed the gleaming future of the modern state. Subsequently, others sought to transform the new state with a vanguard of subaltern indigenous forces and the power of popular culture in activist films.

Chapters in part III analyze a key site of mass mediation that began to invert the popularization of indigeneity, a television talk show that appeared in La Paz in the mid-1980s as a response to the social crises of the neoliberal period. Coinciding with the opening of commercial television, a recent return to democracy several years earlier carried ideas of the public sphere into television. *The Open Tribunal of the People* provocatively envisioned the popular majority of indigenous and poor citizens in La Paz as political participants representing themselves in the public sphere. As *The Tribunal* yielded the populist political party Condepa soon after going on the air, both the program and the party retained elements of traditional political populism and the mestizo project, yet they were saturated with indigenous visuals and tones that envisioned a new Andean popular national identity.

This book concludes with an analysis of a remarkable site in which the indigenization of popular politics and media has been realized. Producing documentaries and fascinating short feature films, indigenous video makers are reappropriating elements from the circuits of popular culture to serve indigenous cultural projects. While intervening in the production and wider circulation of indigeneity, indigenous video making also has become an ingredient in the self-production of cultures and communities (Turner 1991; 1992; 2002a). My analysis connects the video movement with political movements that are dramatically indigenizing the popular nation from epicenters in the cities of Cochabamba and La Paz and especially the neighboring city of El Alto. From the vantage point of La Paz, this book traces the shifting networks in which Bolivian films, technologies, and filmmakers have been assembled to enact the appearance and disappearance of key locations, histories, and publics in Bolivian media worlds.

▶──

Mediation and Media Worlds

I call the social arena of the mobile and representational media in La Paz the city's "media worlds" (Ginsburg et al. 2002), a term that comprehends the far-reaching connections and vital cosmological stakes of mediating culture across boundaries of difference. If travel is one of the cinema's basic features, then the cinema, or what I have called cinematic media, are vehicles that mediate relations of space and time (Ruoff 2006). While Martín-Barbero argues that the "mediation" of transnational media in circulation has meant an upsurge of new cultural identities and practices, the anthropology of media has elaborated on mediation as a fundamental constituent of social and cultural reproduction. Here, mediation additionally refers to how the products of image making supply objectified representations that people produce of themselves yet which are also ingredients of cultural production itself (Turner 1992, 6), thus providing a reflexive means with which to assess and assert identity in, for example, a national imaginary (Ginsburg 1993, Hamilton 2002; Morely and Robbins 1995). As Terence Turner has eloquently demonstrated in careful analyses of Kayapo video making, "Audio and above all visual media thus become, not merely *means* of representing culture, actions or events and the objectification of their meanings in social consciousness, but themselves the *ends* of social action and objectification of consciousness" (1991, 307).

In the circuit of mediation interposed between means and ends and back again, culture is the medium of representation as well as its product.

Faye Ginsburg also has used the term "mediation" in this broad sense to describe the active connections between Australian Aboriginal media and their social contexts: "If we recognize the cinematic or video text as a mediating object—as we might look at a ritual or a commodity—then its formal qualities cannot be considered apart from the complex contexts of production and interpretation that shape its construction" (1994, 6). Another dimension of mediation follows a Peircian semiotic approach that connects the abstract categories of consciousness and memory with the concreteness of everyday life and experience, as Aaron Fox demonstrates for sound and voice in Texan country music (Fox 2004, 35). By problematizing the distinction between process and product, and material and immaterial, the anthropological idea of mediation necessarily pushes the frame of analysis beyond the interpretation of media texts and their reception, or the examination of their formal and material capacities, and extends to the wider social networks and practices and circuits in which media worlds are suspended. Foregrounding mediation forces us to recognize that objects and their circulatory systems are not necessarily conceptually distinct or even materially disparate. In this book, I specifically want to show how the circulatory systems of media are technologies and social processes in which "things" such as film texts, national cinemas, and recognizable publics of varying scale and specificity stabilize and appear (Gaonkar and Povinelli 2003, 386). All the connective qualities of mediation described here imply that forms of circulation inhere in media practices and suggest that our analysis must travel too.

By moving beyond media texts, the anthropology of media has changed the status of media from a taboo topic to "what counts" in anthropology (Ginsburg et al. 2002a, 2–3). This wider frame includes popular discourses surrounding media and its ancillary products (Dickey 1993; Liechty 2002); criticism and trafficking, as Fred Myers has shown for Aboriginal art worlds (2002); the social and material spaces of media venues (e.g., Abu-Lughod 2005; Armbrust 1998; Crawford and Hafsteinson 1996; Hahn 1994; Larkin 2002, Mankekar 1999); sites of production (Abu-Lughod 2005, Dornfeld 1998; Ganti 2002), the implications of media for the formation of nation-state (Abu-Lughod 2005; Askew 2002; Mankekar 1999; Wilk 2002; Yang 1997); or the force of the circulation of "small media" (Sreberny-Mohammadi and Mohammadi 1994 ; Schein 2002; Spitulnik 2002). The anthropology of media puts ethnographic traction on the debates on power and mass mediation (e.g., Askew and Wilk 2002). Taking on the worldwide dissemination of mass media (Spitulnik 1993; Dickey 1997; Peterson 2003), ethnographers have sought to locate elusive and mobile audiences (Bird 1992; Radway 1988) and have located viewers within media institutions themselves (Ang 1991). By emphasizing the plural readings produced across diverse sites of reception in media circuits, Ien Ang (1996) demonstrated how sites of reception are substantial sites of cultural production and resistance. Ethnographies of mass media have also studied production as a process within which to locate the construction of audiences, thereby demonstrating production itself as a practice of reception or consumption (Dornfeld 1998, Ganti 2002). Another valuable approach has been Lila Abu-Lughod's work in Egypt on televisual melodrama and national development (2005); her ethnography moves across sites of television authorship, production, texts, and reception to reveal the permeability and crucial connections between production and consumption. Anthropological research has also turned to indigenous media makers who have taken up small-scale media technologies and techniques of storytelling as forms of cultural activism and collective self-production (Dowell 2006; Ginsburg 1993, 1994, 1995, 1997; Michaels 1994; Turner 1991, 1992, 2002a, 2002b; Wortham 2002). Across the range of studies of viewers and production of mass media, too wide to mention comprehensively here, media anthropology has made an explicit attempt to overcome the conceptual splits that stem from the categories of the marketplace that divide social process between production and consumption.

As Toby Miller et al. (2005) and Barry Dornfeld (1988) have shown, the presumed divide between production and consumption has given rise to debates on the effects of mass media and resistance to it, thereby casting the culture industries and their audiences as intrinsically opposed across the dividing line of the marketplace. Yet Miller et al. call for blended disciplinary perspectives that consider media as forms of representation and experience as well as products of political and economic structures, specifically because they travel across time, space, producers, and publics (5, 42). In this book, I take up this proposition and use circulation as a frame to overcome the misleading bifurcation between political and corporate structural conditions, seen as production, and the cultural meanings within them, seen as consumption. Although there has been much attention given to the unequal distribution and traffic of media from several perspectives already mentioned, I propose a view that conceives of circulation as more than a passive media delivery system. I share Martín-Barbero's view of social process as mobile and involving the mediation of culture within interconnected circulatory matrices that contain "the obstacles and contradictions that move these societies" (1993, 187).

Indeed, it is attention to cultural circulation that underlies his vision of how mass mediation does not break down into binary oppositions that can reflect the actual plurality of social experiences in mediated worlds. Because mediation connotes processes of cultural circulation, I argue for the value of theorizing both production and consumption within the material and social processes of transmission, translation, transculturation, and transfiguration—which all entail mobility.

▶

Studying Circulation

The circulation of cultural forms and practices has become a productive scenario for critical cultural and social theory.[4] This can be seen in the proliferation of anthropological works, too numerous to cite here, that take as their point of departure the traffic and resignification of culture across boundaries and the sweeping transformations associated with capitalist globalization, decolonization, immigration, and new social movements. The significant contribution of the anthropology of media for analyzing these historical forces has been the transformation of the view of culture from a static and bounded concept to the processual and transcultural, foregrounding the deterritorialized, unbounded, heterogeneous, and contested processes of objectification and struggles over cultural forms set in motion (Ginsburg et al. 2002, 3–4; Schein 2002; Spitulnik 2002; Wilk 2002; Yang 1997). Yet as Greg Urban reminds us, culture "is always already in motion" (2001, 15); if the fundamental anthropological definition of culture is not only whatever is socially learned but also that which is socially transmitted (2), then mobility has always inhered in the very idea of culture. Furthermore, if culture is inherently mobile, it is always already transcultural—traveling, arriving, displacing, and recombining, and therefore neither unitary nor strictly global nor local—a point that is visually registered in my photography (Figure 1). Yet the persistent conceptualization of the local as culturally distinct, visible, resistant, and small-scale underlies a problematic opposition in which global forces are considered acultural, homogeneous, and transcendent, as Anna Tsing tells us (2000). One suggestion Tsing makes is to study the very conceptualization of these particular scales, such as global and local, as parts of historical projects. But such attention to the imagination of "scale-making projects" must also involve studying the very movements that take place between locations of varying scales once they are constituted; we need more attention on the practices, machineries, images, and discourses regarding circulation itself. Considering circulation as an issue for anthropological attention, George Marcus suggested that "the global arena is itself constituted by [such] circulations" (1992, xiii). To be able to claim this constitutive capacity, we need to do more than think of circulation as an intermediary or a passive delivery system or as materializing and having meaning only upon arrival to contexts of exchange, consumption, or criticism. We need to specify the material infrastructures, their temporal and spatial dynamics, and how they are read. What does circulation encompass and perform? In short, what does circulation actually do?

The scene captured in my photograph of *The Lion King* and the Devils is a conspicuous performance of circulation, a staged intersection of Hollywood film and national heritage in which the vitality and mobility of culture is flaunted, framed, regulated, and embodied. This spectacle provokes the kinds of questions I explore regarding the expressive and reflexive practices entailed in cultural circulation. How are the paths organized along which media travel, who directs them, and how are they staged to draw attention? How are the publics along their routes envisioned and how do they apprehend the itineraries of cultural circulation? How do narratives about worldwide media distribution form public scenarios in which the forces and struggles for public making, representation, and sovereignty take place? Finally, how is the work of media makers forged in (and displaced from) specific matrices for the circulation of technologies, financing, and support networks? And do junctures reveal the dynamics between specific cultural circuits? By drawing from the dynamic mobility and spectacular performativity seen at these public spectacles in La Paz and from the intrinsic movement in audiovisual media, these questions constitute this book's broadest concerns with the performance of circulation.

The steep city canyon of La Paz is a particularly rich arena for generating the questions about indigenization and circulation that I take up here; and, to be sure, the terrain of the city's "media worlds" is neither self-enclosed nor level. As a city in which key social distinctions and hierarchies—from nationality to urban social classes—are marked in mobile popular parades, where Hollywood film traffic dominates the screens, where political struggles regularly seek to halt or intervene in politics through road blockades and mobilizations, and where popular ritual practices are all efforts at managing circulations, La Paz vibrates with an astounding array of performances that are self-consciously enacting circulation. In tracking the mobilities and far-reaching channels of this moving terrain, my own fieldwork involved less a strategy of localized dwelling and more a series of travel encounters (Clifford 1997). In the following sections of this introduction, I retrace the routes of my own ethnography

Figure 2. In La Paz, "the Center" at the bottom of the canyon is a privileged site of commerce, government offices, and cultural institutions. The surrounding urbanized steep canyon walls are lined with the popular neighborhoods *(barrios populares)*.

through the circuits of media worlds in La Paz and back to the United States to further draw together some of the main issues addressed in the trajectory of this book.

▶

Ethnographic Circuits

Beginning in the Archives

It was my search for exactly the films that were visibly absent on the Prado that had brought me into position to take pictures of the scene of *The Lion King* and the Devils in 1994. When I arrived in La Paz more than eighteen months earlier, on what was my third research trip, I prepared for a year of ethnographic fieldwork on cinema in Bolivia, seeking to study how filmmakers and their audiences have used film and video as instruments for the imagination of the nation-state. Starting at the Cinemateca Boliviana in La Paz, I found its staff welcoming and its archives well organized with abundant documentation of the remarkable histories of filmmaking in Bolivia. In those archives I was able to explore an intertextual field resembling what Mark Liechty calls a "media assemblage" (2002, 31) of films, publicity, and photos as well as the public discourses about cinematic interventions that have shaped and contested how Bolivian filmmakers and critics represented their nation-state, its cultural differences and inequalities, and its relation to the international system. In spite of the absence of a Bolivian film on the Prado during the parade in 1994, the Cinemateca sheltered a rich social history of Bolivian films connected to the competing and successive historical projects of nation making.

In the archives, I traced the impressive range of film styles and social projects to which filmmakers have been committed. Working with and creatively combining forms of documentary, testimonial, and narrative realism, Bolivian filmmakers have sought to reveal key social cleavages, forms of subordination, and hidden cultural realities. From a number of divergent ideological positions, Bolivian cinema has been conspicuously shaped by indigenism, an artistic and philosophical emphasis on representing the country's majority indigenous populations and their significance in the national imagination. More to the point, the archives provided a media assemblage of evidence of the popularization of indigenous imagery. That is, the ways in which indigenous culture was incorporated into national popular movements led by an emergent mestizo and non-Indian bourgeoisie aiming "to recapture Indianness to grant themselves, and their nation, non-European ancestral warrants. . . . Striving for a dignified imperialism-resistant basis for a new kind of nation-building, they revalued 'native' collectivism as a forerunner to socialism" (Abercrombie 2003, 180–81). As chapter 3 describes, the earliest narrative cinema in the decades of the 1920s and 1930s had used theatrical actors to play nonindigenous and indigenous roles, thereby staging their adoption of Indianness, but the cinema was transformed with the works of iconic figures such as Jorge Ruiz, recently honored by the Smithsonian and known as "the father of indigenous Andean cinema," discussed in chapter 4. In the works spanning his career beginning around midcentury, indigenous peoples played themselves in films that combined narrative storytelling and documentary while communities were cast as collective principal protagonists. These styles would be taken up in the 1960s in the revolutionary filmmaking of Jorge Sanjinés and the Ukamau Group, also discussed in chapter 4, who self-consciously organized their own modes of film production as movements toward the anti-imperialist social transformations their films attempted to bring about; they also sought to develop a popular film aesthetic that would connect with how nonprofessional actors and viewers from indigenous and mixed backgrounds apprehended their own worlds. In the popularization of indigenism between the 1920s and the 1980s, images of Indianness were inserted into circuits of popular culture and populist politics that extended beyond Bolivia.

From the beginning, Bolivian films and filmmakers circulated widely in Latin America and Europe, entering into and intervening in what Deborah Poole calls the "Andean image world" (1997). In her fascinating study, she shows how nineteenth-century Andean photography shaped and coincided with modern forms of objective vision and scientific abstractions of physiognomic racial differences. Yet, when *indigenista* filmmakers, artists, and actors in the early-twentieth-century Andes took up image making (de la Cadena 2000; Poole 1997), they replaced racial images of static Indianness (Demelas 1981) with romanticized cultural scenarios in which they could adopt Indian positions for themselves. Further, there was also an appetite for the Andean image world in Europe among romanticists and bohemians (Poole 1997, 176–77), and soon after, socialists. As part of the twentieth-century Andean moving-image world, Bolivian films won acclaim at festivals across Latin America and Europe including Cannes, and they have influenced other political and socially committed filmmakers around the world and have attracted a number of filmmakers to immigrate to Bolivia. Bolivian filmmakers themselves have traveled worldwide and developed collaborations with well-known filmmakers in the United States, Mexico, and across Latin America, sometimes while working in exile from Bolivia.

Despite this influential and vibrant history, filmmaking in Bolivia has not achieved an industrial or even consistent level of production or mass circulation but is episodic and artisanal and could be characterized as what Hamid Naficy calls an "interstitial mode of production," situated between a number of funding sources, technologies, and cultural institutions (2001, 46). For this reason, histories by Bolivian experts on the national cinema have been organized around pioneering figures and the films that have resulted from their struggles to produce films. Yet the trajectory of *Circuits of Culture* is not intended to be an encyclopedic chronological history of Bolivian cinema. In addition to my own historical research at the Cinemateca Boliviana archives, interviews with filmmakers, and my fieldwork in La Paz, there are several excellent comprehensive detailed accounts by Bolivian film scholars from which I draw, including Pedro Susz's impressive account of film circulation during the years 1975 to 1985 that demonstrates the crucial question of distribution (1985); works by Alfonso Gumucio Dagron (1979, 1982), Carlos Mesa Gisbert (1979, 1985), José Antonio Valdivia (1998), and a comprehensive book in English by José Sanchez-H. (1999) provide much detail. Rather than reiterate their histories, this book is a selective analysis of specific films and filmmakers as key sites along the pathways in which Indianness has traveled in the Bolivian national imaginaries envisioned in filmmaking.[5] My emphasis here on filmic media worlds resembles Poole's term "visual economy," which analyzes "the role played by images in circulating fantasies, ideas and sentiments" (1997, 6). Whereas she privileges moments of image production in photography, arguing that "production determines circulation" (10), this book foregrounds the circulatory practices that inhere in moving images and their production. Focusing on the materialities of motion picture media, I concentrate on the particular practices, material matrices, and discriminating discourses about circulation that are inherent in moving images and at the venues through which they travel and which they may be obstructed from entering.

The archives in the Cinemateca demonstrated that an understanding of Bolivian cinema films and their episodic public appearances would have to address Hollywood's presence and the forces shaping the circulatory systems of media worlds in La Paz. The Cinemateca documented that since the mid-1980s, commercial U.S. cinema and television had occupied most of the media and screen space in La Paz, with more than 80 percent of the screened titles; the remaining 20 percent came from the other Latin American countries and Europe (e.g., Mexico, Brazil, Argentina, France). To sharpen this discrepancy, the commercial Hollywood products held a much higher percentage of time on the city's screens, showing several times a day for weeks in some instances (Caballero Hoyos et al. 1991; Susz 1985). The national cinema production had been stalling across a decades-long lack of state support on the one hand, while cinema audiences had been declining on the other, conditions that were widespread across Latin American "audio-visual space" (Martín-Barbero 2000, 38). In the Bolivian case, where more people had televisions than landline telephones because televisions were cheaper to install, there was a rapid decline in moviegoing in the wake of the economic crisis for film distributors during the period of hyperinflation in the early 1980s, followed by the sudden appearance of commercial television, and soon thereafter, the circulation of legal and pirated VHS tapes. In the 1990s, Bolivian films were seldom exhibited in La Paz, with the exception of a biennial series of films at the Cinemateca Boliviana and a short television series on cinema. While several films were released in 1995 and 2003, only three films were released in theaters in each of those "boom" years. 2005 was an unprecedented year in which six films were released, although not all had their debuts in Bolivia. Many of these new works were coproduced with significant funding from Mexico and Europe; several were made by non-Bolivian filmmakers or in coproduction, and a couple were strategically "denationalized" (Hjort 2005, 161), exposing few identifiably Bolivian markings in order to propel them into wider distribution circuits beyond Bolivia. While these films were publicly marked as coproductions, my research in the Cinemateca revealed that since the outset of filmmaking in Bolivia, films marked as part of the national cinema contained their own international elements.

The history of the cinema in Bolivia combines filmmakers, film theories, materials, techniques, and technologies, as well as financing from a variety of sources moving across Latin America, Europe, and the United States. As a "global assemblage" (Ong and Collier 2005), the "national cinema" of Bolivia has multiple determinants and linkages much wider than the frame of the nation-state, which is not only the case for Latin America (e.g., Noriega 2000) but for Hollywood as well (Miller et al. 2005; Acland 2003). In their global concept of the cinema, Toby Miller et al. trace a wide division of cultural work connecting states, multinational corporations, regional customs unions, international clubs, international civil society, and international governance (2005, 46). With these transnational connections, I theorize the expression "national cinema" (in this case, "Bolivian cinema") as a frame for the practice of assembling the multiplex elements that are brought together in films. The cinema has an internalized relation not only with private and international forces but with state financing as well, a relationship that has been especially potent in some Latin American cases, especially in explicit projects of modernization (see Johnson 1993; Martín-Barbero 1993; and Simis 2002). As I will trace out in chapter 3, "the national" has been used as a filmmaking scenario (cf. Page 2005) in which social and critical discourses about filmmaking sought to define locally made films "as national," often against commercial Hollywood. Rather than privileging individual filmmakers as the principal subjects behind the scenes, as in U.S. media discourse (Urban 2001, 209), writers frequently described films as national expressions, the quality of which could be judged to assert Bolivia's uniqueness and status as a modern nation-state in the twentieth century. This book is not a critical account of the corpus of a "national cinema" that draws on historical "context" to interpret media texts. In my analyses of particular films, I explore the historical forces, material capacities, and social practices that aggregate in "texts" that are suspended in the circulatory systems of media worlds.

Filmmaking as Circulation

By the time I emerged from several months of archival research in the Cinemateca, it had become clear that film, television, and video projects had to be understood within matrices of circulating film technologies, techniques, financing, distribution paths, and social ideologies. I was struck when I learned that there were fewer than twenty movie theaters dedicated to showing new films in the entire country of more than eight million people, making the problem of distribution acute for filmmakers seeking to enter the constricted circuits of cinema. As soon as I began to talk with filmmakers about their work, I understood the significance of the dynamics of circulation for their history. Early in one of my first discussions with filmmakers, in 1993, Jorge Ruiz discussed the impact of the Hollywood distributors:

> They really block distribution because they have monopolies. Here the distributors distribute North American films. And all over the world. Look at Argentina, look at Brazil. It's the same thing in these countries. But more in this country where we don't have our own market. Brazil makes its own films, Argentina also, because they have a market from which they can pay their production costs.

Ruiz pointed out to me that he never had a problem with distribution, but this was because he navigated many of his documentaries into the flow of commercial films by having them screened before commercial features from the United States or Mexico. Other filmmakers such as Jorge Sanjinés sought to subvert the dominating presence of commercial cinema that obstructed national filmmakers from accessing screens by contesting the narrative styles of Hollywood and entering alternative paths of circulation with political films. The challenges of distribution quickly surfaced when filmmakers chronicled the barriers they faced in getting their films into distribution circuits and onto screens.

Filmmakers described the obstacles they confronted in putting together financing or obtaining materials and equipment; there was not much state support in Bolivia for importing the needed materials. During my visits, filmmakers revealed new projects they were imagining, and in one instance I regularly visited with a filmmaker who was holding rehearsals for a project that eventually would not be produced. As filmmakers recounted their production strategies and plans to me, they described how their projects were shaped by the resources they could obtain in order to shoot as well as how they were connected to arrangements for distribution afterward. They situated the moment of film production along a series of connected narrative paths in which the constituent parts of their films were moving. As Charles Acland has written, "Production, distribution, and exhibition, as the broad divisions of the film industry apparatus, present a narrative path for the film commodity as it moves from conception to consumption" (2003, 229–30). In their own narratives about their work, filmmakers described production as if it were a moment on an assembly line along which moving film stock is exposed to materials and ideologies that are also in motion and then consolidated and packaged for distribution further down narrative pathways to audiences (cf. Beller 2006). Within this understanding of filmmaking as circulation, filmmaking as well as distribution and its publics are formations and practices that entail narrative forms.

Film Distribution as Media

The problem of circulation that arose prominently in my archival research and in my interviews with filmmakers piqued my curiosity about the organization of transnational and intra-urban film distribution in Bolivia and among publics in La Paz. When I began to interview the first of several national distributors and theater managers, I heard complaints about the new mass media circuits that arose following the appearance of commercial television in the mid-1980s and then the proliferation of pirated films on videocassette. These distributors also discussed the challenges of forecasting the moviegoing public's changing interests; against that uncertainty, they conjured up striking views of the social topography across which they directed films through the city's cinemas. In their "urban imaginary" (LiPuma and Koelble 2005), the city was inhabited by remarkably exaggerated characterizations of distinct publics plotted on its vertical social topography. I call the map they plotted "the cinemascape," borrowing from Appadurai's notion of "–scapes" (1996); it is the terrain in which the ranks of urban social classes and cultural formations are associated with specific film genres and theaters located in particular neighborhoods and elevations. During my interviews, as I began to recognize the contours and selectivity inherent in film distribution, it appeared that the locations on the map the distributors drew were also effects of the mobility of films across the city's theaters and social spaces. As Acland adds to his account quoted above, "Clearly, the mechanics of the film business involve not only the making of movies but also their delivery to an audience, the gathering up of that audience, and the provision of a site for the film encounter" (2003, 229–30). In narrative paths, the films were telling stories about how theaters halt and enclose their mobile publics, who are, after all, also known in English as "moviegoers." I too was attending different cinemas and tracking the routes of films as they traveled through La Paz during this research. Like the distributors, people I met along the way used specific movie theaters and film genres to identify themselves and others in a city in which social stratification corresponds inversely to elevation.

■───

The Circularity of Circulation, or the Publics of Circulation

In addition to the spatiality of film distribution, I emphasize the timing and selectivity in the trajectories of film circulation as the narrative elements for the public reflection about its own place in the circulation of culture. Examining film distribution as a cultural medium in chapter 2, I argue that moviegoing publics in La Paz are suspended and come into being in events, film screenings specifically, along the circulatory systems of cinematic media. In their concept of "cultures of circulation," Benjamin Lee and Edward LiPuma (2002) take circulation in a direction that I had explored earlier (Himpele 1996b), considering how distribution involves reflexive, performative, and discursive practices that objectify and constitute the very publics to which cultural forms are distributed; circulation "always presupposes the existence of their respective interpretive communities, with their own forms of interpretation and evaluation" (Lee and LiPuma 2002, 192).[6] By tracing the circulations from which publics precipitate, I follow the contours of the urban social imagination. I draw from Charles Taylor's use of this term as "the ways in which people imagine their social existence, how well they fit together with others, how things go on between them and their fellows, the expectations that are normally met, and the deeper normative notions and images that underlie these expectations" (2002, 92). Taylor also specifies that although elements of the social imaginary may resemble and even originate as social theory, that imaginary is a wide symbolic matrix composed of shared images, stories, and legends that key certain social practices as salient sites for historical agency, diminishing and occluding some while fixing on, enlarging, and arranging other ideas and practices in sequences. These forms circulate among large groups of people who comply and contest using its terms, thereby making the imagination inseparable from everyday practices, institutions, and history making. As Michael Warner has written, "The public or citizen state is the field and the effect of the organized circulation and broadcast of social discourse" (2002, 62). Where the circularity of circulation occurs, then, is in the moment when moviegoers appear at the movie theater box office as a public of circulation. By tracing the distribution and mediation of films and filmmaking, I delineate the pulsing circuits of film traffic that connect the city's imagined urban publics.

The relationship between circulating narratives and affiliation offered by Benedict Anderson's "imagined communities" thesis (1983) has centered on considering the modern nation-state as a simultaneous interpretive community of anonymous readers of mass-produced novels, maps, and newspapers. Perhaps nowhere more than in the anthropology of media have we concretely explored the imagination in social life as opened up by Anderson's thesis and taken up Arjun Appadurai's claim that "the imagination has become an organized field of social practices" (1996, 31). In ethnographies of media, Anderson's focus on earlier print forms has been usefully and critically transfigured to the present cinematic and televisual forms of cultural production and reflection (e.g., Lee 1993; Abu-Lughod 2005; Hamilton 2002; Ginsburg 1993, 2003; Schein 2002; Mankekar 1999; Dornfeld 1998). While the dissemination of media is crucial to Anderson, Appadurai, and ethnographers of media, this book seeks to advance our understanding of the dynamics and discourses of cultural circulation itself by specifying the uneven social terrain in which publics are formed and the selective and exclusionary circuits in which media and their publics travel. It illustrates how film distribution delineates narrative paths in the social landscape in La Paz, linking together and avoiding locations, temporally slowing and speeding, toward endings imagined at the outset, and arranging into sequence the sites and publics of circulation. A major effort of this book is to establish that the circuits of cinema, broadly defined, constitute a social imagination as much as the textual vehicles that travel them.

My analysis of the discursive constitution of the publics of circulation is combined with archival and ethnographic attention to the materiality of the circulatory infrastructure of built locations that channel films through the city. With this combination, I expand on the idea of a performative view of circulation (Lee and LiPuma 2002) in which publics are prefigured vis-à-vis circulation by considering the spectacle and social drama built into the idea of performativity as seen in theaters, film stock, and the cityscape. Like the categories with which specific transient publics are imagined and ranked, movie theaters also serve as concrete sites at which specific publics are brought into visibility. For one, the visible and physical architectonics of the movie theaters and the genres of films they offer encode the status of the moviegoers who attend films there.[7] I argue that the box office is a scene of exchange between publics and distributors. If tickets provide access over a perceptible boundary to the interior of theater buildings, the built space of movie theaters contains and segments moviegoing publics so that they can be apprehended isomorphically as "a public" having the same apparent fixity of the buildings they enter. Miriam Hansen has argued that in the United States, narrative cinema offered a "universal language" that assembled urban masses at shared events where they would assimilate and become national citizens in theaters (1991). I will show that in La Paz, to the contrary, this unity was not sustained in film circulation or in theaters across the city where moviegoing publics are ranked and differentiated as they are held in suspended animation. By focusing on the materiality, ephemerality, mobility, and selectivity of circulation of both publics and films, instead of presuming their apparent fixity as things that travel, I view the publics of circulation as events or happenings that come into view along with the films and screenings they show up at. This is also a way of saying that people have significant social lives beyond the theater, especially in La Paz.

■———————————————————————————————

Displacing the Cinema

The routes of my own work inevitably expanded and passed through popular festivals and exchange networks in the streets as well as family rituals and fiestas in what are called the "popular" neighborhoods of La Paz. The streets are the city's first circulatory system, and those running through the unofficial markets where urban social networks converge are crucial junctures of cultural mediation and social tension (Albro 2000; Buechler 1997; Seligman 1993; Wiesmantel 2001). As Thomas Abercrombie has insightfully described such sites, "it is this *interface* that determines the cultural whole" (1991, 95). No single social space or practice can be said to be fully determinant of urban identities, no single zone fully encompasses the others, and they do not stack up to a unified cultural logic. I call the contemporary formations that meet and surround this axis the city's "popular publics" (Albro and Himpele n.d.), urban popular classes consisting of these interconnected middle and lower poor classes with an identifiably Andean orientation.

As I was venturing to discuss moviegoing and films with people at cinemas and in the popular neighborhoods where I lived and visited, my questions about reception were frequently displaced as they redirected my attention to their networks of social events and festivals, weddings, baptisms, soccer, or their work, which all clearly outweighed cinema for them. After all, these events were "mass media" topics of conversation and controversy as much as films and television are in the United States. More than a few people told me that they rarely if ever go to the cinema for both social and economic reasons. So in addition to field notes on how people made, watched, and distributed films, my notebook computer was also filling up with descriptions, interviews, and my own emerging notions about these spectacles. To be sure, folklore parades, neighborhood patron saint festivals, parties, and rituals were more crucial and continuous sites of social and cultural production than cinema. These tensions between the cinematic mass media circuits and the matrices of popular culture and media reveal how local spectacles mediate the cinema by displacing it with practices and paths through which the popular classes practice circulation (Himpele 1996a).

The director of the Cinemateca Boliviana, Pedro Susz K., who has studied cinema in Bolivia, also observed the cinema's peripheral position:

> This is a country where there is not a single magazine about cinema and in the bookstores you practically cannot find any books about cinema. Where the criticism is practically relegated to the newspapers, which have little circulation. So there is little information and there is little development of the cinema. . . .
>
> In the collective imagination, cinema is not at the center and it can be proved in the Bolivian novel. In the Bolivia novel, it practically doesn't exist. It's a very different thing in Argentina, Brazil, Mexico. Cinema is part of the imagination, like you said, in the United States and France. Here, there are other elements of a society less fragmented. Here the fiestas, the ritual, the get-together with friends, are more at the center of life. (personal communication, August 4, 1993)

In these circumstances, it could seem misleading to study cinematic media as a site for tracing modern historical projects in Bolivia. Yet Hollywood blockbuster debuts appear as stories on the front pages of major national newspapers in La Paz, typically measuring their proximity to their debuts in the United States as if they were quantifying degrees of modernity in temporal units; similarly these major papers have a cinema section in their Sunday editions, such as "Cine Mundo" (Cinema World) in the newspaper *El Diario,* which promises "up-to-date goings-on in film and summaries of the best productions." Such discourses that index specific circulation dynamics reveal how the movement of cinematic media is a diagnostic site for how publics delineate national modernity, as chapters 1 and 2 demonstrate. Nevertheless, the cinema is displaced by other forms of popular culture.

Unlike Mexico or Egypt, for example, where television has been the "salient institution" for producing the modern nation-state (Abu-Lughod 2005, 7), in Bolivia the widespread and diverse mass media of festivals and folkloric events are more clearly prominent. Despite this contrast or, better, because of the narrowness of the circuits of cinema in Bolivia, the cinematic media are an excellent place to focus on and follow mediation and representations of Indianness as historical projects. In most films made in Bolivia, popular rituals, festivals, and parades appear as key narrative turning points or as settings. Filmmakers who have captured the magnitude and meanings of these cultural performances on film have self-consciously represented and attached them to specific historical projects and urban social spaces. Indeed, in an inversion of Martín-Barbero's sense of the term, filmmakers have "mediated" the wider forces of indigenous and popular culture by incorporating them into the cinema. So in addition to *The Lion King* from Hollywood, the "national cinema" that was beyond the frame of my photo was also displaced by the Devils, popular culture, and its spectacles of Indianness.

With the twenty-first century, La Paz and Bolivia itself have become proportionally more indigenous than when the republic was founded in 1825, according to official categories (Greishaber 1985, 59). Between 1900 and 1952, and against the expectation that Indian immigrants would assimilate and disappear in modern cities, the indigenous population expanded to become the majority population of La Paz and Bolivia. This coincided with a shift in census categories from economic and racial categories to visible ethnic features, now including "two types of 'Indians,'" those with indigenous clothing, occupation, or language and those who lived and worked in traditional rural communities (Greishaber 1985). Ideologues of the national revolution of 1952 similarly did not foresee that Aymaras and Quechuas would not assimilate to a Western-oriented mestizo national culture. As these immigrants to the city after 1952 succeeded as entrepreneurs and workers, they invested their new wealth into enhancing their cultural systems and increasing their status in it, rather than assimilating. This new parallel middle class of urban Aymaras has used festivals, expensive clothing, and costumes to perform their Indianness and flaunt their status among the ranks of immigrants and cholos and against a parallel middle class of Westernized mestizos (Himpele 2003). Viewed as a corporeal series of moving images, festivals and parades have been crucial vehicles in which new urban Andean publics have gained social prominence as indigeneity and indigenous movements have come to define the popular national project.

During my research, the indigenization of urban publics and media

Figure 3. The serial imagery of cholas dancing the Morenada constitutes social networks, status, and gender representations of Bolivian Indianness that compete with the dances of Westernized mestizas.

appeared in everyday life on a highly successful prime-time commercial television talk show taped in La Paz, *The Open Tribunal of the People*. In a setting saturated with folkloric music, Andean ethnic tones, and the charisma of its nonindigenous host, people from the indigenous and poor sectors in La Paz appeared as participants in a public sphere representing themselves. No doubt the broadcast of these powerful images did sustain the paternalist indigenist history of popularizing Andean Indianness, as I will show, but *The Tribunal* also went beyond and registered the possibility of an alternative historical process—the indigenization of popular media and politics. While I was studying the cinema, *The Open Tribunal* was the only local film or televisual program in continuous circulation that people in the popular classes of La Paz were engaged with nightly and gossiped about daily. Accordingly, my ethnographic trajectory led to the network studio and, as it turned out, promptly in front of its cameras.

■ ───

Ethnography in the Matrix (1996)

Just hours after arriving home from my first visit to the daily taping of *The Open Tribunal* in central La Paz earlier that day, I was taken aback when I saw the thirty-second commercial for that evening's broadcast:

"We are definitely the best!!! Tonight, a North American anthropologist visits us to study *The Open Tribunal,* a unique example of alternative communication across the entire world [fast music and announcer's voice over twoshot of Jeff Himpele and television cohost Adolfo Paco].

[Close-up to clip from Jeff speaking] ". . . a constant direct connection with the people that the Bolivian cinema does not yet have because . . ."

[Announcer's voice over wideshot] "Tonight, after your soap opera *Three Destinies.*"

[Radio Television Popular network logo and music fade in]

Hoping for permission to do research at the program, I considered myself aligned with the other participants seeking assistance from *The Tribunal,* yet I was drawn into appearing on the program with cohost Adolfo Paco as a tacit condition for my work there (for a detailed discussion of my appearances, see Himpele 2002). My appearance privileged me to bestow the program with international significance; either way, my image authenticated the program's rhetoric about itself that had gone so far as to galvanize a neopopulist political party led by its host and network owner Carlos Palenque. Seeing myself as a participant in his project and as a coming attraction made me apprehensive about the field relations this might be foreshadowing. Seeing myself on the screen, I realized that I was inside the matrix of media circulation that I had been studying for several years.

Moving from radio to television during the commercialization of televisual space in the mid-1980s, the nightly *Open Tribunal* offered social aid to the poor while serving as the stage for the neopopulist political party Condepa led by the program's host, Carlos Palenque, publicly known as "El Compadre" (the Godfather). Palenque's charismatic presence, musical voice, and promises of assistance for problems brought to him by the city's urban indigenous downtrodden made the program voyeuristic, hypnotically seductive, and crudely manipulative all at once. Admittedly, I had been initially skeptical about the program while doing my earlier research on filmmaking, and I was somewhat puzzled by its success. I became fascinated when I talked with audiences who put the program, El Compadre, and their publics, including themselves, in an ambivalent light. He was either finally going to solve the problems of "the people" or he was manipulating the poor, or both. For audiences, as well as for me, the discourses about the show's participants and its avid viewers made media and power the foremost issues, and yet it seemed that the sharp lines of opposition between the terms of debate on media power (i.e., active audiences versus powerful media institutions, or between resistance and domination) were collapsed each time a new visitor stepped in front of the camera.

At the program taping the next day, I appeared with Carlos Palenque himself. Later, when I viewed a tape of *The Tribunal* broadcast, I watched him maneuver and encircle my authority in order to establish his own. He told viewers that he would chat with me, and then the screen cut to me, the anthropologist taking notes behind one of the studio cameras. By the time I met with him on the air, I had gotten over the fact that he had been watching me in the back of the studio and that he had obligated me to appear without any advance notice. Further, this unrehearsed on-air moment was the first time I would talk with him! Palenque reintroduced me to the television audience, greeted me with a smile, and asked about the results of my work thus far. I first thought it a strange question for the second day of my research, but I quickly realized that he was asking me to provide a favorably sweeping judgment. In this precarious public exchange, I could not make critical judgments about how he channels individual crises into the totalizing narratives of his own project, but I also wanted to avoid endorsing him.

"Well, anthropological work is a bit . . . it takes a long time and one cannot make conclusions very quickly because one has to be very sensitive. . . ."

"Of course. Of course," he broke in approvingly. At that moment, I became aware of one of his techniques, how he cuts off people in order to insert his support of them.

". . . to all of the details. For the anthropologist it is in the details where the conclusions lie, so for now . . ." I continued, tactically evading the question while staying within its frame.

He pushed me: "But right now, in general, taking a first glance at things, what results do you have up until now?"

"What I see now is, for example, that *The Open Tribunal* has had an important impact in La Paz, and that the people feel a direct connection with *The Tribunal* and that they can come directly to the studios to participate."

"And they can express themselves with absolute freedom."

"That's what they say, yes. Exactly."

As I watched this conversation on television at home, I sensed I was being used to enhance the program, with both of us fixing on *The Tribunal*'s unique practice of offering social aid, yet I was surprised to hear myself again repeating its own discourse about its unique openness, accessibility to the urban poor, and popular social authority.

While my ethnographic work was informed by my own prior work in U.S. television news and video production and more recent projects in ethnographic filmmaking, I learned firsthand the specific moral dynamics that organized televisual production in *The Tribunal*'s studios. I took part in an open-ended transaction in which I would maintain prestige for the show in return for the assistance I wanted in doing research there. As I elaborate later in chapters 5 and 6, the program is built from a chain of such encounter scenes, each one organized around ritualized greetings and unequal exchanges of historical agency, specifically, prestige for the promise of visibility and aid. Examining how exchanges from everyday life bear on mediated interactions, my analysis supports what Mankekar (1999) and Abu-Lughod (2005) find among television viewers in India and Egypt, respectively, or Miller's (1992) essay on U.S. soap operas in Trinidad and Naficy's analysis of Iranian television in Los Angeles (1993), which show that mediated exchanges are more complicated than scenes of binary negotiation. Watching my own appearance, I learned the "public secret" that participants, workers, and viewers had already known: this was a performance that represented an unspoken cultural strategy of complicity and collusion. In fact, I had known this, having engaged these kinds of exchanges when navigating social relations across the city.

As I watched myself in the transmission, it seemed the more I struggled to separate my project of social representation from Palenque's, the more they appeared to converge, evoked by the on-screen image of us standing beside each other and facing the viewing public's gaze. In a flash of recognition, I saw myself as Palenque, and I knew why I might have disliked him—he was an embodiment of the repressed anthropological other constituted by all those critiques of the omniscient controlling voice! In the vertigo I experienced as I watched the screen, I recognized myself in the same moral sphere of engagement with the people I was studying and who were also monitoring me. I began to ask myself if my ethnographic solicitation and editing of informants' voices was different from Palenque's elicitation and cutting off of participant's voices while he praised their protagonism. Do we appropriate images of suffering and testimonial narratives as our own cultural capital or to mobilize popular sentiment and solidarity (Kleinman and Kleinman 1997, 1)? What of Palenque's authoritative voice that orders social crises into his narratives for people watching at home? This seemed to be close to the heart of the ethnographic project: in our attempts to provide a cross-cultural frame we employ peoples' lives in narratives of varying scales that are meaningful for our own audiences at "home." I desperately sought to remind myself that anthropology's goals are not to commercialize and dramatize suffering in brief meetings but to produce sustained analyses of social processes that look beyond rather than stay constrained by given frames of reference. In my position as a viewer at the convergence of my own and Palenque's lines of sight that converged on the public at home, I knew that the scene did not simply turn the tables on ethnographic authority; it parodied and imploded it.

Couched in the contours of the televisual public sphere, my appearance in the matrices of media circulation poses the challenge that there is no neat separation between media ethnographers and media producers on the terrain of cultural representation. To interpret this scene, I have drawn from an image that Faye Ginsburg vividly makes in the idea of a "parallax effect" in which ethnographers and media producers are situated alongside one another while each directs their vision and produces their own representations of the same social phenomenon (1995, 65–66). When viewed together, these juxtaposed angles of vision raise questions that stem from the public mediation of ethnographic work. Barry Dornfeld's reflection on his ethnography of the making of a PBS documentary series reveals how his fieldwork in the public sphere entailed negotiating stances toward cultural producers who are well aware of what ethnographers are up to (1998, 21) and who produce similar "ethnographic" representations themselves. Further, he shows that in the shifting between positions as observer and participant, feelings of obligation and duplicity emerge by becoming part of the social hierarchies created through media institutions. The immediacy of carrying out media ethnography in the public

Figure 4. The author in an interview on *The Open Tribunal of the People* with the television host and populist political leader Carlos Palenque.

sphere forces ethnographers to sort through the dynamics of field relations with others who also converge upon "culture" and with whom they
may be complicit in making sense of localities (Marcus 1997), on the
one hand, or, on the other, with whom they may isomorphically employ
spatial practices that produce their localities and their publics as ethnographic fields of affiliation (Appadurai 1996b; Clifford 1997; Gupta and
Ferguson 1997).[8]

New Popular Publics

In this ethnography, based in La Paz, *The Tribunal* is an arena of transition in the production of new Andean popular publics that formed in its
electronic networks disseminated across the city and the televisual public sphere. It is at that point in the trajectory of this book, in chapters 5
and 6, that we will hear *The Open Tribunal*'s televised nostalgia for what
were perhaps the final gasps of the popular project that had pursued the
fantasy of national cultural synthesis *(mestizaje)* that one might say died
coincidently when Palenque himself did, unexpectedly, in 1997. Studies
of popular politics during the proliferation of neoliberal reforms in Latin
America have claimed that "the popular" as we have known it has diminished, its potency "exhausted" with the crisis of the sovereignty of the
nation-state in transnational economies (e.g., Williams 2002; Masiello
2001). Yet the conjuncture of commercial television, *The Tribunal,* and
the political party Condepa registers a proliferation of Bolivia's regional-
ized popular publics and politicians contending for a prevailing definition of the nation during the social crises of the 1980s and 1990s (Albro
1998). Unlike Bolivia's earlier unifying national project, however, the new
popular sectors that have materialized in La Paz exhibit clearly urban,
Aymara, and Quechua identity, voices, and issues; they mark the political
emergence of a culturally conscious urban Andean popular public. The
argument I develop here is that these popular publics have been brought
into view as they achieved public visibility through the circuitry and social
networks of televisual mediation.

This indigenization of media worlds in La Paz is the subject of part III
of this book, which focuses on how television framed and brought into
relief a discernible yet heterogeneous urban majority, a public that was
very present but also elusive. Metropolitan La Paz–El Alto is a distinctive
region in Latin America where a vast majority claims Indianness as part of
their collective identities. Even though 80 percent of Bolivia's almost nine
million people speak indigenous languages or self-identify as indigenous,

Indianness has long been a defining and legitimating feature of claiming Bolivian citizenship even for *criollo* whites or urban mestizos who patriotically play at being Indian in folkloric pageants, as Thomas Abercrombie has shown (1991, 119). In national festivals and parade dances, memories of Indianness are popularized and embodied as national habitus (cf. Connerton 1989) as well as heritage (see Figure 3). The question of just who are the "Indians" is a misleading question, if not an intricate, situated, and elusive one.[9]

The highly contextual and slippery meanings of urban identity were evident to me in La Paz, especially in the neighborhood of San Pedro where I resided. The mixed residential and commercial neighborhood of San Pedro is a popular neighborhood more established and prosperous than those above. It is one of the older neighborhoods not far up the city canyon from the center of La Paz where many households are within a generation or two of their family's arrival from rural towns and countryside. The older rural-born generation and newly arrived immigrants are often called *gente del pueblo.* This term refers to the city's popular classes but specifies that "the people" come from rural communities known as *pueblos,* thereby collapsing the rural into the term for "the people," the root for "popular." San Pedro's population includes the city's laborers, lawyers, engineers, students, teachers, prosperous indigenous entrepreneurs and their families, and vendors in the informal markets. Many are bilingual speakers of Spanish and Aymara or Quechua and practice combinations of marked indigenous and Catholic rituals and beliefs. Yet rather than verbally self-identify as Indian or indigenous, most people represent their social status and cultural identity through clothing. Older family members often tacitly identify as indigenous Aymara or Quechua if they were born in the countryside by using clothing styles to mark their place of birth. They may be called *cholos,* usually a pejorative term, or the diminutive *cholita* (feminine) or *de pollera,* to refer to women's expensive wide-layered skirts. Their daughters who are born in the city use Western dress *(de vestido),* their mothers say, because Western clothing is cheaper and they don't want their children to face the social discrimination they faced as indigenous immigrants. For themselves, this urban-born generation views the term "mestizo" as a pejorative racial term for "mixed blood," despite movements to render it in cultural terms earlier in the mid-twentieth century (see Barragán 1992; Sanjinés 2004). Beyond their own households, the popular sectors across the city of La Paz are intimately tied together through networks of ritual kinship (coparenthood or *compadrazgo*) and their mutual exchange obligations. These plural identities and alliances laced across the city complicate the image of two clearly opposed social blocs, such as a bloc of non-Indians or even wealthy white elites opposed to an "indigenous bloc" who participate in folkloric events of Indianness (Abercrombie 2003).

After a night of hard drinking and dancing, many cholo/as and non-Indians in the city may say that "mi indio salio" (my Indian came out). By using the term "Indian," they internalize a colonially defined category of uncivilized otherness (see Abercrombie 1991), but they also demonstrate that single linguistic categories or hyphens cannot capture the shifting layers of identities as convincingly as drinking delineates a path to their own indigenous pasts (Abercrombie 1998; Bouysse-Cassagne and Saignes 1993).

The fine social distinctions among the urban popular classes are often amplified into invidious discriminations in everyday life, especially against those who are from the Andean countryside (see Gill 1994; Weismantel 2001). If single linguistic categories are always potential pejoratives, then a plurality of social identities escapes the unity and fixity implied by linguistic categorization. The Bolivian historian Rossana Barragán has suggested that the popular classes seem to be better understood or described as "a group with an 'identity' defined more implicitly by its conduct than explicitly in its consciousness" (1993, 102), meaning that identity is expressed "emblematically" or "tacitly" in a visual realm such as clothing, profession, topographic space, or neighborhood. Thus, the social landscape is ranked in inverse relation to urban elevation on the city's canyon walls, with the higher neighborhoods and even the sprawling immigrant city of El Alto on the canyon brow associated with those recently arrived from the *campo* or the rural Altiplano beyond La Paz and El Alto and marked as indigenous and popular.

The Tribunal was a crucial site for the formation of new indigenous and popular publics from these areas of La Paz, framing and forming them as a mediated event on a program broadcast across the cityscape, as chapter 6 describes. In the view I take here, popular culture is not a fixed category therefore, but a frame that moves across "a space or series of spaces where popular subjects, as distinct from members of ruling groups are formed" (Rowe and Schelling 1991, 10). This analysis of the formation of popular publics in film circulation and in TV media events takes issue with Néstor García Canclini's regard for the "staging of the popular" in the circuits of popular culture and mass media as offering a simulation of historical agency (1995). I take up this question of historical agency ethnographically and consider whether the televisual circulation of popular classes has meant their political disappearance. My episodic view of these popular publics also revises Nancy Fraser's more structural critique of

Habermas's idea of the public sphere in which she argued that there were "competing publics from the start" (1993, 7), subordinate publics who inhabit "actually existing" alternative public spheres. Nonetheless, Fraser's point that "people participate in more than one public, and that membership in publics may partially overlap" (18) certainly matches the heterogeneity of popular publics in La Paz that I have described. The unfixed plurality of these "new social subjects" and conflicts (Laclau and Mouffe 1985) coincides with regional shifts in Latin America called the "rediscovery of the popular" (Martín-Barbero 1988, 453), the turn to identity politics (Hale 1997), social movements grounded in cultural struggles (Alvarez et al. 1998), and the popular publics that form in associational networks (Chalmers et al. 1997; Emirbayer and Sheller 1999). Yet rather than revealing "submerged" forms of resistance (Melucci 1988; Scott 1990) or even asserting the distinct "newness" of the specifically cultural terms of political action (Edelman 2001, 296–98), the issue I focus on in examining the mediation of popular publics is how cross-cutting social differences and cultural life worlds of urban Andean publics have been fashioned, comprehended, and strategized since appearing in the frames of televisual mass media and populist politics.

The populist Condepa party and *The Open Tribunal* appeared alongside the populism of official "neoliberal multiculturalism" (Hale 2005; Postero 2005) in the Law of Popular Participation, a decentralizing political reform that arguably honed the state's capacity to assimilate difference into ambient clientelist political structures (Ayo Saucedo 1999). Yet both set the stage for imagining an indigenous and popular Bolivia defined by cultural differences rather than sameness, forging a national imaginary that ultimately could not be realized under existing political structures. Like the political reforms, Condepa's centralized authority and entrenched clientelism may have both propelled and delayed the transformative processes mobilized around "indigeneity" already underway in the dominantly indigenous neighborhoods of La Paz, but especially El Alto.

The Paths of Indigenous Media

The concluding chapter of this book discusses the indigenous video movements that emerged in a political environment in which indigenous popular movements have risen and made demands that are indigenizing the politics and the profile of the nation. Beginning in the 1990s, as indigenous politics became decisive for Latin American national politics (e.g., Van Cott 1994 ; Warren and Jackson 2002) and indigeneity gained political value among new regional and transnational organizations and movements, indigenous video centers have achieved alternative paths for media production and circulation in Bolivia. Members of the Center for Cinematographic Education and Production (CEFREC) based in La Paz have produced short fictional feature films that combine indigenous ways of knowing with representational strategies that both incorporate and challenge styles from the dominant mass media. As indigenous video makers mediate popular and media cultures, they open up possibilities for indigenous "cultural futures" (Michaels 1994). Unlike the media worlds that represented twentieth-century popular projects that attempted to achieve modernity by assimilating and rendering invisible the hybridity of the nation-state to achieve a purer modernity (Latour 1993), these video makers are staking their claim in the present and the future by engaging with the multiple cultural combinations and transnational networks that the state could not contain, hide, or homogenize. Just as indigenous political movements are indigenizing popular politics and the state's relation to transnational corporations, video makers are indigenizing popular culture and media with their own transcontinental networks, opening new venues for cultural representation in national and international channels of distribution. To be sure, indigenous movements have their critics and their complexities, as Kay Warren shows (1998). I argue that the visible circuits that enable their wide-ranging engagements imbue indigenous media with cultural vitality and political value.

My own work with several CEFREC video makers began when I found myself in the path of their travels to screen their works in New York and across the United States in 2002. I worked assisting them as a guide and translator when they were hosted by the National Museum of the American Indian (NMAI) to present their works there and at New York University, and I joined them on a video tour to museums, Bolivian cultural groups near Arlington, Virginia, and a film festival in Taos, New Mexico. My work continued in other visits they made to the Native American Film and Video Festival at the NMAI in 2003 and the First Nations/First Features Festival at the Museum of Modern Art in 2005. Grounded in our meetings and travel in the United States, where our paths crossed, the discussion of indigenous video that concludes *Circuits of Culture* closes the ethnographic itinerary that had begun with my fieldwork on media and popular culture in La Paz. Now that Aymara and Quechua filmmakers and their works are traveling in transcontinental media circuits, the traditional popularization of Indianness is overturning, like a Möbius strip exposing its reverse side, and revealing ongoing projects to indigenize the circuitry of popular media and national politics.

I The Cinemascape and the Publics of Circulation

[1]   *Film Distribution as Media:*
   Mapping the Urban Imaginary

▶

The Travels and Transfigurations of Dracula

On the eve of 1993, Dracula descended from the sky and arrived in Bolivia
on board an American Airlines jet at the international airport in El Alto,
the indigenous immigrant city sprawled on the dusty flatlands overlooking
the wide and steep canyon bowl of La Paz. Securely bundled inside several metal canisters, he cleared customs and continued on his itinerary. In
spite of the dense population of this city, and even with his own appetite
for circulatory material, he decided that El Alto would have to wait and
promptly swooped down along the curving expressway to the city center
of La Paz at the bottom of the canyon. Dracula may be insatiable, but he
is also a histrionic creature and desperately seeks attention. Waiting for
the right moment when his first public appearance could take place most
prominently as well as profitably, he remained in his canisters and lurked
for several days inside the offices of a film distributor on the Prado.

The Paseo del Prado is a wide promenade, with fountains, statues,
green manicured shrubs, and flower gardens, that runs along the center
of the main boulevard at the bottom of the city canyon. On the streets
facing the Prado are expensive hotels, travel agencies, bookstores, art and
shopping galleries, airline offices, restaurants, high-rise apartment buildings, a state university, and two first-run movie theaters. The Prado is also
a highly visible and symbolic stage for patriotic and folkloric parades,
where images of the country's origins and its cultural uniqueness are concentrated and exhibited in pageants. Given the Prado's prominence as a
public stage, it is also the space of loud social protest marches, frequently
made by people from the poorer areas above the city like El Alto and the
Altiplano who cannot afford to live or buy anything down near the Center.

During the civic holidays and the strikes, when the nation-state is either being performed, claimed, or contested, everyday traffic and life appear to be suspended in order to reveal and direct attention toward the moving images on the Prado.

The Prado appeared motionless on the morning of the New Year's holiday of 1993, except at the Cinema Monje Campero, where people had been lining up at the box office. Above, a wide billboard advertising Dracula's "Great Debut" that day spread his image and name across the front of the building like bait. On the sidewalk in front, Aymara women began to set up tables to sell potato chips, soda, and candy. At the head of the line to the box office inside, a dozen unemployed people who had arrived earlier were buying the eight-boliviano (4.49 bolivianos were worth one U.S. dollar at that time) tickets for the best seat locations to resell later to the eager moviegoers shut out of the sold-out screenings, extracting a profit from the increasing desire to see Dracula at Bolivia's largest and best-equipped movie theater. They enticingly offered, "There are no more tickets. I'll sell you two tickets for twenty-five bolivianos, with seats close to the screen." Most of the viewers who came to see Francis Ford Coppola's *Dracula* at the approximately 1,100-seat theater were professionals, bureaucrats, entrepreneurs, and their families who work in nearby retail stores and government offices and live in high-rise apartment buildings nearby or in the luxury homes in the elite neighborhoods farther below the Center. Extracting vital circulatory material each time a new crowd entered, *Dracula* inhabited the Monje for seven weeks, long enough to set the record for the longest-running film exhibition at the cinema.

Dracula then began to move from the bottom of the city back up the canyon wall to the Cinema Roby, a large theater on the Plaza Garita de Lima in the busy commercial streets and neighborhoods of the city's popular classes of indigenous and mestizo families. His large banner, which had hung on the Monje Campero announcing his Great Debut, hung above the theater doors. Along these streets surrounded by markets and shops, the city's cholo immigrants (urban Indians born in the countryside) live and work as merchants in family businesses and as importers and resellers of official and contraband goods and produce. Many sidewalk vendors who work here descend from poorer neighborhoods higher along the steep canyon wall; they eat their meals, care for their children, and organize their social and political lives in the street markets and dance halls surrounding the Garita plaza. Two weeks before arriving at the Roby, however, Dracula had already begun to replicate and circulate in these surrounding street markets in blurry images and muddy sound on pirated subtitled videocassettes. Color photographs of the official movie poster

Figure 5. A scene depicting *Dracula*'s seven-week grand debut in Bolivia at Cinema Monje Campero.

served as labels slipped inside the clear plastic shrink-wrap of the original blank VHS tapes. As if Dracula could move across time and space as he wished, his replicas were finding their way into peoples' homes, while the official film of *Dracula* went on to other large cities in Bolivia for several weeks and then returned to La Paz in March.

Just a few blocks up from the Center, *Dracula* reappeared for another debut in La Paz in the Cinema Plaza on the Plaza Murillo, the well-kept city plaza surrounded by the ornate state government presidential palace and parliament halls. He was seen by professionals and bureaucrats and their families who work here and shop in the glitzy gallerias. After the Cinema Plaza, *Dracula* spent several months traveling upward through the city's smaller and cheaper cinemas in the neighborhoods that line the wall of the city canyon where aged prints of comedy, police, action, B-grade martial arts, and pornographic films from the United States and Brazil circulate until they are too worn to be projected or sold. By now, months of traveling, great debuts, and extracting vital circulatory material from others were beginning to leave their marks on him. The accumulating scratchy images and fuzzy sound track inscribed on him at his sites of extraction became tell-tale signs of his travels.

For audiences along *Dracula*'s route in La Paz, his deteriorating image and sound quality indexed how long he had been traveling along a path that mapped out the inverse relationship between the city's elevation and its social classes. With each new appearance at another cinema along his itinerary, he was rising upward from the bourgeois city center at the bottom of the urban canyon, through the small theaters in the poorer and peripheral neighborhoods, to the higher elevations, where he obtained less circulatory material than at his earlier stops. While the contours of the urban social topography became clearer as he moved upward, they were inscribed on him and Dracula found himself slowly deteriorating. To make matters worse, he also found himself anxiously competing for the attention he craved.

On a Sunday midafternoon on the sidewalk outside the Cinema Esmeralda, women set up tables to sell various pieces of electric, plumbing, carpentry, and masonry hardware. Careful not to be pushed by the slowly descending bus and car traffic in this neighborhood filled with street markets, streams of people walk by the cinema carefully as they step past browsers and vendors occupying the sidewalk. The Esmeralda was previously an open produce market before concrete walls were poured and a corrugated tin roof was laid across the top, a small ticket office added, and seats and projection equipment brought from Brazil. A father, mother, and their three young children enter the theater. For ten bolivianos (about

2.25), the family will see *Dracula* along with *Universal Soldier* and *Home Alone 2*. A fifteen-year-old Aymara domestic worker enters with her boyfriend. As they walk into the theater laughing, they carry some potato chips and two liter-size bottles of Paceña, the ubiquitous local beer. The children run around the theater laughing, and after a few minutes of telling them to be quiet, the parents concede. Three Aymara cholas, dressed in heavy multilayered gathered skirts, enter and take their seats together. They are celebrating the birthday of one of the women who has not been to a cinema in eight years, and they quietly chitchat through the screening. They will stay for only a little more than an hour and then leave to get a meal a few blocks upward. In the early evening, they will attend a rehearsal with other older members from their dance group for the parade in the Gran Poder, the citywide festival that is only two months away. Like two of these three women, many of the twenty-seven spectators inside are not reading, or cannot read well enough, all the subtitles on *Home Alone 2*. They chat and gossip about others in their dance fraternity, and at times they stop and laugh at the spectacle of slapstick action set in exotic New York. The father gets up and plays with the children outside on the patio of the theater. The cholita and her boyfriend drink, snack, whisper, chuckle, and touch cheek to cheek; they only see each other on Sundays, which is her day off, when she can leave the Center household she works in. During a lull in the laughter and action in *Home Alone 2*, many in the audience turn their attention to the screen, where the main character enters his room in a luxurious Manhattan hotel. The hotel room is palatial and exquisite; the screen is illuminated with the excessive wealth of the North. The adult spectators collectively ogle and gasp at the extravagance. Throughout the afternoon's triple-feature, however, people enter and leave and scatter out into the city, derailing the attention sought by the train of moving images.

I also break and go outside to meet José, the theater manager, who had moved to La Paz from Lima ten years earlier. He explained to me that *Dracula* had done very well in the City Center, but its poor performance here at the Esmeralda was due to the fact that people in these neighborhoods have very little money to spend. He also went on to describe the uniqueness of the public:

> *Dracula* had a [waiting] line when it debuted at Monje Campero. It's a good film. It had good recommendations. But not here in the Cinema Esmeralda. It's for a type of people from the lower parts of the city. But the people here, they go in to see the film, and they do not understand the conflict, they leave. They do not understand. Here we'll show *Dracula* only a week. Here the people are very unique. . . . Bring to this cinema a "Van Damme" film

and the people come. And *las chinas* [martial arts films] and the people will come also. Before we could show anything oriental, but the taste of the people is changing. Now it's variable. So we are showing different types, one for kids, terror, and an action film. You have to know the parameters of the people to show what they like in this zone.

Evident in José's account are vital connections between knowledge and difference that organize *Dracula*'s itinerary through the city, as he describes how audiences apparently decline in their interest and ability to fully comprehend certain film genres as *Dracula* moves up the city's steep incline. According to his whereabouts, Dracula typically captures his audiences' attention by drawing on his own intrinsic mutability, his capacity to transform into diverse forms. Yet his publics are manifold too and here they don't sit still, so he cannot fully know their expectations or sustain their attention for long. Worse yet, as the circulatory matter he seeks begins to dry up, Dracula finds himself materially deteriorating. In another two years of touring other cities in the country, including El Alto, where he first landed, his biography in Bolivia will close. Under his contract with a Hollywood agent, he will be recaptured by the distributor in La Paz and then burned and melted away; he seems destined to be destroyed by the locations of his own gaze and the source of his vitality. Yet Dracula has also already begun to take on other incarnations. Although they are less fruitful, his official and pirated video replicas have been proliferating since his arrival. As the story goes, Dracula never dies and in some form he will reappear elsewhere.

To absorb the shock of his inevitable disintegration and eventual humiliation, however, Dracula pursued the maximum circulatory material and attention earliest in his travels. He believed that the value of circulatory materials corresponded to their sites of extraction and so too the social status of their associated publics. Strategically, he needed to know how to navigate across the city's heterogeneity in advance of his first appearance. When he arrived in La Paz, then, he required an atlas that plotted the different moviegoing publics in the city; moreover, he needed an itinerary for moving through places that might best sustain him. Though he had been here before, in 1958, it had been a while and there were no guarantees. For an itinerary and some certainty, he needed a local travel agent who "knows the parameters of the people" and could act as his guide.

▶ ────────────────────────────

Film Distribution as Media

The paths and timing of film traffic in La Paz are directed by film distributors who refer to their own imaginary maps of social differences to prepare itineraries for films that circulate through specific venues in the city. From their offices near the center of the city, they look up and across the social landscape to create itineraries for film circulation based on their views of audiences and which films attract them. In the following sections of this chapter, I engage with film distributors and their publics to explore how their social imagination of this heterogeneous city, or the urban imaginary, is immanent in discourses regarding the circulation of filmed commodities, on the one hand, and, on the other, how the mobility and materiality of circulation infrastructures index and rank particular moviegoing publics. Film distribution, to be sure, is not a passive conduit between consumption and production. This chapter shows that film distribution is an active medium in several senses: First, it is an institutional practice of mediation that guides films between production and exhibition. Second, it is a medium of social discourse, composed of spatial plots and temporal narratives and events into which people insert themselves as mobile subjects. Third, as a spatializing practice, distribution entails an infrastructure that is discursive and material at once, through which people are propelled and channeled toward sites that conjoin social space, films, and publics.

As intermediaries between film producers, theater exhibitors, and audiences, film distributors seek to secure themselves in unstable circumstances at the conjuncture between production and consumption. Buying in order to sell, film distributors operate like banks positioned between financing and payment, controlling the circulation of film and money. How do they securely control the conditions for their profit, sustain their own institutional reproduction, and mitigate their own financial risks through the control of circulation? While the risks for the distributors in Bolivia are different from those for the international distributors in the United States, the major U.S. distributors have greater control over the flow and selection of films that Bolivia distributors receive, as I will explain. Similarly, while national distributors have the same circulatory control over the theater owners, larger Bolivian distributors also own theaters, which they may legally do in Bolivia. This means they are able to deliver audiences for the films they distribute (see Chanan 1997, 191).

The risks and instability for distributors and media institutions are due to their fundamental uncertainty about their audiences (Ang 1991). Their potential audiences are not essentially unified, circumscribed, and stable publics with necessary viewing practices; they are mobile moviegoers. Ang writes that as media institutions "desperately seek" audiences, they freeze, objectify, and contain the circulation of audiences within taxonomic categories. To ensure institutional success, as Ang shows, media institutions do not passively "know" their audiences as if they were waiting to be registered and reeled in. As she writes regarding television institutions, they formulate their knowledge practices toward "making the audience visible in such a way that it helps the institutions to increase their power to get their relationship with audience under control, and this can only be done by symbolically constructing 'television audience' as an objectified category of others that can be controlled, that is contained in the interest of a predetermined institutional goal" (Ang 1991, 7). If theaters can be seen as material containers in which specific types of mobile audiences are suspended, become visible, and encounter films placed there to lure them inside, then, to recall José's account of audience specificity outside the Esmeralda, "to know the parameters of the people" is a crucial practice for distributors who envision how specific audiences pertain to specific theater locations. In the uncertain circumstances in which they operate, media institutions construct and identify specific audiences by reflecting on the wider social or urban imaginary—the framework with which people imagine their own social existence.[1] For media distributors, this includes the mutual social, material, spatial, and temporal boundaries, locations, and expectations that organize the social field they share with their audiences. Though not uniformly, moviegoers reflect on their locations in the city's social imaginary when they view themselves as plausible audiences.

In order to trace out these multiple sight lines, I build on Ang's emphasis on how media institutions make publics visible through their arrangement in fixed categories. But I continue to pursue my interest in the mobility of film traffic and film's transient audiences. How are the divided interests and manifold social positions of audiences aggregated in the itineraries of film traffic? How does circulation fuse and make audiences cohere and appear? How do distributors attempt to regulate the mobility of films across time and space through clearly defined built locations where audiences encounter films? How are social identities fixed at theater sites along the public itineraries of film circulation, and how do publics read them? Edward LiPuma and Thomas Koelble have argued that the hemispheric interconnections converging at Miami make that city an exemplar of how a "culture of circulation" constitutes the urban imaginary, "a culturally imaginary space that is created in and through the relationship between these forms of circulation and the practices of stabilization to objectify the city as a totality" (2005, 154). In La Paz, where social class and cultural identity are emplotted inversely with steep gradations in altitude and distance from the elite city center, films' debuts and their subsequent trajectories through theaters mark, divide, connect, and rank social differences along the city's canyon walls. It is this punctuated movement of filmed commodities in their travel itineraries that organizes the urban imaginary, I argue, by fashioning narratives into which film distributors and audiences insert themselves and others as subjects. Yet as much as the pathways of films form narratives, film distributors also stage the settings in which they maneuver as they select, link, and cross elements of the social imagination. It is within theaters in these narratives that specific publics of circulation eventuate.

Michel de Certeau's (1984) writing on spatial practices in cities is especially useful for understanding how film traffic traces out the contours of the social imagination in narrative form, since for him both narrative and its locations are formed through movement. Like others (e.g., Lefebvre 1991; Deleuze and Guattari 1983; Hardt 1998) interested in pursuing a post-Foucauldian account of modern social space in terms that cut through the sorted matrices of rigid and disciplinary cells, de Certeau describes how styles and rhythms of walking subvert the planned, angular, and disciplinary space of modern cities. Like speech acts, these "spatializing practices" rewrite the city; they are inscriptions that reconstitute urban space as they travel through it. As they move through space and time, spatializing practices "traverse and organize places; they select them and link them together" (115). Inherently selective, paths through the city skip and diminish some spaces while they pause at and fix upon others, erasing and diminishing while magnifying other places as they travel both space and time. As de Certeau writes, "A space treated in this way and shaped by practices is transformed into enlarged singularities and separate islands" (101). Mobility creates its own locations in the process of dividing and ranking spaces. Yet, "What the map cuts up, the story cuts across" (129). Rhythmically connecting plural, dispersed, and uneven social spaces, furthermore, spatial practices select and string locations together as a narrative path through the city. This narrativity reconfigures places as punctuated temporal moments, or episodes. The coherence of the elements of narrative, even if connected by social antagonisms that never totally resolve, is enabled through the discriminating temporal and spatial terms of the wider frame of social imagination.

De Certeau's emphasis on mobility as a signifying practice complements other approaches that have shown how spatial practices follow laws of motion (and apparent motionlessness) that ensure the accumulation of capital (Lefebvre 1991) or its mirrored processes of destruction and de valuation (Harvey 1989). De Certeau, however, was interested in revealing the elusive and unquantifiable spatial practices of pedestrian movements that subvert the modern spatialities of coded partitions, vertical layers, and power channels produced with capital. My use of de Certeau draws from his analytic emphases on the performative and narrative forms of spatial practice and turns them back onto the spaces of a modern urban scene created by film circulation.[2] Specifically, distributors direct the traffic of films through a selected series of venues over time in itineraries that are based on their knowledge of the city's "plot"—its set of historical circumstances, locations, and the identities of its different publics. The film itineraries they script not only assemble heterogeneous and incompletely knowable elements into coherent and knowable publics; they also imagine them as singular and mobile publics who can be steered to theaters set up to attract them.

If social imagination is immanent in film circulation, and circulation is a framework through which the city is imagined, known, and traveled, then circulation founds its spaces for practical action. By founding, I mean both the creative act of "providing space for the actions to be undertaken" as well as the space that is created for practice, the nominative form of the "field which serves as their base and their theater" (de Certeau 1984, 124). It is within this performative circularity of circulation, along a terrain de Certeau fittingly marks as theatrical, that film itineraries inscribe stories seemingly waiting to be told about fixed locations like cinemas and their specific publics, who also appear there as stable types who belong to them. Through these fixations, theaters and their publics appear as both "enlarged singularities and separate islands" (de Certeau, 101), formed as films travel across the city containing and joining together their subjects and locations.

If films move through narrative paths, then cinemas are plotted as spatial events within a narrative order, much like film debuts are temporal events within a chronology. This inseparable fusion of emplotted spatial elements and temporal processes is captured in Mikhail Bakhtin's idea of the chronotope that orients narrative genres in the novel. Moreover, Bakhtin says, "the chronotope is the place where the knots of the narrative are tied and untied" (1981, 250). In these terms, theaters are chronotopes in which diverse publics and divided interests are assembled into a unity. And while their unity is a tentative one that holds at least the possibility of unraveling as audiences scatter, chronotopes do frame expectations about what can unfold in an episode and who is involved. Within the narratives in which publics are plotted in film itineraries, as I will show, the publics of these chronotopes, or theater events, can be anticipated and represented as temporally ahead or behind (Wilk 2002; Fabian 1983). Chronotopes dramatically contain and define their subjects, and it is here where they undergo the fantastic flattening and amalgamation of character and the stretching and exaggeration of scale that inheres in the selectivity and timing of narrative paths.

Jerome Bruner writes, "The act of constructing a narrative, moreover, is considerably more than 'selecting' events either from real life, from memory, or from fantasy and then placing them in appropriate order. The events themselves need to be *constituted* in light of the overall narrative . . . to be made 'functions' of the story" (1991, 8). If theaters and publics are events in wider historical processes, then they too must be constituted as immobile places. As chronotopes along the narrative paths of circulation, cinemas are buildings that function to contain, regulate, and conjoin the film traffic and mass publics that move through them. It is the imaginary possibility of viewing the urban social terrain as occupied by static architectural structures that enables the mobile publics they enclose to appear isomorphically as objectified and fixed types, thereby countering a more indeterminate image of them as mobile and plural subjects. De Certeau's distinction between places and spaces (and their parallel pair, the map and the tour; 1984, 117–21) is relevant here. While places are a stable and ordered "instantaneous configuration of positions," space has in view the "intersections of mobile elements . . . actuated by the ensemble of movements deployed within it." His important distinction reveals how both theater buildings as well as the publics they contain can be seen as processes and as concatenations of heterogeneous mobile elements.[3] We can say therefore that film itineraries are not only narrative paths through a series of selected venues; they are narrative operations that convert mobile spaces into fixed places, constituting cinemas as "enlarged singularities and separate islands" in suspended animation, where they function to provide predictable stability and repeatable uniformity.[4] The reiterations of this continuous mobility accrue so that distributors can predict and objectify particular publics as potential audiences for a series of profitable and successive film debuts over time.

Distributors script their itineraries and address their publics from a discursive universe in which it is possible to objectify mobile spaces as fixed places. They also draw from the wider terms of a social imaginary consisting of the same historically available narratives about publics, circulation, and theaters as devices with which people typically recognize particular urban publics. In other words, the publics of circulation do not appear as entirely fictitious, as the exclusive products of *someone else's* imagination. This circularity with which film distribution produces its public is also a more general procedure for bringing publics into being through the circulation of texts. Michael Warner writes, "The circularity is essential to the phenomenon. A public might be real and efficacious, but its reality lies in just this reflexivity by which an addressable object is conjured into being in order to enable the very discourse that gives it existence" (2002, 51). While distributors presuppose their particular audiences, as if differentiated publics appear as already part of the social landscape, those who do show up for a film meet their texts halfway, responding as their respective publics, for the moment, and confirming the social imaginary. Of this encounter, Warner says, "punctual circulation turns these exchanges into a scene with its own expectations" (66). If mobile films and transient publics do intersect and encounter each other in an exchange, then the ticket box office is its scenario. When money is exchanged for access, the moment is quantified and space is put in suspended animation—the building, its public, and the value of the film—except the movie itself. In this moment, the circularity of circulation appears to come full circle.[5]

▶
─────────────────────────────────────

Film Distribution and the Contours of Social Imagination

Carlos Alvarez has worked in film distribution in Latin America for thirty years. He worked in the offices of Fox in Peru and Ecuador until the 1970s and has owned an independent distributor, Cinema Internacional, since 1982. His map of La Paz is a social imaginary of difference that contains an argument that people must see films in their own social spaces:

> It is known that the people from the Center do not go to the neighborhood cinemas because of their location and that the popular classes do not come to the Center. The Center has a public from neighborhoods like Sopocachi, all of the Zona Sur, Obrajes, and Calacoto. Another level. The upper middle class. The people over here [he points out and upward], they are catalogued like *populacho* the masses; public that is part *campesino* [rural peasant]. So the films shown here in the Center, the nominees and prizewinners, are of a different type—finer—they are for a more refined taste. The others have their *cines populares* and go there. Now they have their own "advantages." Here they show only one film in the Center. In the *cines populares* they show triple, double, or continuous. The people want quantity. They can see two or three for one price that does not exceed sixty cents of a dollar. And they are happy. . . .
>
> This barrier between one public and another has always existed. Always existed. On the Montes Avenue, an extension of the Prado, there is the Cinema Mexico, which showed only Mexican films fifty-two weeks a year. Double. They showed two films. If they put the same films in other theaters, nobody went. Or very few people went to that cinema. . . . The people do not mix here in the Center. It's rare. It's very marked, Señor.

Alvarez is among six or so independent distributors who buy copies of used older (more than three years old) Hollywood films, B movies, and independent material for $2,000 to $3,000 and circulate them in the secondary and tertiary cinemas around the country.[6]

Two other national distributors, López Films and ZW Films, have exclusive rights to rent and distribute new Hollywood releases, and each has arrangements with specific "majors," the U.S.–based distributors who take the greater risks of actually buying the films; their rent on the film is a commission based on a film's local income. During the first week of exhibition, distributors remit up to 60 percent of the gross earnings to the U.S. major distributors as their rent for films; then their rent slides to 40 percent over the following two to three years. Local distributors also divide their leases with the theaters on a sliding scale from a 60/40 to a 40/60 percent split. Because the producer-distributors in the United States may set a quota for the first weeks of exhibition so they can pay off their own investment loans quickly in order to pay less interest, it is important to debut films where they will do best commercially in a short amount of time. To maximize profit from the earliest audiences, theaters have urban identities; that is, distributors and exhibitors create spaces—such as the Center—where money is concentrated and the prices can be conventionally higher. This is a system of urban social space that distributors must create and protect, as the distributor Manuel López implies:

> Logically we put the best films in the best cinemas. For example, Cinema Monje Campero always has well-chosen material. Why? Because they [the viewers] are demanding too. And because it is the best cinema in Bolivia commercially and because it's among the best-equipped cinemas . . . If a cinema is number one, we have to try to take care of that cinema. If it specializes in a certain type of material, then we try to give it to them repeatedly.

Revealing the uncertainties of film distribution, however, one manager of a small neighborhood cinema could not explain why film genres are associated with specific cinemas:

> If we show a film from Monje Campero here, it does not work because every theater has its public. Monje Campero does not show *las chinas* [martial arts]. And in the cinemas around here—Madrid, Imperio—they like pure *chinas*. Pure action. Below, they like the social films. . . . The truth is that I have no idea why they like it. But in these zones they like these films.

For other distributor-exhibitors, there are no social differences among audiences of their material. At Cinema Murillo, only a few blocks up from the Center, pornography is usually shown. The managers there told me, "Here there is no class distinction. People who like these films come here from all social classes." In discussions about cinema exhibition sites and their audiences, people in La Paz suggested to me that these managers are guarding their business from being degraded by association with "the lower classes who go there." Yet in contrast with these two readings of attendance there, it was mostly male middle-class bureaucrats and young men whom I observed attending Cinema Murillo. Despite the blurring of classes in discourse about the theater, it is gender differences that are visible.

More certain about the divisions in the cinemascape, perhaps, the president of the successful distributor who handled 75 percent of the new films in 1990, Manuel López of López Films, explained to me how cultural divisions intrinsically separate the audiences:

> The peasants feel forced to come to the city because the style of life is better, relatively. They want to wear shoes. They want to dress like urban people. . . . If he had potable water, if he had gas to cook with, access to electricity, his television, the peasant would not come. We would not have the invasion, the migration of peasants to the city.

López sees assimilation as natural because of the attractiveness of urban comforts and, as he also explained to me, because the government will not redistribute money in the countryside. Here in the city, he said, rural immigrants have no time to go to the cinema and must spend all of their time selling "some little thing. Besides they have a 'super-special'

Figure 6. Cinema Madrid, on a main boulevard through the cholo commercial zones, offers action and martial arts films.

Figure 7. Cinema Ebro is a small neighborhood cinema in residential upper San Pedro that screens a variety of three films for a single ticket up to a year after their debuts in the Center.

mentality." López went on to subvert the linear narrative of urban assimilation because rural and urban native culture determine the extent of their capacity for modern urban life:

> Let's say this country arrives at a moment of fantasy, that it would have money to get everything in the world it wants. First, the peasant does not take care of things. Never is he going to care for things because he is not used to that. If you give him a refrigerator, he'll have it until he breaks it, and if he does, he is not going to be able to fix it. It's complicated. It would be a little difficult.

Alvarez's map of social barriers and López's views on assimilation follow a local model for cataloging and ranking people in the city according to fixed cultural differences and hierarchies. They provide U.S. film producers, who now do more than half of their distribution outside the United States, with local maps of publics and the itineraries for distributing films.[7] The situation is not easily dichotomized for distributors who mediate traffic between theaters and their audiences on the one hand and the major distributors on the other. While the itineraries for films traveling within the city are written by local distributors, choices about which films will travel to Bolivia are made elsewhere. As Z. Willi of ZW Films explained,

> In my case, I depend on the Panama office [of United International Pictures, which distributes Metro-Goldwyn, Paramount, Universal, and United Artists]. That is because Panama distributes to Venezuela, Central America, and Bolivia. So they choose and say, "Take this." And many times I see the list of some of the films available that I have not received. [If I ask for something from it] "It's not worth it," they say, "because it has not done well, the film has done poorly. You will not do anything."

▶
_____

Public Reflections of the Cinemascape

In La Paz film debuts are revealing junctures. Each time the same film debuts is a unique event since each occurs in a theater in a new paying sector of the urban audience who attends films. As a film moves through cinemas on its itinerary, it separates sites of exhibition to which audiences disperse themselves and connects them in a narrative that emplots difference and the hierarchical organization of local terms of class, cultural identity, and urban space. People in the city also reflexively insert themselves into the topological spaces in the itineraries of film distribution to index social and cultural hierarchies and differences. As Reynaldo, a twenty-three-year-old university student, defines the popular classes:

It does not refer to the general public, but to the lower middle class and poor people. . . . They are from zones higher up in the city and further from the Center. The peripheral zones. People who work in the streets. These are people who do not go to the cinema, for example, because they do not have the money. You will see these people at cinemas like Cinema Mexico, where they show Mexican films; Cinema Center; or Cinema Murillo. They cost three bolivianos and some show two films for the one price. There are all types of films shown: action, comedy, and martial arts. I do not know why so many people like them. Eventually the big movies go there. First, they debut at a cinema like Monje Campero, then they go to a smaller cheaper cinema.

Marcos, fifty, a professional engineer who lives near the Center, uses cinema locations to encircle the psychology of immigrant classes:

The people from peripheral zones that go to the neighborhood cinemas go because they have less self-esteem, they are humble people *(gente humilde)*. Those cinemas are cheaper and not as nice as the others. . . . On Sundays they are filled with the *cholitas* [young Aymara women domestic employees] who have Sundays off.

And Andrea, a thirty-two-year-old teacher who lives in an older popular neighborhood, used cinema culture to define elite social status:

I had a friend at the university from Calacoto [in the elite Southern Zone]. She always used clothing styles that she saw in movies. During a movie she would say, "Look at that outfit," and then go have the same thing made. The Southern Zone is another world. People down there—probably because of their economic position—are oriented toward the foreign. Clothing, music, film, and a way of life—going to the supermarket, for example. You will not see them playing folklore music. It really has to do with where you are born. They have the attitude that they are better than the rest and do not associate with us. All the classes up here have more in common than any of us do with them—the same music, ways of dressing, and ways of thinking.

Andrea's account of her friend from the wealthy Calacoto neighborhood evokes how clothing may be used to cohabit the space of Hollywood media culture. While this practice represents an immediate social boundary for Andrea, people also position themselves within narratives of film itineraries that mark out shared national subject positions. The arrival of Francis Coppola's *Dracula* at the Cinema Monje Campero in Bolivia occurred only a week after its arrival in Buenos Aires, for example, but the event was a month and a half behind its U.S. debut in November 1992. Indeed, the well-known trickle-down story of the movement of films outward from the Monje Campero in the city center reiterates an old colonial story about cultural traffic between codependent centers and peripheries. As Richard Wilk has written regarding television programming in Belize, pre–satellite era media delivery systems served as "timekeepers" for a colonial modernity in which the staggered arrivals of programs denied coevalness, ranked social groups and concentrated wealth (2002); this bolstered the bourgeois class and its definition of the country as culturally dependent. While proliferating bootlegged video copies simultaneously subvert colonial paths and temporalities in Bolivia, social discourse about films nevertheless foregrounds the traffic of official copies of films to Bolivia and through the circuit of theaters in La Paz.

In the public narratives in which they are embedded, film debuts provide spectacular evidence of the wider circuits traced out by the transnational cultural traffic in which Bolivians are emplotted near the end of pathways of commodities designed, assembled, or sometimes even used earlier and elsewhere in industrial and wealthier countries up in the "advanced" North. When people comment, "Bolivia is always behind," for example, they translate national affiliation into a narrative marked by limits to coeval status with other more "advanced" locations. "Bolivia will always be the child of the United States," some people say regarding the delayed appearance of films and other commodities, as well as about their currency's slipping exchange rate against the dollar; the saying also implicates these movements within larger structures of political and economic subordination from North to South. Bolivians also sarcastically remark that their worn-out military passenger airplanes were donated by the United States "as if they were gifts." The "gifts" and the commodities in this hand-me-down flow lose value in each exchange as they descend ranks within a circulatory regime that obtains quicker and larger profits in the earliest points of transaction. Paper currency itself wears out with circulation and use in La Paz, taking on a dirty and vulgar sheen so that it loses value. It is quite common for official stores and offices as well as market vendors to reject even slightly torn or crumpled currency in transactions. In the same way, degrading films and pirated videos move on from each preceding use, marking each new public as temporally "behind" and socially "beneath" its preceding publics who had the interest and/or the social status to obtain access to them earlier. Within these contemporary international neocolonial circuits, to extend Ana López's (2000a) formulation of early-twentieth-century Latin America, modernity and "progress" arrive in Latin America first as a fantasy in the vehicle of cinema, as subsequent chapters will describe.

Distributing Hollywood: Film Genres and their Publics

Global distribution from the Hollywood majors has overwhelmingly re-placed films from "national cinemas" whose circulation began to decline in the 1970s following the expanding television industry and the start of "blockbuster" financing. Social discourses of distributors also sustain the circulation of films for the Hollywood majors through their configura-tions of local audiences. I asked distributors if they thought that U.S. films alienated people from their own culture, as leftist filmmakers in Bolivia had argued forcibly for years. Unsurprisingly, no distributor claimed to be the agent of U.S. expansionism to me. Manuel López and Z. Willi pointed out that some films had spurred "superficial" fads in dancing, hairstyle, and clothing for short periods. López said that rap music was briefly popu-lar among youth who traveled to the United States and knew its dances and among some children who saw *Ninja Turtles* films. Salsa, he said, was introduced in Bolivia in the film *Salsa,* but the dance is still not generally very popular here. Willi pointed out that people often say, "The foreign is always better," but in terms of cultural alienation, he said,

> Not necessarily from the United States, but across our own borders. No. I do not see the U.S. films as alienating. But I see it in Mexican films, for ex-ample. . . . If you see the TV series *Chavo del Ocho* and you hear the people here say, "You are in the right!" or *"chavos,"* then people are changing how they speak. That is alienating! [He laughs.] Because it is changing how people speak.

As the smaller popular cinemas add more Hollywood reprises to their programming, special effects in the major blockbuster films are replacing what the independent distributor Carlos Alvarez called "the spectacular material" of martial arts and B-movie violence. For Alvarez, the effect of the higher investments in the exhibitionary aspect of cinema since the 1970s has been that Hollywood films have achieved the earlier fantasy of a "universal language" (Hansen 1991): "The American films are more assimilable, I would say, here in Bolivia. They are assimilated more. The public apprehends them faster. That is why the films are more successful."

Z. Willi, president of ZW Films, explained the increase in Holly-wood films in "two aspects": the crisis in Mexican cinema and the over-saturation of Mexican films that appeared on the private TV channels that opened and began transmitting in the early 1980s. As a result, he said, the cinemas have had to use Hollywood films to compete with and distinguish their programming from television. Willi reasoned that people also would get bored with that material because of its increasing circulation in the cinemas and on TV. In his reading of the shift to Hollywood films, however, he also sees a change in peoples' motives:

> What do they look for in cinema? Few people go intending to analyze the film. The majority go for a distraction. We live in a country that has a lot going on, many problems. So to go to think in the cinema is not agreeable. The majority looks for something agreeable, to relax for a moment, to reduce and get rid of stress. For a moment.

Willi argued that the quality and distraction that audiences now look for is found in commercial Hollywood films: "For me American cinema is its technique, its focus on some things, with a lot of technique. That is, very well made." The American version of a story of the survivors of a plane crash in the Andes was much better made than its Mexican version, he said. He believes audiences are captured by the technical quality and special effects of Hollywood cinema. "By using modern equipment and computers they can do anything, effects that are incredible."

Similarly, seeing the visual exhibitions of Hollywood films as a sign of finance capital, Manuel López observes that the increased distribution of better Hollywood films among popular cinemas means a concurrent improvement in the mentality of audiences:

> Until fifteen, twenty years ago, Bolivia was a market where the Mexican films worked very well because the public was accustomed to it. The mentality has been changing slowly. . . . I think there is a change because the people are getting used to seeing a certain type of film. The quality of American cinema is always better than the Mexican cinema. As one gets accustomed to American cinema, one leaves the other. Why? Because the other has no quality, the other has had all the same actors. It does not have much innovation. There is no one type of film that one wants to see. As one North American has told me, [in English] "The people are so smart." The public is very awake now.

López adds that the "smarter public now can choose to see a film . . . it can laugh at. They are not going to see a film that is ambiguous, where you have to think after seeing the film. You leave and you cannot understand some things . . . like European films." Each of the distributors perpetuated the hegemonic definition of cinema as diversionary entertainment, rather than defining it as a medium for social analysis and critique as filmmakers in Bolivia have.

Distributors' images of audiences' capacities also addressed the replacement of Spanish-speaking films with English-speaking and Spanish-subtitled films. The audiences, some distributors pointed out, are more literate than before and are now accustomed to reading Spanish subtitles. Carlos Alvarez observes,

I understand that the public has accustomed itself to subtitling, to the "sub-titles" of the films. The people do not know how to speak it, they do not know how to read it fluently, but they are accustomed to the English phonetics. It is the actor that talks in English, in fact. Many people do not need to look at the words. It's enough that the actor is American and English to be preferred. I have distributed a mountain of Russian films, but under one condition, that they are dubbed in English. Dubbed and then subtitled. So the Russian, spoken in Russian and translated [subtitled] does not work.

Whereas people in white upper and middle classes read subtitles and watch dramatic narratives and character dilemmas, many people in the immigrant and popular classes told me they read very little of the subtitles, and most popular discourse about films is about their exhibitionary rather than narrative qualities. Because of their visual narratives and special effects, action films are the most popular, interesting, and worth the money to see in a cinema, people explained to me. I found that action films are the most popular in video stores across the city as well. The manager of the official video store Erol's in the middle-class Sopocachi told me that violent and action films were very popular in La Paz because they differed from the lives of audiences:

Clearly people prefer the films with violence and action. It is because there is not much violence in Bolivia. The streets are tranquil, unlike those of Mexico and the United States, for example. There are protest marches and other incidents here, but it is generally a peaceful place.

Though he mentions popular protest, his view of urban audiences does not associate violent films with the potentially threatening immigrant masses lining the canyon walls above. He twists around the violence of action films to define a peaceful city (La Paz) by contrast. Further, well-to-do men in La Paz characterized an "Aymara psychology" among the popular classes as "closed" and "inexpressive," despite the visible popular protest marches and festivals that move through the Center. In this social imaginary, the popular classes who see the same, or possibly more, action, terror, and martial arts films cannot be incited by them because of an apparent innate passive psychology.

The City as Film Festival

Narratives about the pathways of film circulation are examples of what Anna Tsing calls "circulation rhetoric" (2000). In this case, the social discourses of distributors and publics also articulate what Greg Urban calls a "metaculture" (2001) that propels and directs cultural media along specific itineraries. For example, in his book on Danish cinema (2005), Mette Hjort shows how the Danish film movement Dogma 95 explicitly addressed issues of circulation by creating a metaculture about their works beyond the films' content and plot in order to intensify interest and boost their films' ability to travel globally. In this chapter, I have focused on how distributors and their publics speak about circulation and insert themselves and others as subjects in the narratives, or biographies, formed by the itineraries of films in motion, thereby attaching specific publics to particular locations in the circuits of cinema. In La Paz, moviegoers who appear at movie theaters momentarily become the publics of these narratives about circulation, closing a circuit between the historical world and urban imagination.

To close this chapter, I return to its point of departure on the canyon rim above La Paz, commonly known as the *ceja* (brow). From the immigrant neighborhoods high above the Center, the buildings below are monuments to the authority of those who occupy its offices, but they also appear as a miniature and peripheral city, its excesses perceptibly diminished and displaced, its gazes upward reduced to a glimpse and a glance.

Figure 8. La Paz viewed bifocally: alternate sightlines downward toward the center of La Paz from the canyon rim and upward from the Center toward the popular neighborhoods above converge on a mirrored office building in the Center of La Paz.

Quite vividly, the glitzy Center of La Paz has emerged as a central crucible of technology, politics, capitalist accumulation, and transnational media in twentieth-century Bolivia. From inside the high-rise buildings clustered in the bottom of the canyon, with neighborhoods virtually revolving around them, the view strikingly suggests the image of the power center of a panopticon, the well-known metaphor for the apparatus of the invisible and omniscient gaze of modern authority that has informed the gridded spatial organization of Latin American urbanism (Goldstein 2004 and Rama 1996). Yet while the media institutions located here seek to know, objectify, differentiate, and make their audiences visible, distributors in the Center are fundamentally uncertain about them (Ang 1991). They cannot see their audiences directly nor monitor them constantly; ultimately, they can only guess at the desires and activities of their publics. Under these circumstances, as if in a mirror, the looking relations simultaneously run in the reverse direction: The populace is imagined to include spectators whose vision is directed toward the display of concentrated capital and media power. The spectacle of theaters like the Monje Campero, *Dracula*'s traveling Great Debut banner, and the gasp at the wealth on the screen in the Cinema Esmeralda are all reflected here. Indeed, the awards at the annual "Llama de Plata" film festival in La Paz are given to the distributors who circulate the winning films. If the modern city is an event or a spectacle, as some have suggested, then in the imaginary of film circulation it looks like a film festival.[8]

Along the circuits of film distribution in La Paz, attention runs both ways and the regimes of surveillance and spectacle coincide (see Crary 1990). In what Tony Bennett calls an "exhibitionary complex" (1994), power and regulatory forces are on permanent display that not only incorporate and reverse the orientation of the panoptic gaze but also form "a technology of vision which serves not to atomize and disperse the crowd but to regulate it, and to do so by rendering it visible to itself, by making the crowd the ultimate spectacle" (131–32). In these visual relations, as Bennett (126) argues, crowds see themselves mirrored as both subjects and objects, and thus they regulate themselves as the ambulatory publics that observe, in both senses of the term, particular kinds of exhibitions. Media institutions are not only "desperately seeking the audience," using their own categories to map the cinemascape anonymously and visibly objectifying the populace in order to know and control it, as Ang wrote (1991); they are desperately seeking attention too, staging their own attractions to set in motion audiences who will make themselves visible and distinct as publics at the moment they appear at their pertinent cinemas. In short, distributors "put on a show, and see who shows up" (Warner 2004, 82).

At their conjuncture, a cinemagoing public isomorphically becomes as much an ephemeral event as the films they show up to see, both delimited by the architectural space of the theater and the duration of the event and both assembled from disparate sources beyond the moment. If a modern Latin American city can be viewed as a visually arresting spectacle (Goldstein 2004), then in this reading, the modern arrangement, with its control center at the bottom of the canyon bowl, can be seen as a panopticon as much as a central stage in a performance arena.

This chapter argues that the mobility of culture and publics through modern urban spaces must be theorized in terms of their arrangement and visibility in space and time. In the narratives of circulation, films, distributors, and theaters display the itineraries and locations they have inscribed in the cinemascape as spectacles (Today! Grand Debut!) to which they seek to attract their imagined publics. Reading these itineraries, audiences maneuver their own mobility, assemble, and become visible as publics at the sites of exhibition where they momentarily pertain—and then scatter.

▶

Arrival Scenes

Announcing one of the earliest public cinema exhibitions in the center of
La Paz in 1904, the social column of the newspaper *El Comercio* flaunted
the "cinematograph" itself as the arrival of a new kind of machinery:
"'The apparatus . . . is ultra-modern, up-to-date, and it will be a spectacle
worth seeing'" (in Dagron 1982, 32). Rather than by storytelling, and
unlike photography, the attraction of early cinema featured its technological capacity to present brief scenes composed of images in continuous
perceptual motion (Gunning 1986).[1] The technologies and experiences
of perceptual movement became a defining feature of twentieth-century
modernity in forms such as railroads and department stores (Schivelbush
1986), shopping malls and cinemas (Friedberg 1993), and, in other ways,
money (Simmel 1900). These mobile systems for transporting commodities and representing modern capitalist relations, to follow Henri Lefebvre
(1991), are infrastructures that mediate and conjoin other kinds of traffic and power. In this sense, the cinema projector ("the apparatus") was
connected to a wider circulatory system as soon as it was plugged into the
infrastructure of electricity. As an extension of the power grid, the cinema
turned the city's new electric infrastructure into a spectacle that shed light
on the uneven and selective distribution of power, in both senses of the
term, along key lines of difference. The movement of electricity through
urban locations undermines a view of cities as bounded and static collec-
tions of discrete autonomous buildings (Palus 2005, 185). Yet if electric
current reveals the city's internal motion, it also points to material connections to wider infrastructures of power at the turn of the century. Electrification in La Paz developed as part of the "empires of light" (Jonnes 2004)

created with corporate capital as well as it was plugged into corporate global media systems controlling the early transcontinental telegraph cables (Pike and Winseck 2004). Embedded in these infrastructures, the cinema opened up and channeled relations between viewers along worldwide commercial circuits and colonial trade routes. Yet even before electrification, the travelogue films that dominated early cinema were performances of visual motion that registered the worldly travels of itinerant showmen along these routes (Ruoff 2006). The cinema apparatus has put the distribution and infrastructures of modern forms of power on visible display.

As in much of the world, cinema exhibition began in Bolivia amid the arrival of agents from the Lumière Brothers film company of France, who had dispersed on an enterprise to record and exhibit films around the world and then return to European audiences with fifty-second films of exotic places, many of them colonies. Their agents traveled with cinematographs, hand-cranked, wood-encased devices invented in 1896 (just as Bram Stoker was finishing writing *Dracula*) that could exhibit, shoot, and develop films. The Lumière Company combined production, distribution, and exhibition within a single integrated manually powered machine. While there was nothing new about where the Lumière agents traveled—along established colonial pathways—they reconfigured these trade routes and circulatory infrastructures into circuits of communication through which cinematic looks and affiliations were exchanged and forged across the world. These itinerant showmen occasionally added films of local views to their exhibitions of European films held in private homes and other semiprivate spaces of the La Paz elite families. Most of the earliest exhibitions in La Paz were held in the elite Teatro Municipal and in homes of the criollo upper classes (Dagron 1982, 32), who considered themselves to be an extension of European civilization. A newspaper announcement in 1907 proclaimed a program of short films as the "Debut of Scenes Never Viewed . . . The Latest from Paris." By expanding what Deborah Poole (1997) describes as a transatlantic Andean photographic image world to include motion pictures, the circuits of film traffic also became channels through which viewers could visually forge and verify imagined affiliations with counterparts in other capitals and cities such as Paris and New York.

By the second decade of the twentieth century, biograph or itinerant exhibition companies began to rent space to install Edison's new electric-powered Vitascope in the center of the city. The emerging cinemascape was being plugged into the infrastructure of electric current, and its limited distribution along power lines of class and culture. The small *biógrafo* theaters showed short single-reel imported "silent" films, most of which were from the Lumière Brothers and the Pathé Brothers, also of France, which had acquired Lumière patents in 1902 and were rapidly opening offices worldwide (Cook 1990, 49). Until the First World War, the Pathé Brothers dominated the world film circuits by industrially manufacturing projection equipment and distributing films throughout the European colonies and the Americas. To compete, Edison and U.S. film distributors began to package their machines with pirated copies of Lumière films, but with the credits and references to the French companies removed (Susz 1985, 35). Yet once the *biógrafos* became popularized and the flow of films increased and settled in rented theaters across the cinemascape, the initial elite status of the cinema permanently declined.

With the settlement and popularization of cinema, elite families held onto their definitions of privileged art and class practices—music, live theater, and literature—where literacy in Spanish and European languages was a mark of their status. They complained that while Buenos Aires had performances by live actors, it appeared to them that La Paz merely had cinema (Susz 1990, 32). Cinema was not art, they declared, but merely a diversion and a "spectacle without cultural value" (in Dagron 1982, 45). As films began to circulate through the city's peripheral zones the status of cinema degraded for the elites. For as the popularity of cinema was expanding in the social spaces among rapidly expanding immigrant, middle-class, and laboring publics, films came in contact with urban spaces where mestizos and urban Indians were romanticizing, flaunting, and mounting indigenous heritage and culture as potent political forces in La Paz. Within a century, these new popular and middle classes would emerge as protagonists of Bolivian modernity.

This historical chapter explores how these new urban publics were assembled in the built spaces and international circuits of cinema in La Paz from the twentieth to the twenty-first centuries. How did the contours of the broader cultural movements and class antagonisms in the emerging capital reflect the location, architecture, and itineraries of film? Responding to the expansion of the city's population up the canyon walls, municipal authorities arranged and classified the cityscape with centralizing models of urban planning in which social status declined with distance from the city center (Goldstein 2004, 8–9). While the compartmentalization of space is a powerful form of ordering publics, I examine how film traffic moving *across* these urban social spaces and *through* theaters also stabilized publics during a period of rapid urbanization and modernization. In that La Paz became Bolivia's capital city, enmeshed in the networks of film distribution extending beyond

Bolivia, I trace the emergence of built environments and publics that eventuated from circulating films, technologies, trade practices, and political ideologies and movements. If the infrastructure of film circulation regulates the mobility of the rising popular classes in the capital city, then what are the *counter*itineraries of piracy and popular culture that divert the dominant circuits of cinema?

This chapter also asks, how does the unevenness in the spatiality and timing of circulation bear on the national project? In Bolivia, the cinema may have coincided with new modern temporal and spatial modes of travel and perception and even may have been instrumental in forming a visual mode of collective self-awareness that consolidated a longing for national affiliation that could be asserted to mark modern status (López 2000a, 53), but the actual infrastructures for media circulation hardly connected a synchronous or horizontal national "community" (Anderson 1983). First, cinema in Bolivia was a foreign import that presented experiences of political and economic modernization located elsewhere well before such structural changes were adapted as actual historical projects (López 2000a, 48; Schelling 2000, 24). Second, cinema might have imagined and placed consumer modernity on the horizon as an accessible attraction, but its uneven circulation made that modern life a possibility for selected groups in La Paz, as already evidenced by the specific itineraries of film traffic in the city discussed in chapter 1. Here, I trace how the emergence of the network of theaters in the cinemascape in La Paz reproduced social asymmetries rooted deeply in the experiences and infrastructures of colonialism and the national project. By calling attention to social status, the traffic through the cinemas created a field of spatial simultaneity and temporal discontinuity between social groups, marking the extent of proximity and participation in modern commodity capitalism in narratives of *uneven* national progress.

▶──

La Paz Becomes the Media Capital

As the cinema was arriving at the turn of the twentieth century, along with new infrastructures of capitalist modernity such as railroads and telegraphs, La Paz was emerging as the new political and economic capital of Bolivia. As a tin-mining oligarchy was replacing the powerful silver mine barons to the south in Sucre (Klein 1992, 158–63), the Liberal Party regimes fostered the rise of a new educated, professional mestizo middle class to manage the private and expanding state enterprises, including the army, as they sought to modernize the state. The reorganization and expansion of the hacienda system under President Montes also displaced many indigenous Aymara- and Quechua-speaking families on the rural Altiplano. Settling in the higher parts of the city canyon in the peripheral parishes, which were much lower than today, these new families began to engage themselves in expanding nonagricultural activities such as artisan work, unofficial trade and merchandising, wage labor, and positions in the growing private, government, and military bureaucracies (Barragán 1990). The rapidly growing city of more than 50,000 combined agrarian with new manufacturing sectors as the economic and cultural center and political capital of the state appeared to concentrate in La Paz, which became a potent crucible in the circulation of new mestizo nationalist ideologies.

After the elite Teatro Municipal gave its last biograph exhibition in 1911, cinema construction grew fastest in the city blocks surrounding Plaza Murillo to attract members of the new professional middle and working classes. As the construction of permanent cinemas expanded, however, spectators were dispersed along the two sides of the Prado that runs along the bottom of the city canyon. Cinema Biógrafo Paris was located on the Plaza Murillo, the new de facto Bolivian government seat, to serve the widening strata of private and government professionals. Its fierce competitor El Cinema Teatro was just a few blocks below and advertised itself in lavish terms: with "'hygienic conditions, it is open and ventilated, and its films are varied and excellent, its exhibitions perfect'" (Dagron 1982, 48). The owner of the Teatro also built the Cinema Popular almost directly across the Prado on Calle Sagarnaga at the foot of the street markets operated by rural-urban networks of immigrant Aymara vendors, artisans, and agricultural traders and their mestizo families. The distribution of theaters in the Center and the popular neighborhoods corresponded to identities that reflected the deeply entrenched "rural" and "urban" dichotomies that were already splitting the city along the Prado: laboring mestizos and immigrant cholos on the western rising side, and criollos, criollo mestizos, and *blancos* (whites) on the east and descending to the south. By the mid-1920s, there were four permanent cinemas operating in the city blocks around Plaza Murillo, all showing films mostly from U.S. producer-distributors (Dagron 1982). Despite the assumptions of the rising ideology of *mestizaje* (cultural mixing) that immigrants would assimilate into Western modernity in the city, a rigid race and class hierarchy continued to divide cinemagoers in urban space. Since urban professionals considered immigrant Indians more civilized than their rural counterparts, they saw the immigrant neighborhoods and popular zones as possible sites of assimilation and modernization (Barragán 1990, 233). Furthermore, Aymaras and Quechuas were tacitly not permitted to enter the Center of the city. Apart from the Cinema Popular, only one other cinema (Cinema Colón, now the Cinema Center) opened in the lower elevations of the immigrant and working-class side of the city in the 1930s, due to the worldwide Depression hitting the exposed markets of the Bolivian mining economy.

At their position in circuits of international film distribution, distributors in La Paz faced few regulatory barriers in importing U.S. and European films (Susz 1985). While the Bolivian distributors and spectators may have aligned themselves with their bourgeois counterparts in the United States and Europe, the U.S. film distributors considered Latin American audiences to be composed of "'the very poor or uneducated,'" and they sent used, scratched, and incomplete film prints to this market (Usabel 1982, 12–13). Hollywood film companies quickly filled the emptying global distribution paths used by Pathé after World War I ruined the European economy. They replaced the French and Italian distribution in Latin America and the European colonies (Donaghue 1987). Since films were amortized in their domestic U.S. market, all the foreign income earned by Hollywood films was profit, which afforded the increased industrialization of cinema and, aesthetically, a new industrial standard with expensive synchronous-sound films made in sound- and light-controlled studios. By 1922, the United States "controlled" 95 percent of the South American market, 95 percent of Australia's; 85 percent of continental Europe's; 85 percent of Britain's; and 8 percent of the Far East (Usabel 1982, xv). In Paceño cinemas, reprises of films from U.S. studios occupied the most time on the screens; yet 61 percent of the 180 films that circulated in 1921 were new releases from the United States (Susz 1990, 30), while the balance consisted of older European and some Latin American films.

While inexpensive short newsreels made in Bolivia were placed as preliminaries to the commercial features (see chapters 3 and 4), cinema was frequently maligned in the press and it was characterized and regulated within moral discourses of the government and press-controlling elite in the context of rapidly expanding popular sectors. The first of a number of government agencies to do so, an "inspectorate of spectacles" already had been policing the importation and exhibition of French and U.S. films since 1908. Theater exhibitions, especially those attended by children, were monitored by on-site police who were given discretion to censor the exhibition of films. It was not only the immoral content of films that posed a moral threat, however. Beginning in 1918, municipal inspectors and censors controlled prices and decreed that theaters sell tickets for specifically numbered seat locations, a practice that continues today, to preclude theater owners from selling more tickets than they have seats. The Biografo Paris was caught selling tickets to the same film twice by simply renaming a film for subsequent exhibition. An office for the "Judge of Spectacles" was established to inspect the quality of film copies and to regulate theater practices (Dagron 1979, 52).

Paralleling municipal censorship, Paceño newspapers owned by aristocratic families also discriminated against films. They could affect the popularity of individual films; in 1927, three films were censored merely for their titles (Dagron 1979, 55). Cinema was blamed as the cause of bad eyesight and poor health and considered a corrupting influence on children. In 1921 a series of negative and scandalous articles in *El Diario* blaming cinema exhibitions for a flu outbreak resulted in the temporary closure of La Paz cinemas. Such responses can be interpreted as an effort by the criollo government and press to contain the growing mestizo middle-class professionals now attending the new "biógrafo" cinemas in the elite Center. In the immigrant neighborhoods rising up the canyon's western wall, the press was also maligning the patron saint festivals, such as the one in the parish of Gran Poder, whose festival was gaining citywide visibility by the 1920s (Albó and Preiswerk 1986). Both cinema and the festival parades comprised spectacular scenes of moving imagery that challenged the dominant criollo narratives of national identity (Himpele 2003).

If visual spectacle was one attraction of the cinema, the envelope of the event extended to the material architecture of theater spaces as well as the performances of the moviegoers themselves. A ticket to a filmed commodity included the experience of its exhibitionary space that encircled and designated the social status of spectators such that attending the cinema became a middle-class-status event. My own visits to cinemas in the Center confirmed that they were (and some still are) large public spaces with ornate spacious lobbies redolent of wealth and luxury. In an attempt to evoke the declining aristocratic theatergoers or to sell the atmosphere of aristocracy to the new professional middle classes, the owners of the Cinema Biógrafo Paris installed next door what many elder people recalled to me as "the best café ever in Bolivia" with a lavish interior and delicious pastries. Inside the Paris, prices rose for seats to further distinguish spectators who were willing to pay for higher seats in the more prestigious balcony. By performing urban status, by being "seen" at the cinema, a middle-class "public" consolidated as such, yet as a differentiated crowd, until they left the theater and dispersed.[2] If the built space of movie theaters contained and segmented moviegoers as "publics" who were apprehended isomorphically with the apparent fixity of the theater buildings, their moviegoing publics were held in suspended animation and marked with the status of the buildings they entered.

Beginning in the early 1920s, according to Susz (1990, 31), as the cinema became increasingly popular, marks of status and quality were attached to the national origin of films, with the new U.S. narrative films at the top. That their national origin identified films drew significance from the emerging world system of self-determining nation-states. Attempted with the scheme for a League of Nations at the same postwar moment, the system of nation-states was subsequently made real as a diplomatic organization with the formation of the United Nations after the Second World War (Kelly and Kaplan 2001, 9–11). And the fact that U.S. films were considered highest status films after World War I points to the actual hierarchies among the imagined horizontal "communities" of nations as well as the powerful ambitions of the United States. Neil Smith argues that South America was the earliest site of U.S. dominance and investment after the 1823 Monroe Doctrine (2004, 54). In the spirit of that doctrine, theaters were emptied of films in distribution from Europe and Latin America during the Depression and were filled instead with new films and reprises from Hollywood (Dagron 1979; Armes 1987).

In the mid-1930s, a recovering world economy renewed the global expansion of the Hollywood studios but also reinvigorated production in some European, Asian, and Latin American (especially Argentine and Mexican) industries with new and expensive sound technology, which again raised viewers' expectations for having the newest modern technology. This meant an aggressive renewed interest in distribution in the Latin American market and a flood of new Spanish-speaking films from the United States (Usabel 1982, 125–50). During the 1930s, Hollywood's new sound films were associated with the U.S. Good Neighbor Policy to diffuse revolutionary nationalism in Latin America, to secure access to its markets in the post-Depression years, and to beat German competition. To do so, U.S. studios opened their own theaters in some of the largest Latin American cities and directly sponsored the industrial development and creative activity of the Mexican film industry (Usabel 1982). Although U.S. producers distributed films dubbed in Spanish, the strategy was generally rejected among Latin American audiences because of regional dialects in Spanish.[3] Hollywood studios also attempted to improve their own images and their images of Latin Americans with "imported" Latino actors in new films for Latin American distribution, but this replicated the problem of regional accents (Usabel 1982).[4]

When World War II began, the European Axis distributed propaganda films across Latin America until the United States entered the war.[5]

During the war, however, a shipping blockade prevented many U.S. films from reaching South America, and Hollywood's presence declined on the screens. Without any local productions to show and with shipping lanes in the Western Hemisphere blocked, screens in Bolivia and Latin America were opened up to lower-status Spanish-speaking Mexican and Argentine films (Usabel 1982, 164–65).

During the tin boom in Bolivia during World War II, the Western bourgeois middle classes of La Paz expanded positions in business, newspapers, and government, and some opened local film distributorships and new theaters. By that time, there were approximately twenty-five cinemas in the country, eleven of them in the Center of La Paz. By the 1940s, neighborhood patron saint festivals and "folklore" parades were displacing cinema as the central modern technology of representation, circulation, and economic and social production in the city. As a distributor from United Artists noted in a letter to the home office in New York at the time: "They [Bolivians] observe the usual church holidays and their big fiesta 'Carnival Days' is observed for one week in March and is celebrated by prolonged drinking and dancing and as a result the box office suffers" (in Usabel 1982, 227).

After World War II, Hollywood-based companies obtained a monopoly in Europe and Latin America in the distribution of their own and of European films. Many practiced block booking, in which exhibitors were required to rent less-successful titles in packages with the most successful features. The Sherman and Clayton antitrust laws were actively pursued to prevent monopolies through the vertical ownership of production, distribution, and theaters within the United States, as with the "Paramount Decrees" of 1948 that legally severed distribution from exhibition. The MPAA's foreign offices were reorganized as a legal offshore cartel—the Motion Picture Export Association of America (MPEAA)—and without any government participation it began to negotiate on its own with foreign governments, distributors, and exhibitors by setting prices, allocating customers, allocating distribution rights, and defining the terms of the import and export of films, even calling itself "a little State Department" (see Wang 2003).

In the postwar period, the MPEAA operated as a front, opening protectionist barriers to accommodate U.S. corporations in an emerging world order of trade regulations and conventions among self-determining and decolonizing nation-states backed by uneven military powers and perceived dependencies (see Kelly and Kaplan 2001; on film distribution, see Wang 2003). Eric Johnston, economic adviser to Eisenhower and president of the Motion Picture Export Association, claimed, "Our films occupy more than 60% of projection time in foreign countries . . . our films keep open more than half of the cinemas that give people work and are a factor of economic support" (in Susz 1985, 56–57).

At the same time, distribution income from foreign markets became vital to recuperating and accumulating investment capital for the Hollywood industry; by that time it represented 40 percent of theatrical revenue (Donaghue 1987, 146). The U.S. government explicitly considered cinema to be an apparatus for visually promoting commerce in a wider array of U.S.–produced merchandise and democratic ideologies. That is, cinema would be a principal instrument in the instruction of "socially acceptable behavior—the behavior of consumerism" (Allen 1980). Permanent cinema exhibition had settled at the confluence of other image technologies, already well established in European and North American countries that were integral to the making of an international consumer middle class. Like cinematic display, new department stores opening in the city center in the buildings adjacent to the cinemas also presented views of commodities organized for the mobile customer moving through panoramic space (Schivelbush 1986). Along with other products of industrial capitalism, cinema and its field of commodity culture were the tickets the urban-born middle classes needed to access "modernity." In order to participate in the emerging cosmopolitan consumer class, it was crucial that consumption was contemporary in order to keep up with "progress." To meet the demand for the latest films, underground pirating networks formed to distribute copies of films, but many of them were of poor quality. The telltale scratches and poor sound quality devalued the event for audiences and the films were sent on to the cheaper neighborhood cinemas higher in the city's poorer zones. Moreover, along with Hollywood depictions of Indianness, the fantasies of consumer modernity from the North were circulating through theaters and new shopping centers around the city. Yet the country itself was still entrenched in virtually "feudal" political and economic structures.

If cinema was deployed as a vehicle of postwar capitalist modernity in which nation-states were imagined and organized as independent and simultaneous communities and symmetrical trading partners, in order to avert atomic war as a means of politics it set up terms for globalization whereby "only corporations, not nations are free to pursue dreams of domination" (Kaplan and Kelly 2001, 59). In this scenario, twentieth-century decolonization in Asia and Africa would ostensibly correspond to the revolutionary projects in the most feudal of Latin American states. In Bolivia, the revolution in 1952 was framed as the liberation of "the Indians" and their incorporation into a new modern democratic popular

nation-state. If this twentieth-century moment entailed the universaliza-
tion of historical time, the reinvention of history and of futures, it was
then that narrative would become a dominant vehicle for circulating the
"imagined" nation across simultaneous publics, constituting them as a
national interpretive community (Anderson 1983). The problem is the
actual asymmetrical topographies and asynchronous temporalities constituted in the narratives that guide circulation in capitalist modernity. It is
clear that the cinemascape in La Paz was built with neocolonial trenches
between the mestizo commercial center and the immigrant neighborhoods lining the canyon walls. It was tacit knowledge that immigrant and
rural Aymaras and Quechuas and their urban-born children, depending
on the clothing they wore, were not to enter the central plazas and the
Prado. Cholos as well as peasants were persistently treated as obstacles to
national progress and modernity (Demelas 1981; Greishaber 1985); those
who reproduced their rural cultural practices and dress in the city could
not leave their lower status.

In 1952, armed urban laborers and miners, peasants, and a left-
of-center middle class won a bloody revolutionary coup for the MNR
(National Revolutionary Movement), toppling the criollo tin oligarchy and
valorizing the twin ideologies of modernization and *mestizaje*. The ensu-
ing reforms ostensibly shifted the state into the hands of the new mestizo
bourgeoisie in La Paz. The tin mines were nationalized and a year later
the Agrarian Reform re-privatized hacienda lands and attempted to redistribute them to indigenous people who prior to the revolution had been
bound to work on haciendas in debt bondage; state money was poured
into health and education reforms in order to assimilate indigenous communities; and Indians were granted full citizenship, and the few who were
literate gained the right to vote. The social discourse of national populism
and indigenism was, however, set squarely within traditional official party
politics and the language of class protagonism; the term "Indian," for
example, was replaced by *campesino* and continued to refer to rural peasants with an agrarian mode of life.

Despite the revolutionary expectation that mestizo nationalism,
urban migration, and expanded market relations would produce a unified national middle-class culture, the numbers of people appearing in
the midcentury census category as "Indian" had been growing in La Paz
since 1899 (Greishaber 1985). At the same time, mestizo social discourse
began to shift the definition of indigenous from phenotypical categories
such as facial features to cultural indices such as language, dress, ritual,
and practices. Attracted to the city in order to *progressarse* (to progress
or improve oneself), people arriving in La Paz met with marginalization,

poverty, and, for many young women, abusive work as domestic servants in households of the Westernized middle class (Gill 1994). In their precarious position as urban immigrants, many continued to supplicate the panoply of indigenous natural spirits and Christian saints in relations of exchange and sacrifice and in neighborhood patron saint festivals. Rather than assimilate, furthermore, immigrant cholos sustained their indigenous cultural identities through clothing, festivals, and practices while adding layers of urban and Western affiliations. Many cholo families in La Paz achieved prosperity through mercantile capitalism, mediating the unofficial commodity and agricultural networks. Displaying their new wealth with expensive clothing and ostentatious festivals, cholos distinguished themselves as prosperous *and* modern in contrast to their rural indigenous circumstances. The once peripheral neighborhoods above the official Center, especially those around the Gran Poder parish, emerged as a vibrant commercial center for the unofficial markets and became the pivotal cultural and political center of the urban Aymaras and Quechuas. From the stratified urbanization that followed the 1950s, parallel if not rival mestizo-criollo and indio-cholo urban middle classes emerged (Himpele 2003). These emerging parallel social and cultural divides split the cinemascape into discernible upper and lower sectors.

With the cinemascape entrenched by these social divisions, distributors could repeatedly debut films to new audiences at a series of cinemas.

Figure 9. Overlooking the Center, Buenos Aires Avenue is a main avenue running along the canyon wall through well-to-do cholo neighborhoods.

In this context, marked and ranked theaters cannot be read as locations for the powerful generalizing forces and normalizing narratives associated with modernity, as in the United States (Hansen 1991). Susan Buck-Morss has explored cinemas specifically as sites of mass assimilation for immigrants in the United States in which uniform subjects were formed as part of a crowd, as "*one* viewer, infinitely reproduced" (1994, 53) whose fixed attention toward the same screen is physically anesthetizing so that "kinetic activity is reserved for the 'objectified' screen-bodies" (57). This unitary formation of corporality and subjectivity is typically disrupted at neighborhood cinemas by the divided attention and constant activity inside the theaters in La Paz as well as the continuous traffic in and out. In the film texts themselves, according to Miriam Hansen (1991), narrative cinema was defined as a "universal language" celebrated to assemble its "spectators" in a context where urban masses could assimilate and become standardized citizens in shared communicative space, a democratic public sphere. While films produced and exhibited with these techniques of addressing viewers were said to unify the diverse crowds into modern national subjects (Martín-Barbero 1993, 151), in Bolivia this unity was not achieved in the circulation of films. Publics at the Center of the city were seen as "ahead" of the "backward" popular sectors of cholos and Indians who lived above them. This temporality did not proceed at a uniform speed; furthermore, those who were behind were unable to catch up and assimilate, as indicated by the distributor López's imaginary peasants who, upon moving to the city, were incapable of maintaining their own refrigerators. Each time audiences showed up at popular neighborhood cinemas, they met the films directed toward them halfway, dramatizing and reinforcing the fixed differences that distributors held about them. With the ongoing formation of parallel indigenous and mestizo urban social space, the dominant narrative trajectories of films in circulation in La Paz continued to constitute the city as socially vertical and spatially continuous but temporally and culturally discontinuous.

In the 1960s and 1970s, the city continued to expand in opposite directions. The wealthiest middle-class mestizo families were moving into warmer parts of the city, lower than the Center itself, in the tree-lined Zona Sur (South Zone), while new immigrants were filling in the higher elevations along the canyon wall. Near the Plaza Murillo in the Center, older theaters closed as the Universo and 16 de Julio on the Prado were built to show "finer" English-speaking musicals as well as some Mexican and Spanish films. As arriving immigrant families were displaced further from the Center and upward to steeper and poorer "peripheral zones" of the city, rural immigrants were also settling in El Alto, the flat shantytown

Figure 10. Women resting at the *ceja,* the brow overlooking La Paz in the immigrant city of El Alto.

on the canyon rim above La Paz that has become Bolivia's second largest city after Santa Cruz.

Most of the theater construction in La Paz expanded in the established prosperous immigrant neighborhoods below, in Tejar, Ch'jini, and Gran Poder; the largest theater was the Cine Roby. These neighborhood cinemas are smaller and architecturally indistinct buildings rather than ornate movie palaces emulating European architecture. Yet because these smaller box-style theaters have less acoustic reverberation, the sound quality of dialogue is better. However, the seats are smaller and harder and reflect the social context of the exhibition site: if you are tall enough, your knees press the back of the seat in front of you. Some of the cinemas in the higher neighborhoods have hard benches rather than seats. Only a few cinemas in the city were constructed with heating, and some neighborhood theaters do not show films at night because it is too cold. Inside these spaces, the telltale scratches, tears, and audible static that accumulate from heat and friction in projection equipment are inscribed on films and register the social distances that the films have traveled across the city's projectors and publics. These material transfigurations of film material indicate the friction in the moments of stabilization along the circuits of film distribution. Following the revolution, the dispersion of films across the cinemascape "had formed circuits where certain types of films were shown in certain theaters," recalls Walter Guerra, owner of a small distributor and the prosperous popular cinema Universo. In the Center, Cinema Scala imported and showed Argentine films; the Cinema Monje Campero also exhibited Argentine as well as Mexican and Spanish films. Meanwhile, the neighborhood cinemas began showing martial arts, Mexican, and other B-grade action films. The cinemascape continued to be marked in terms of the national origins of films displayed on the colorful billboards above theater entrances.

In the late 1970s and early 1980s, a combination of the political and economic crises in the Argentine and Mexican cinemas, Bolivian hyperinflation, and political instability, along with the introduction of private television programming on multiple private channels, led to a 50 percent decline in movie theater attendance. The first Bolivian television station was operated by the state government in La Paz in 1969, and it was not until the early 1980s that color and private television stations were authorized and began to operate, though with a majority of foreign programming (Rivadeneira 1988; Rivadeneira and Triada 1986). At that time, private media companies operated satellite dishes to receive news and entertainment channels from the United States, sometimes "pirating" and reediting incoming material to be packaged and broadcast as commercial local programming.[6] Most stations also repeated commercial programming, and now a high percentage of programs are dubbed films, sitcoms, entertainment news, and telenovelas that are produced in the United States, Mexico, Venezuela, Chile, and Brazil. By defining the network or distribution channel during program breaks with images of traditional regional and cultural distinctiveness, networks interpose themselves as the site of mediation for distinctly "Bolivian" viewing publics.

Within these global programming flows, Bolivian television essentially started up in the midst of an era of what Jesús Martín-Barbero calls "mediation" (1993), even though the state had had a monopoly on television since 1969 (Rivadeneira Prada 1988). He writes about the use of television and cinema in the Mexican national project that tied national development to communications; the goal of this populist project was the formation of homogeneous national citizenry through the massification of popular culture and emphasis of class identity in order to reconcile the opposition between labor and capital. The development of transnational mediations began in Latin America around the late 1960s and was intensified by the early 1980s. Following foreign debt crises, the diminishment of national economic strength, and the delegitimization of political parties among the urban popular classes (i.e., poor and working classes), the mass media appealed to the popular sectors as the means with which to form new identities and popular struggles that could fill the political vacuum in popular representation (Martín-Barbero 1993, 182; Lazarte 1993). Moreover, the coinciding swift liberalization of national economies and the opening of commercial media markets meant that cheaper external transnational mass media programming also entered and dominated the delivery systems of television and cinema. In fact, regional trade agreements among Latin American countries (e.g., MERCOSUR) contain minimal national quotas or limitations against imported programming in the new Latin America "audio-visual space," thereby protecting "culture" with policies that privilege conceptions of culture as national patrimony and elite art (Martín-Barbero 2000, 42; García Canclini 2001).

Occurring on the heels of Bolivia's jolting return to democracy in the early 1980s, the emergence of a commercial televisual public sphere as a perceived space of mediation between publics and the state also merged the Latin American sense of the popular with that in the North, where popular culture is synonymous with mass culture.[7] When transnational media enter everyday life and routines through mediations, Martín-Barbero argues, popular culture becomes a field textured by both seduction and resistance, connected by new hemispheric loyalties of complicity and opposition; new kinds of plural social actors and popular subjects emerge who may not conform with earlier political formations organized around singular identities, such as class (1988, 453, 462). In La Paz, the appearance of new popular publics at this time took on a distinctly Andean orientation. After the expansion, private conglomeration, and regionalization of Latin American televisual circuits in the 1980s (Sinclair 1996), which coincided with the shift in the homogeneous popular national project toward a "pluri-cultural" one, as it was officially called, there was a dramatic increase in participation in neighborhood and citywide festivals and parades. Cinema managers across the urban cinemascape appropriated (or were appropriated by) the popularity of these spectacles. On the first weekend of Carnival in February, some neighborhood cinemas are modified as large dance halls that compete for business by hiring local bands and national folklore music groups. "The business has always dropped during this period, so we do it to make up for that," the manager at Cinema Murillo told me; he added that it is also one way to compete with pirated videotapes. The Cinema Mexico rents out its space to Radio and TV Popular Channel 4 for the live production and transmission of its all-afternoon Saturday variety television show *Sabados Populares* (Popular Saturdays), attended by audiences from the popular classes who fill the theater to participate in contests and to see live national folkloric and Latin American musical performances.

Returning to the crisis in Latin American cinemas and the expansion of television in the 1970s, Hollywood also saw the percentage of its films exhibited in theaters in Bolivia drop below 50 percent by the mid-1970s (Susz 1985, 149–61). But the drop in new Latin American and Hollywood films was soon made up for by films issued by new transnational and wealthy U.S. distributors who had survived the 1970s global political economic restructuring with multimillion dollar "blockbuster" strategies. By investing heavily in stars and special effects, and with a renewed blitz in global distribution by simultaneously debuting films in several large capital cities at once to ensure immediate returns in order to pay less interest on the bonds put up for the initial production, distribution circuits were negotiated before production began. Thereafter, Hollywood films rose steadily to beyond 77 percent in the 1990s (Cinemateca Boliviana). It is important to recognize that the percentage of films shown in a period does not take into account the disproportionate amount of time that films occupy on screens through repeated daily exhibitions and the sequence of appearances throughout the city.[8] Between the increased demand for cash by the international distributors seeking to finance blockbusters and the decline in moviegoing, genres, screens, and publics were increasingly compartmentalized into sequences in order to control and access publics who could provide as much income as early as possible in a film's movement through its life. As Hollywood films began to dominate screen time, locations in distribution circuits became marked by their position in the sequence of a film's debuts and by the genre of film they show, rather than by the national origin of the films. Cinema Mexico and other neighborhood cinemas, which had shown predominantly Mexican films to the popular audiences in La Paz, began exhibiting reprises of U.S. releases in the early 1990s.

The increasing uniformity of films screened in La Paz coincides with new forms of differentiation on the cinemascape. Five busy theaters around the Center debut new films from "the majors" (the major transnational distributors from Hollywood) and run a single film during three or four daily projection times. Only Monje Campero has kept successful films for up to seven or eight weeks, and the large theater was recently divided into two theaters with 750 and 380 seats. The neighborhood cinemas now show a package of two or three films together and have begun mixing in a single day the martial arts, B-action films, and reprises of major U.S. films all for one price to lure in the public. Films in circulation tend to stop in the neighborhood theaters only for a week or less because business declines quickly and a higher percentage can be earned for a distributor by sending it to a new debut elsewhere. The cinemascape in La Paz now has a parallel if not secondary Center in the prosperous cholo neighborhoods

Figure 11. Cinema Monumental Roby, the busiest of the popular cinemas, is located at a major traffic intersection in the well-to-do neighborhoods that are the hub of social and commercial life among urban Aymaras and Quechuas. Located near the starting point of the city's festival parades, Cinema Roby offered the movie *Geronimo* as a student dance group passed by performing Indianness in the Gran Poder parade.

Figure 12. Months after its stay at Cinema Roby, *Geronimo* appears at Cine Imperio, located in the nearby commercial zones and street markets.

surrounding the Cinema Roby. Films often tack from the Cinema Monje Campero to the Cinema Roby and then back to the Plaza Murillo in the Center, on to the popular neighborhood cinemas, back to Cinema Roby, and on to the small neighborhood theaters. This movement disrupts a trickle-down transit that might otherwise be a linear continuum of social identities and declining status from white to mestizo to Indian, or in broader strokes, Western to Andean, going up the city canyon.

The present trajectories emplot narratives of antagonistic multiple urban centers from which concentrated wealth can be extracted rapidly. They reveal the mutual antagonism (rather than a neatly oppositional domination and oppression) between parallel middle classes (Himpele 2003). Nevertheless, film distributors continue to read the subjects of their itineraries as inherently differentiated and culturally superior and subordinate publics, now in terms of the genres of films they see. Omitting the national identity of films, as well as the Cinema Roby and neighborhood cinemas, Carlos, the manager of Cinema 6 de Agosto, mapped out for me the current scenario in the Center: "Each cinema is exclusively characterized by types of films. For example, Cinema Monje Campero is characterized by action, Cinema Universo by action, Cinema 6 de Agosto by comedy, suspense, and terror, at Cinema 16 de Julio, finer films." The contours of the cinemascape in La Paz are delineated by film traffic through its arena of marked theaters; along the way, the location, comfort, price, and prestige of exhibition sites decline as urban altitude rises, and with them, the status of their respective publics.

▶ ————————————————————————————————————

Imagined Communities: Asynchronous Circuits and Uneven Terrain

Colonial and industrial experiences of material and perceptual mobility such as railroads, ships, telegraphs, and of course the cinema continue to be celebrated as icons of modern and national life (Simmel 1990; Schivelbush 1986; Friedberg 1993; Charney and Schwartz 1995). In Bolivia, the cinema coincided with new modern temporal and spatial modes of travel and perception. As an instrument in forming a visual mode of collective self-awareness, it consolidated a longing for national affiliation that could be asserted to mark modern status (López 2000a, 53), as this recent news item in the newspaper *La Razón* demonstrates:

A Multiplex of 10 Cinemas for Cochabamba

At the center of a spectacle, a multiplex opened with 10 theaters. US $6 million was invested. The President cut the red tape.

   The modern multiplex Cinema Center was inaugurated last night in the city of Cochabamba, in the middle of a spectacle that, alongside the debut of the film Superman, had music, a parade of models from La Maison and many fireworks. (May 26, 2006)

This appearance of a ten-theater multiplex, celebrated as a significant national event, reveals the asynchronies in the infrastructures for media circulation for Bolivia as a national "community"—"a solid community moving steadily down (or up) history" (Anderson 1983, 31). Of course, anthropologists, among others, have raised some of the difficulties in Anderson's thesis, such as the "deep horizontality" and simultaneity of "imagined communities" (e.g., Kelly and Kaplan 2001; Lomnitz 2002; and on national media specifically, Abu-Lughod 2005), and have considered alternative arenas of public performance not centrally mediated through commodity capitalism (Abercrombie 2003). As I have traced here, the emergence of the circulatory network of theaters in La Paz reproduced social asymmetries rooted deeply in the experiences and infrastructures of colonialism and the national project. When it comes to the selectivity and temporality of dissemination in actually assembled circulatory systems, the distribution of films within and to Bolivia reveals significant asynchronies in the coordinated simultaneity that Anderson's argument imagines within and among nations moving together steadily forward through universal historical time.

On the uneven terrain of La Paz, through which national modernities are distributed and adopted and through which the trajectories and timing of cultural circulation pass, temporality ranks some publics as temporally behind and socially above and below others (cf. Fabian 1983). In other words, the traffic through this cinema infrastructure reinforces spatial contiguity but temporal discontinuity. This contradiction signals the extent of proximity and participation in modern commodity capitalism within temporal narratives of *uneven* national progress. First, cinema in Bolivia was a foreign import that presented scenes of political and economic modernization located elsewhere well before such structural transformations took place to diffuse it (López 2000a, 48; Schelling 2000, 24). Second, the cinema might have imagined and placed consumer modernity on the horizon as an accessible attraction, but its circulation made that modern life a possibility for selected groups in La Paz as delineated by the specific itineraries of film traffic themselves in the city. Given the publicness of the timing, selectivity, and exclusions that constitute these narrative paths, which is reflected in social discourses about circulation (see chapter 1), one can wonder why the imagined communities thesis stops at an account of the development of the idea of horizontal and territorially sovereign national communities (national states) when historically the circulation among and within national formations has been characterized by vertical social hierarchies and permeable boundaries. In a later work, Benedict Anderson sought to open up his thesis to national communities "no longer confined to interiors of already existing nation-states" (1998, 131). Yet the notion of synchronization seems to persist, such as in his account of the arrival of the scientific census to Central Java in 1920: "Doubtless this came a bit late in world time, but not terribly late" (123). My interest is in this asynchronous slippage, however minor, and the ways in which the timing of the adoption of new governing techniques takes on public meanings.

One way to read Anderson's work itself is as an instance of Anna Tsing's idea of "circulation rhetoric." The ease with which we invoke circulation to characterize "new" imagined collectivities and global interconnections, she suggests, implies a false contrast with a stagnant past of disconnected premodern localities that have been superseded by the current mobilities of globalization (2000, 346). At stake in Tsing's consideration of "circulation rhetoric" is the identification of circulation with ideologies of corporate expansion and market-based social models that obscure and justify inequalities; at the same time, she points out, circulation has oriented emancipatory projects seeking to break down oppressive social barriers (336–37).[9] She renders contemporary rhetoric about circulation, with its characteristic emphasis on fluidity and "flows," as a visual field with a blind spot obscuring crucial struggles and frictions in carving out specific channels of circulation through social terrain (337).

▶ ────────────────────────────────────

Counteritineraries

If film circulation channels dominant social forces, then political struggles and alternative social formations are also embedded in the counternarratives of cultural distribution (Himpele 1996a). Though similarly operating as traffic that moves in itineraries through topographical space, neighborhood and citywide folklore parades not only incorporate and displace dominant cartographies of social difference and the itineraries running through them, they are spectacles that pose challenges to the ordering power of sequential narrativity itself (see Himpele 2003). Though film distributors have commented on the effect of festivals on their work, at least since the 1940s, their focus is on the circuits of cinema where the key challenge is the competition that they face from video piracy that subverts and drains the official circulation of films as well as the staggered "colonial time" with which distributors bolster their social position (Wilk 2002). Distributors, theater owners, and video store managers told me that videotapes and videocassette machines circulated among families and friends are the major challenge to their businesses, even in the Center of the city. According to a study by the Cinemateca Boliviana (Cabellero Hoyos, Carranza, Ramiro, and Barragán 1991), most people see films on television or on official and pirated videocassettes at home because of their economic circumstances—a sign of widespread unemployment and contraband importing among the tens of thousands who seek to survive in the post-1985 neoliberal regimes. Contraband commodities flow into Bolivia by truck from Peru, Chile, Brazil, and Argentina. Some trucks are regularly met by Bolivian customs at borders and pay corrupt officials between US$1,000 and $2,000, depending on the size of the truckload, in order to continue on to the city. A law against contraband videotapes and unofficial businesses was passed in the early 1990s, but instead of precipitating a "video crackdown" (Hamilton 1993) the laws have not been fully executed.[10] In the mid-1990s, a radio report quoted a state economic minister as saying that it was better to have the unofficial markets filling the sidewalks than to have the unemployed and poor in the jungle training to be guerrillas. While contraband merchants are often scapegoats for wider structural problems, the once-scorned unofficial markets were also praised by neoliberal governments who claimed that the unofficial markets throughout "civil society" could absorb social problems.[11]

Tapping the rules of neoliberalism, the distributor and Cinema Universo owner Walter Guerra said, "The unemployed who sell the videos are also operating in a free market like we are, but they must do it legally." He explained to me that he had contacted the Motion Picture Association of America for help with the piracy problem in Bolivia, but he remains caught in the middle. As he spoke of his own position in this scenario, he depends on the rules of the free market at the same time as he sarcastically commented on discourses of modern development. He told me that he said to the association, "If you sell us the official videos for less, with the same laws of the marketplace we can make the pirates leave. But the response is 'No.' But they are the great geniuses. We are underdeveloped. They know what they are doing."

While Guerra and other distributors continue to employ a neo-colonial framework to circulate films, the debuts of pirated films on videotape reverse the class correspondences and itineraries of official film circulation and exhibition. While there are sidewalk video vendors in the Center, many La Paz neighborhoods (and El Alto too) have small "video clubs" whose walls are lined with shelves filled with pirated copies of official subtitled U.S., Mexican, and martial arts films that come as contraband from Chile. "The same day that the films debut in Puerto Rico, with Spanish subtitles or dubbed in Spanish, or if they debut in Miami or in California also in Spanish, the first pirated copy exists here twenty-four hours later. These come through Panama," Guerra explained to me. A pirated film can be available on video in the unofficial street markets before its debut in an official theater in the city center, offering the fastest access to world debuts to the popular classes and those who shop in the unofficial markets.

As with films, the itineraries of video copies are registered within the frame and sound themselves, telling tales about where they have been. In contrast, the official videotapes from the Erol's video store appear to viewers to have no such technical "distortion." Pirated videos are typically copies made from copies of an "original copy." Videotape duplication is a process of recording electronic signals to a new tape, a process that degrades the technical quality of each newly recorded videotape by adding audiovisual noise, oversaturated colors that "bleed" beyond their outlines, and, after several copies, tracking problems that are not correctable because of an unstable electronic control track (electronic pulses that serve as the "sprocket holes" that time the movement of the tape). Like the exhibitions at neighborhood cinemas, pirated tapes have two or three movies

Figure 13. Video vendors can be found in the center of the city (as seen here) as well as in the markets in the higher elevations, offering pirated films to multiple urban audiences often preceding official theatrical releases.

on them since they are recorded at low tape speed to make them fit on a single cassette; as a result, the image and sound quality are further deteriorated from the slow tape speed. The itineraries of pirated copies of copies seen in the smeared images, the unstable tracking, and muffled sound may not matter to most viewers since what is lost in quality is made up in quantity, lower price, and accessibility. While the correlations between image quality, price, comfort, and the prestige value of film exhibition sites do follow entrenched neocolonial hierarchies of film distribution, the timing and circuits of film debuts in what Brian Larkin (2004) calls the "pirate infrastructure" reverse and fragment the available neocolonial narratives that dominate official circuits of film distribution.

▶

Nonlinear Time

In order to mitigate the risks that underlie film distribution and produce capital instantly to cover the financing for production, synchronous film debuts are now coordinated across widely dispersed global locations (Acland 2003, 234) and reported in newspapers as worldwide events whose magnitude and value is augmented by their simultaneity. For much of the twentieth century, films from the North were circulated in Bolivia in staggered "colonial time"; often, already-used copies that had been screened in the United States were refurbished with Spanish subtitles and sent southward. Or, if they were not too worn from their play in another Spanish-speaking country, they would go to Bolivia directly from there. Challenging this Hollywood-centered trickle-down narrative of film traffic, Walter Guerra told me that his Cinema Universo debuted the 1993 action/sci-fi film *The Fortress* before its U.S. debut. Occasionally, he explained, U.S. distributors send films in advance to Bolivia and to other countries as a marketing test, a sign of the fundamental uncertainties about audiences. When *The Lion King* debuted at the Monje Campero in 1994, it was highly publicized as an event that was occurring only one week after its debut in the United States and, as it turned out, months ahead of most of its European debuts. *The Fortress* and *The Lion King* mark the beginning of a significant shift away from the neocolonial narratives of film distribution at the national level in Bolivia as the distributors, who are aligned with their multinational corporations, reconfigure the time and space of flows as they seek to stay ahead of the pirate circuits and beat them to debuts.[12]

Currently, it is common for multiple copies of films to arrive in Bolivia for concurrent debuts in as many cities. In stark contrast to the single copy of *Dracula* that toured Bolivia in 1993, nine copies of *The Passion of the Christ* were dispatched to Bolivia in March 2004, one month after its first world release, and it debuted at once in the three cities of La Paz, Santa Cruz, and Cochabamba. In La Paz, *The Passion* debuted and ran simultaneously in the city center at the Monje Campero and the Cinema 16 de Julio, which are only several blocks apart on the central Prado. Newspaper reports about the event said little to nothing about the film's narrative, yet anticipated record-setting attendance and described the facilities at each theater. "Both the 16 de Julio and the Monje Campero guarantee the public comfort and the latest in audiovisual technology. The Cinema 16 de Julio has Dolby sound and DTS that will provide quality and security at all of its screenings. The Monje Campero surely has the only theater with digital and 3-D Dolby sound" (*La Razón,* March 25, 2004). Appearing in Bolivia one month after its first debut in the United States and a week after debuting in several other Latin American countries, a shorter ninety-minute VCD (video compact disc) of the film was already available. In May 2004, the $200 million film *Troy* debuted virtually uniformly worldwide and in the largest cities of Bolivia. The film's synchronous global dispersal reflects a mirror image of how the film was assembled from scenes produced at disparate sites in Malta, London, and Mexico into a single narrative vehicle. *La Razón* reported that 9,000 copies of *Star Wars 3* premiered in a worldwide event on May 18, 2005. At the Monje Campero, where a midnight screening was held, and at 16 de Julio, the tickets for the sold-out premieres went on sale weeks earlier on May 1, dramatically extending the timing of the exchange relationship at the box office, providing capital for distributors and exhibitors well before Darth Vader landed in the country. Yet a year later in 2006, *Superman* arrived from Hollywood weeks after its U.S. debut.

These debuts are signs of an overall shift away from the linear itineraries of global media delivery in colonial time, although much of the traffic flows through colonial channels and hierarchies, toward a collage of relatively close yet unpredictable release dates that resembles the palimpsest of televisual programming in Bolivia. This shift in film itineraries over the course of the twentieth century signals a decline in linear itineraries as a mode of identifying and assembling publics and a rise in discontinuity and mixture as forms for reconfiguring the space and temporality of the media worlds of diverse worldwide publics with multiple global and national sentiments and affiliations (Acland 2003, 237). Current plans to construct a sixteen-theater multiplex in La Paz by a Spanish transnational company would make it the largest multiplex in South America. If the international infrastructure and itineraries of film traffic do not cohere into the same linear narratives and centralized disseminations that stemmed from an earlier colonial imaginary as they did over the past century, they do not necessarily represent even the beginnings of a global and homogeneous temporality; they represent a shifting, indeterminate, dispersed, and multicentric system related more to events and the asymmetrical give-and-take of trade negotiations and shifting political terrain.

*II   Cinema and the Social
      Imagination of Indigenism*

[**3**] *The Visible Nation:*
Excavating the Past,
Projecting the Future

▶

National Cinema, National State

Historical narratives of national cinemas differently reveal and exclude
the uneven political, global, and technological determinations of both the
cinema and the nation-state. Consider the following accounts of Bolivian
cinema:

> During the 1920s, films were being produced in every country of Latin
> America. However, only Mexico, Argentina, and Chile made some notable
> contributions to the art of silent film making. Most films were trials, experi-
> ments. Without a film tradition, without experienced direction, without
> technical facilities and financial support, Latin American film makers could
> not create excellent works. (Usabel 1982, 7)

> Bolivian cinema? It is behind. Everything here is behind, but because it is
> slower, the lifestyle here is better. The Bolivian cinema is like we are in the
> year 1930. 1930!!! Look at the U.S. films. They are using modern computers
> to make incredible special effects. That's why people like them. (Businessman
> in La Paz, 1994)

> "'Latin American cinema had finally come into its own.'" (in Stephen Hart's
> 2004 *Companion to Latin American Film,* regarding recent films from
> Brazil and Mexico that had achieved wide international distribution and
> critical success, quoted by Joanna Page [2005, 306])

These academic and popular accounts exclude and privilege certain cinema histories by binding their terms as a singular temporal and
spatial narrative, marking certain regions as "behind" the achievements
in the North by projecting the experience of turn-of-the-century industrial modernity in the United States inappropriately onto Latin America.

Moreover, as Ana López writes, such progressive narratives also obscure the "complex global interactions . . . contradictory and ambivalent transformative processes that would mark the later reception of sound cinema and other media" (2000a, 48). To add to López's point, these narratives conceal the plurality of their conditions; that is, how cinema histories have been shaped through control over the international trajectories of production and exhibition equipment through the same transcontinental channels in which other commercial products, social ideologies, and political alignments were also circulating. Yet as Joanna Page warns in response to Hart's triumphalist account she cites in the third quotation above, critical praise for contemporary internationally coproduced films privileges the market and the movement of international capital while downplaying the trend of state involvement. Further, the narrow focus of these accounts keeps a wide range of media practices "off the map" (Ginsburg et al. 2002a, 14), conceals the asymmetries in cultural exchange, reproduces the invisibility of films ostensibly not made with such resources, and overlooks the difficult conditions that limit production and distribution in less celebrated instances across the region. Finally, this emphasis occludes production practices and circuits of exchange that are not primarily organized around the commodity form. All these tensions point to how, in addition to the uneven material access to international distribution, financing, and technologies across Latin America, film histories and criticism themselves have been a salient discourse in which the narratives and locations of national cinemas emerged.

Film scholars have shown that in Latin America and elsewhere "national cinemas" were from the outset the products of the transcontinental mobility of cinematic technologies and of filmmakers themselves, yet these projects have been fashioned in resistances, engagements, and struggles for resources and for screen time in increasing tension with Hollywood corporations (e.g., Noriega 2000; Hjort and Mackenzie 2000).[1] Consolidating the disparate and heterogeneous elements for producing and exhibiting films within the frame of a "national cinema" makes claims that materialize these elements in nominal form; that is, they make the cinema an objective and stable entity. As Andrew Higson writes, "To identify a national cinema is first of all to specify a coherence and a unity; it is to proclaim a unique identity and a stable set of meanings. The process of identification is thus invariably a hegemonising, mythologizing process involving the production and assignation of a particular set of meanings and the attempt to contain, or prevent the potential proliferation of other meanings" (1989, 168).[2] With a focus on public discourses concerning the national cinema in Bolivia, this chapter shows that the national cinema closely emerged and intersected with the forces and forms that were defining the national state itself. For in addition to resistance to the increasing command and control that Hollywood corporations had over the mobility of and access to the elements of filmmaking and circulation, the compelling idea of a national cinema also grew in Bolivia during the emergence of the hegemonic international world system of nation-states, imagined to be horizontal communities, that manifested in the formation of the United Nations (see Kelly and Kaplan 2001).

In situating the emergence of Bolivian national cinema in the linked schemes of politics and social discourse, this chapter is critical of viewing national cinema and films as singular entities or national allegories, as Jameson regarded "Third World" texts (1986). The idea of allegory as a mode of analysis suggests that there are hidden conditions of national significance and form that run parallel to the wider circumstances of the nation in the larger international system. Both Aijaz Ahmad's critique of the linguistic limitations and privileges of the idea of national allegory (1987) and Ismael Xavier's criticism that shows that Jameson's implicit periodization does not hold for Brazilian cinema or Latin America (1997), however, reveal that "national allegory" is one interpretative framework among a number of historically situated possibilities. I argue that the idea of national cinema is deployed as a strategic scenario or a controlling frame within which films are materially and meaningfully assembled from multiple determinants in projects of self-definition. This composite cluster that national cinema frames is an assemblage (Deleuze and Guattari 1983 [1977]; DeLanda 2006). As Ong and Collier use the term, "An assemblage is the product of multiple determinations that are not reducible to a single logic. The temporality of the assemblage is emergent. It does not always involve new forms, but forms that are shifting, in formation, or at stake" (2005, 12). Assemblages emerge in compound and multistranded processes that "vibrate," to use a Deleuzian term. While the term "assemblage" most saliently implies heterogeneous materialities, forces, and forms, I also use the term "event" somewhat interchangeably but to key the ephemeral dimensions of public performance, sociality, affect, and the selective and contingent strategies that are enacted. As events and assemblages set into motion and draw together mobile elements from disparate sources, they form locations along the pathways of circulation at varying scales. As assemblages, then, films produced in Bolivia are more than allegories that resemble the discourses and forces that constitute the circumstances for the national cinema, and as events they are more than reflections of the nation-state as a historical project. Rather than running parallel to each other allegorically, films as well as nations represent emergent assemblages or events that function to connect and intertwine international circulatory matrices. In this perspective, both the nation and global structures are connected as an assemblage in which the idea of the national cinema is one strategy of stabilization.

If the national cinema and its films have appeared in popular struggles to both participate in and combat the worldwide traffic in the cultural and economic forces of commercial film production and distribution (Birri 1985), the specificity of a national cinema also formed in the circuits of finance and political economic regulations enacted by the state. "[T]he boundaries of cultural specificity in cinema are established by governmental actions implemented through legislative frameworks, industrial and financial measures on the economic level, the gearing of training institutions toward employment in the national media structures, systems of licensing governed by aspects of corporate law, and so on" (Willeman 1995, 25). This common infrastructure of the national cinema and the state can be traced through their convergent paths, "the chain of relations and exchanges which develop in connection with films, in a territory delineated by its economic and juridical policy" (in Hjort and MacKenzie 2000, 5). Both the nation-state and its national cinema are conjunctions of multiple assembly lines that are the pathways through which strips of currency and film stock travel. Intertwining money and the cinema, as we will see in chapter 4, the Bolivian state became a source for the fantasies of political and commercial modernity by being envisioned as the scenario in which these fantasies could be realized; like the cinema, the nation-state itself became an instrument and an object of modern desires.

This chapter will sort through the mobile elements, regulatory frameworks, and nationalist discourses that were assembled in the twin frames of national cinema and the nation-state in early-twentieth-century Bolivia. Filmmakers and exhibitors struggled against and complied with state regulations, moral pressures, and international monopolies as they appropriated new cinematic techniques that laid the groundwork for a new mestizo social imaginary. As political and economic power in Bolivia grew in La Paz among the expanding mestizo middle and working classes, *mestizaje* (cultural mixture) grew to national significance as a social ideology in which the cultural traits of indigenous ancestry were tipped toward a positive valence. By popularizing indigeneity, "Indian" populations that had been silenced and subordinated became recognized as national citizens, yet they were romanticized in popular culture. Artists had been calling for more "national" artworks that reflected the culturally mixed reality of the country in order to repel the "parasitic" United States (perhaps most evidenced then by the onslaught of Hollywood films), which had been "sterilizing the Bolivian spirit" whose uniqueness and authenticity were being located in Indianness. The twentieth-century indigenist movement was widely dispersed in sociology and painting, but the prestigious narrative media of elite national culture were literature and theater, which supplied the stories that were adapted for cinema. Another key site in which the cinema was inserted into these movements was in the press, which became a crucial force in the mobilizations that led to the 1952 revolution.[3] This chapter examines the social discourses on cinema in newspapers in which cinema was considered an instrument of modernity and a vehicle of the mestizo social imaginary. These discourses cast Bolivian cinema as a technological medium that could track the nation's modern progress mainly as a form through which scenes of the nation's indigenous past and vital essence could be registered. As this chapter will argue, at stake in these public discourses on the viability and progress of the "national cinema" was the modernity of its metonym, the nation–state.

▶───────────────────────────────

Situating Bolivian Cinema

As a technology of cultural reproduction and mediation, cinema is as much the product of the forces of twentieth-century modernity as it has been an instrument in assembling them.[4] As I describe elsewhere in this book, twentieth-century modernity in Bolivia was first experienced in scenes of fantasy in the films that traveled through Bolivia and presented scenes from industrializing countries elsewhere to the North and in Europe. The arrival and circulation of cinematic technologies preceded, if they did not accompany, the formation of modern technological infrastructures such as railroads and the telegraph (López 2000a). If modernity was marked by the experience of these new forms of circulation, the cinema uniquely put them on display at the same time that it was a visual attraction for its own mobilities—moving pictures and travel itself (see Charney and Schwartz 1995).

With backgrounds as mercantilists rather than industrialists, the bourgeoisie in La Paz directed its capital toward the formation of an exhibition infrastructure for imported films rather than risk local productions. During the formation of commercial cinema outside the United States, the advantage of this business strategy was that, as Roy Armes points out, "distribution consistently brings a steady profit, though at the cost of dependence on imported products. Distribution profits continued to be derived from imported films regardless of whether there is any local production or not" (1987, 166). Making production difficult and expensive, the Motion Picture Patent Company (known as the Trust) formed in 1909 by Thomas Edison had made Eastman film stock (the only maker at the time) virtually unavailable to anyone outside of the nine-member Trust of two French and seven American companies.[5] In these circumstances, access to production and exhibition materials in Bolivia depended on alignments between European immigrants to Bolivia who owned biógrafos and had their own relationships with U.S. and European distributors who were all linked to Edison's Trust. If the cinema featured mobility, many of the earliest filmmakers were recent immigrants who were themselves mobile subjects.[6]

Exhibitions of the early films made in La Paz during the first decades of the twentieth century combined fascination for the cinema machinery itself with views of one's social setting projected on the same screen with scenes from other parts of the world, creating a new cinematic imaginary from the locations displayed in the montage of scenes. Ana López argues that such international juxtapositions on screens in Latin America fed a "need to assert the self as modern, but also and, more lastingly, as different, ultimately as a national subject" (2000a, 53). In this engagement, filmmakers in La Paz responded with their own scenes of national distinctiveness and modernity: government and society elites; local streets and the government plaza (Plaza Murillo); cinematic views of the nearby Andean valleys *(yungas)*; Lake Titicaca; archaeological sites; railroads; civic events, and especially military projects and processions. One early film was made in honor of U.S. president Calvin Coolidge, whose state department had been trying to resolve the continuing hostilities between Bolivia and Chile (the latter had won Bolivia's entire sea coast in the War of the Pacific two decades earlier). Many of these films were made by Luis Castillo, a man remembered as sober and "'very representative of the middle class of La Paz'" (Dagron 1982, 101). In the name of morality, local official censorship and pressures by the press initially favored films that mirrored the documentary aspect of the cinema established by the Lumière films because they were educational. These early documentary scenes consisted of thirty- to ninety-second clips that emphasized modes of presentation rather than storytelling.

The first narrative-style film made in La Paz was made by the ambitious Italian-born Pedro Sambarino, a filmmaker who moved to Bolivia after working for two years in Buenos Aires, where he had arrived in 1923 as an itinerant filmmaker working for the Lumière Brothers. In 1924, Sambarino edited short documentary film clips together and exhibited them with a live "guide" in the theater to tie together the scenes with narration. His documentary *Por Mi Patria* (For My Country) was designed to evoke the spectator's patriotism as its announcement asks: "'What are the ideals of the people? How to prepare to achieve them?'" (Dagron 1982, 63). If the cinema fed desires for both the modern and the national that would take narrative form (Anderson 1983; Bhabha 1990), this was especially heightened for filmmakers who had immigrated to Bolivia and sought to define their new national affiliations. As films began to take narrative form in works by immigrant filmmakers, they envisioned the nation from a non-native viewpoint, as both exotic, vis-à-vis its Indians, and erotic, as an object of desire (see López 2000b, 47).

Just before World War I in 1912, the distributor Paramount joined eleven production companies to vertically control production, distribution, and exhibition; exhibitors were required to rent lesser titles in packages with the most successful features, thus ensuring income from all its products to the monopoly. The films coming to Bolivia from Hollywood and Europe (France, Italy) were produced in the medium of industrial capital's techniques and technologies and driven by a "star system." Between 1912 and 1915 the cost of producing a two-reel film jumped from a range of $500–$1,000 to one of $12,000–$20,000. Since their films were amortized in their domestic U.S. market, the foreign income earned in Hollywood films was profit that funded the industrialization of cinema and, aesthetically, a new industrial standard with expensive synchronous sound films produced in sound- and light-controlled studios. By 1926, the entertainment and narrative modes of cinema, supplemented (and eventually surpassed) by an enlarging sphere of ancillary commodities, had replaced the commercial exhibition of scenic documentary views and vaudeville acts. As Hollywood narrative films became hegemonic in Bolivia, official pressure and the newspapers called for national films to match the production values and narrative forms of the Hollywood films. Instead of positioning the Bolivian films alongside narrative features, there was a call to insert cinematic storytelling into a wider history of progress, which meant combining cinema and narrativity.

Yet from the beginning Bolivian "national cinema" was "born under the sign of censorship," in the words of the Bolivian film historian Alfonso Gumucio Dagron (1979). The first full-length filmic narrative, *La Profecia del Lago* (The Prophesy of the Lake), was prohibited from exhibition on the day it was to debut in 1925. The film tells of an elite woman in La Paz who falls in love with an Indian domestic servant *(pongo)* on her hacienda. Perhaps because it was based on a true story, as Dagron suggests, it clearly touched the racialist lines in criollo social discourse and its elitist attitude toward cinema. The film only received references in the press when the government ordered the filmmaker José Velasco de Maidana to surrender the film to be burned. Many years later, when Alfonso Dagron spoke with Maidana and his wife in Houston, Texas (Dagron 1979), they recalled that Maidana had protested the government's order by threatening that he would burn himself along with the film. Apparently, the film was not destroyed and an announcement for it appeared in an Oruro (an Altiplano mining city) newspaper two months later. Eventually, Maidana's resistance took the form of self-censorship when he hid the film in the walls of his house.

In the same year as Maidana's *La Profecia del Lago,* newspapers like *El Diario* heralded the first fictional feature film, *Corazón Aymara* (Aymara Heart) as "the beginning of the Bolivian cinematographic art." This was an adaptation of a theatrical drama produced by a German immigrant, Raul Ernst, and was contracted for a German company that wanted to produce a film showing the customs of Bolivian Indians. The film, slightly over an hour in length, was lost, however, most likely taken by Ernst to Germany to fulfill his contract there. As producer, Ernst hired Pedro Sambarino to direct the shooting and he contracted actors from a La Paz theater group to enact the tragic love story demonstrating that the Aymaras were fatalist. The film was shot in La Paz for twenty days and then for several days in the valley of Calacoto in southern La Paz during the Carnival parades in February. In a newspaper interview with *El Diario* on March 25, 1925, Julio Cesar Ibargüen, the director of the actors, described how one evening Sambrino and Ernst had returned to La Paz by car to sleep while Ibargüen and the actors remained in Calacoto under "insupportable" conditions:

> We stayed in a room that was in disrepair. We had nothing to cover us but our clothes that we brought from La Paz. The Indians did not want to serve us even hot water for the thirst that burdened us because we had only eaten little during the day. In sum, it was a very memorable night because the day after sleeping on the hard floor, none of us could move our limbs.

The social distance between the actors and the indigenous peoples off-screen is striking given that the theatrical actors were playing the roles of what Ibargüen called "authentic" Indian characters. Yet these relations of representation exemplify what Thomas Abercrombie (2003) has written about saint's festivals as pageantry in the Bolivian postcolonial predicament during the rise of indigenism in the twentieth century. In folkloric pageants, members of postcolonial elite society dress temporarily in costumes to perform Indianness in order to lay claim to a legitimate affiliation with national territory while at the same time retaining the racial basis of their elite status as non-Indian "whites."

The successful exhibitions and reviews of *Corazón Aymara* suggest that the press favored fictional cinema and the national fantasies and narratives it could play out, seeing nonfiction films as documents of crude "realities" that would adversely affect Bolivia's image internationally. In 1927, for example, two films were made of the execution of one of the three assassins of the Liberal president Pando. In one, *El Fusilamiento de Juaregui* (The Execution of Jauregui), Luis Castillo edited documentary footage of the execution of Pando's assassins. The municipal government immediately accepted the newspaper *La Razón*'s request to prohibit the film because audiences were not accustomed to seeing an execution or a corpse on the screen. The film was prohibited not only because of the explicit content of the film, however; critics argued that the crude images of the country that would be exported would cause a national embarrassment: "'the gaudy details, of the authorities, witnesses, Indians, Indias, the squalid, etc. . . . it exhibits a depressing approach to our justice, it denigrates nationality with the chorus of ragged Indians'" (in Dagron 1979, 54). *El Diario,* where Castillo also worked as a photographer, echoed the sentiment: "It is a graphic document that will be seen as a mournful example of the judiciary procedures of the Republic." Castillo's film was eventually allowed to be exhibited again, with the condition that it never be exported and that the original film and all copies be returned to the national archives. Almost simultaneously, the same newspapers promoted a filmic reconstruction of the same events made by the Austrian-born archaeologist Arturo Posnansky as a film that "must be seen." As the international circulation of films became intertwined with the national imaginary, the authorities and the press took into consideration the comparisons that Europeans would make between themselves and Bolivians looking at the images juxtaposed on the screen. As motion pictures from Bolivia entered the "Andean image world" (Poole 1997) and began to circulate worldwide, only the Indianness performed in fictional films and portrayed by nonindigenous actors could enter international commercial circuits.

A film's capacity for participation in the wider production and traffic of nationhood in cinematic form became a critical mark of progress for the incipient national cinema. Presses heralded the conquest-era fictional film *Wara Wara* (in Aymara, "star") in 1930 as "the first national work" and urged that it was a film the public "must see" as an act of patriotism and entertainment and, moreover, to "support the national industry," thereby inserting the film into the circulatory currency of the state. While reviews in the press proclaimed *Wara Wara* a success, one remarked that its costumes and the overly expressive theatrical gestures in the silent film were comical. Nevertheless, newspapers declared the film worthy of international export. Joining the international circulation of films would have been a considerable achievement for Bolivians for whom narrative films were always imported.

Wara Wara was made by José Velasco de Maidana's short-lived film company, Urania Films. Like *Corazón Aymara,* it was based on a recent theatrical piece, *The Voice of the Quena,* written by Antonio Diez Villamil.[7] The film was shot at archaeological locations around Lake

Figure 14. Reviews of *Wara Wara* (Maidana, 1930) collapsed "the start of national cinema" into the mythic origins of the nation, urging audiences to see the film as a patriotic act. Production stills courtesy of Pedro Susz K. and the Cinemateca Boliviana.

Figure 15. *Wara Wara*, set during the Spanish Conquest, both romanticized and defended the indigenous origins of the Bolivian nation.

Titicaca and in the ornate customs building in La Paz, where central figures in the elite art society (among them a sculptor, a painter, a poet, and a comedian) dressed as Inca and Spanish characters in an invasion-era romance between Wara, an Inca princess who had escaped the Spaniards, and a Spanish conquistador, Tristán. In the film, Tristán saves Wara when she is discovered by the other conquistadores, who threaten to rape her. Of course the two fall in love. The film reveals the nation's history as the violence of colonialism is converted into a national romance or "foundational fiction" (Sommer 1990). Yet the suggested romance between Wara and Tristán is not the story. The film ends with Wara recalling the horrors of the Spanish military invasion from which she had escaped, which motivates her to reject her lover Tristán. It is not their personal romance that descends from the past into the present, however. Cast as a native Bolivian and available to viewers, Wara herself comes to stand for the authentic nation itself as well as an available image for the national fantasy, thereby exemplifying how woman were seen as bearers of national culture and Indianness (Abercrombie 2003; Albro 2000; for Peru, see de la Cadena 2000). The battles between the Incas and the Spaniards in the film were notably incomparable to the spectacular battles that audiences were accustomed to seeing in Italian epics like *Quo Vadis* and U.S. westerns. While one reviewer attributed this "timidity" to the filmmaker, reviews in *La Patria* praised indigenous peoples for bravery and strength against the colonial violence. Nevertheless, a review from the city of Sucre nostalgically described *Wara Wara* as "the original formation of our roots, shown so admirably with its great force against the conquest of the Collasuyo [highland Bolivia] by the hidalgos of Spain in the 16th century" (*La Prensa,* May 25, 1930).

This presentist anti-imperial echo is also heard when the film was compared by a reviewer with the "absurd Yankee films . . . where artistic intent has been murdered, like all things, by the profane dollar." By distinguishing the national cinema with the status of a unique and authentic "art" rather than as a commodity, reviewers and public discourses contrast the commercial films of the North that surrounded national films in newspaper advertisements and on the movie screens themselves by dividing them into separate spheres of value.[8] As Julio Cesar Ibargüen had claimed earlier, *Corazón Aymara* was made by recognizing an "incompatibility between art and money . . . we don't commercialize art." The social discourses surrounding national cinema do not cleanly reject "foreign" technologies and practices; they claim the position to selectively appropriate and resignify them. Through the discourse of national cinema, reviewers and filmmakers in the urban middle classes positioned themselves as intermediaries of the selection and appropriation of the techniques of the cinema to defend the nation. Like the mythological *Wara Wara,* the national cinema suited a further aspect of twentieth-century indigenism in which postcolonial elites incorporated themselves into images of the past in order to found a "dignified imperialism-resistant basis for a new kind of patriotic nation-building" (Abercrombie 2003, 181). If twentieth-century *indigenismo* saw the romantic popularization of Indianness in which criollo and mestizo elites attempted to resolve their postcolonial situation by "being their own Indians," dancing in carnivals, and playing "Indians" in theatrical costume, films provided scenarios in which they could extend their roots into the national territory.

▶ ───────────────────────────────

Excavating the Nation

When *Corazón Aymara,* the first full-length narrative film permitted to screen in Bolivia, was celebrated for portraying Aymara as protagonists rather than as embarrassing background figures, it marked a populist project to move away from the racialist discourses of Social Darwinism (Demelas 1981) that had kept some Indians bound into peonage on haciendas. Middle-class populism distinguished language and visual markers like birthplace and dress, instead of physiognomic features, and promoted culture-oriented social discourses of indigeneity that could both connect them with and distinguish them from their own indigenous past (de la Cadena 2000). Whereas cultural mixture previously had been regarded as degraded, impure, and an obstacle to progress, *mestizaje* valorized cultural mixture within the framework of a national project. This nationalist-indigenist movement was fourfold: to locate a national "folkloric" tradition; rewrite a common national history; disseminate the nation across shared territory; and inspire the overthrow of a foreign-minded oligarchy and its foreign neocolonial counterparts. For the mestizo middle classes, something like a "national race" would be the end point, not the starting point, of their nationalist (Williams 1989) search for *el hombre boliviano* (Bolivian man).

As political populism merged with popular culture, indigeneity was popularized and commercialized in folkloric festivals, parades, and music as well as in cinema. *El Diario,* long the instrument of the oligarchy that had been maligning festivals in the immigrant neighborhoods as much as it denigrated cinema, remarkably noted the positive impressions of *Corazón Aymara,* suggesting that it presented "the beauty to be discovered, ignored by the Bolivians themselves," in the folklore and lives of the Aymara. The article (July 20, 1925) also noted the everyday dignity seen among Aymaras that hid the hostility of the conditions on oppressive hacienda estates: "The honor, the patience, in the docility, the honor of the trading. Their collective festivals, in this case, have been well exploited and suggests many ideas to the spectator, undoubtedly of sympathy toward the race, which puts its heart into everything."

Cinematographically, *Corazón Aymara* is a "silent film," although it was accompanied by a live piano translation of indigenous music. As Julio Cesar Ibargüen described in an interview, the intention of the film was to show that the life of Bolivian Indians "is not savage like it seems, or like those who presume to know them make us believe."[9] *La Nación* in the mining city of Oruro defined the film as one among "a clamor of shouts of protests" to liberate the indigenous peoples bound to haciendas (March 11, 1926). "While it isn't an easy task to live with our Indians," a review in *El Diario* stated, the film is "the only way to arrive at a full understanding of them."

In the early-twentieth-century indigenist movements, young Bolivian intellectuals were arguing that imperialist European evolutionary social theory had reached a "barrier" in understanding autochthonous cultures and were demanding national sociological studies of the "mysterious" Aymara psychology. But among the literate who were extending their heritage into the precolonial past, the national imaginary was more at stake than "understanding" the Aymaras. In other words, the search to understand the "Aymara psychology" was an archaeological excavation of a national identity and heritage. In its approach to depicting and demystifying Aymaras, reviews of *Corazón Aymara* dwell on personal drama, seeking to expose the internal proclivities and dramas of individual Aymara protagonists. The story takes place in La Paz, on a military base, on a valley hacienda, and at Carnival in Calacoto. As the story is described in the newspaper announcement of the film written by the film's producers:

> Lurpila, the fatalist incarnation of the Aymara. Over her weighs the distrust of her father, Colke Chuíma; the suspicions of Kilko; the wishes of her stepmother Summa Pakara; the loving memories of Kilko; the wishes of the mayor, and the bitterness of her husband Khana Aru, that suspects her of . . . Lurpila fights with everything and against everyone makes her innocence shine. Seen by her stepmother as unfaithful, making her Khentuara distrustful, an inflexible indian as the Romans that punished the indigenous with iron hands, sacrificing their feelings for their dearest ones. . . . Such is the story of *Corazón Aymara,* that will show the sobriety, the docility, and the work ethic of the most hard-working race of Bolivia, presenting at the same time scenes of its rural daily life in the shadows of the highest mountains, Illimani and Illampu. (in Dagron 1982, 71)

Seeking the mysterious but authentic "Aymara psychology" himself, the *El Diario* reviewer wrote that despite its worthy attempt, *Corazón Aymara* fails because of the "European character of its persons . . . its refinement, the culture of its expressions, were not faithful representations of the Aymara Indian." In noting the inauthenticity of the "European" actors, this reviewer reverses the slippage of "colonial mimesis" (Bhabha 1984) in which power is revealed through the differences that appear when the colonized "imitate" the colonizers. Another writer shifts the excavation from an inner Aymara psychology to their common territory, noting how the film succeeds as a "synthesis of the spirit, of the tradition, of the customs of our landscapes" (*La Reforma*, July 14, 1925), "our" being the pivotal term in this context.

The indigenist project of imagining the nation deployed iconic Andean landscapes as theatrical settings for the national heritage. Many of the press reviews of *Wara Wara* and *Corazón Aymara* pointed out how clearly and beautifully the Andean mountains, Altiplano, and lacustrine landscapes appeared projected on the screen. One *El Diario* reviewer of *Wara Wara* makes this attribution clearly in the observation that, in the rural landscapes where the film was shot, "the autochthonous spirit still hangs." As mentioned previously, elite actors in *Wara Wara* had buried themselves in the past with indigenous costumes in order to play out the romance of national origins in this story set among Inca constructions near Lake Titicaca. The same burial and excavation occurred at sites where the national past was constructed as if it were an archaeological site. The cinematic excavation of the national past most directly intersected with archaeology itself when the archaeologist Arturo Posnansky and the filmmaker Luis Castillo collaborated on *La Gloria de la Raza* (The Glory of the Race, 1926). Posnansky, who had immigrated to Bolivia from Vienna in 1904, had reconstructed the monumental stone ruins at the ancient Tiwanaku capital in Bolivia, near Lake Titicaca, and famously celebrated it as "the Cradle of American Man." Censors in La Paz promoted Posnansky's educational film in which he plays an archaeologist who learns the secrets of the Tiwanaku near Lake Titicaca from an Uru Indian, thereby teaching the audience about Tiwanaku and how the Urus, one of the world's oldest cultures, were "decaying" and should be saved. The film also glorifies Tiwanaku and its ancient builders, whom Posnansky portrayed as an Aymara master-race who literally had built the concrete foundations of the nation-state's indigenous heritage.[10] If ancient architectural achievements at Tiwanaku were celebrated in *La Gloria de la Raza,* the film was praised as a modern technical achievement, as seen in its use of miniatures and other visual effects. Like other documentaries, the film was shown alongside imported feature films on a common screen where the advancing project of national cinema could be perceived in the material quality of images: "We are not accustomed to films made in this country that have clarity compared to this. . . . The bright clarity of the photography and the artistic conceptualization in the choice of the landscapes and scenes to be filmed are the principal merits of 'La Gloria de la Raza,'" wrote Marcos Kavlin later in an essay promoting the preservation of films as part of Bolivia's heritage (1958). Praised for its capacity to vividly render the nation's antiquity, the modernizing national cinema was at once a visual register of the modernization of the nation-state itself as well as an index of the indigenous past that modernism conjures up. If history is a "sign of the modern," as Nick Dirks succinctly phrased it, then the cinematic appearance of ruins, *as ruined,* is a potent indication of modernity's arrival.[11]

The appearance of the modern ruins at Tiwanaku on the cinema screens in La Paz coincided with the populist movements to modernize the nation-state while retaining its indigenous heritage. Backed by the growing proletariat strata, state employees, rural immigrants, and the growing middle class, who were all connected to the new tin economy, the populist president Saavedra achieved political success in the early 1920s by promoting a distinctly national culture and seeking to liberate indigenous peoples who were bound to haciendas and blocked from participating in politics and modern culture. By attempting to end hacienda servitude and educate the indigenous servants *(pongos),* he envisioned a prosperous national economy sustained with more consumers and workers. At the same time, Saavedra saw indigenous free communities in the countryside as Liberal reactionaries and he deployed the military to stop Indian uprisings against the wealthy mestizos who were buying up their lands.[12] For some urban intellectuals and ideologues who sought to imagine native peoples as exemplars of a collective national future, "a national community," indigenous peasantries were also seen as dangerous and conservative elements.

During continuous resistance and episodic uprisings by indigenous communities, the new middle-class political and intellectual circles, labor unions, nationalists, and socialists not only challenged the elite oligarchies with foreign interests but they had to reframe the peasantry as the innocent and oppressed autochthonous basis of a strong national culture. In cinema, national folklore, and social discourses, the depoliticization of contemporary Indian communities served the populist design for assimilating them into a project of popular nationalism controlled by the new mestizo middle classes. Depoliticized, community-oriented, folkloric, and pastoral "Indians" would be imagined as the bearers of national history and the source of enduring national strength against external forces in the present. In popular interpretations of *Wara Wara,* for example, the scenes of invasion-era violence were emblematic of the strength of national character and national sovereignty. As seen in the earliest narrative films made in Bolivia, scenes of violence were used not to provoke concrete action but to represent how native peoples had defended the nation. Films made during the Chaco War, however, valorized actual indigenous combatants who were defending the nation.

▶

War and Cinema

Bolivia's disastrous Chaco War (1929–33) against Paraguay was originally intended by an overambitious President Salamanca to be an instrument of morale raising after the defeat in the War of the Pacific, in which Bolivia had lost its Pacific coast, and the devastating effects of the Depression on Bolivia's markets, which were tied to those overseas. Behind the scenes of the war, however, were Standard Oil and Shell Oil seeking to control the oil reserves beneath the surface of the eastern lowland Chaco region. Although the Bolivian government did not seize the propagandistic opportunities offered by cinema for the war, the filmmaker Mario Camacho engaged the setting of the war to make the 1933 narrative fiction *Hacia la Gloria* (Toward Glory). *Hacia la Gloria* was marked as Bolivia's first "sound" film; it added nonsynchronous sound to a film about an abandoned boy raised in the countryside who becomes a war pilot. In theaters, however, the film was upstaged by the sound films arriving from the United States at the time, including one *(Plains of Green)* that included a prewar trek across the Chaco region itself. While Dagron (1979) reports that reviewers had generally negative responses to the film, Marcos Kavlin recalls that the film did "raise national spirit" (1958). Publicity announcements emphasized the film as a sign of national strength: "Monumental debut of the first national sound production, with our best actors, especially Mr. Manuel Sagarnaga, titled 'Hacia la Gloria,' which is a true triumph and that our distinguished public will prize this national endeavor" (in Susz 1990, 59). In public discourses, the production of the film itself was the achievement of a strong national spirit.

Luis Bazoberry's documentary *La Guerra del Chaco* (The Chaco War) about the war was effectively censored in production when it was

Figure 16. Movie poster announcing *Hacia la Gloria* (Toward Glory, 1933). Film posters triumphantly featured technical elements as a measure of the modern status of Bolivian filmmaking—and, by extension, of the nation itself. Photo courtesy of the Cinematica Boliviana.

halted by the Bolivian military. In order to be exhibited subsequently, the original footage for the film had to be reassembled in order to suit the changing political realities and the characters that it appeared to either denounce or support.

Although copies of the film were eventually lost, Juan Peñaranda financed the documentary *La Campaña del Chaco* (The Chaco Campaign, directed by Mario Camacho), which was well received by Paceño audiences and the only Bolivian documentary about the war to be exhibited publicly. As Pedro Susz (1990) describes, *La Campaña* did not receive support from the state, although production in the Chaco was approved by the minister of state.[13] President Salamanca was invited repeatedly to a private exhibition but flatly rejected the invitations. At the beginning of production, raw film stock had to be imported from Argentina, but the customs officials at the border in Villazón charged an import tax that amounted to the entire sum of cash the film crew had with them. Without any of their own money, the filmmakers, Velasco de Maidana, Mario Camacho, and Luis Canelas, worked for forty-five days with their film crew amid the battles on the hot tropical lowlands to which they and the soldiers themselves were unaccustomed. Like Bazoberry in filming *La Guerra del Chaco*, the makers of *La Campaña del Chaco* were subject to impulsive state military leaders. During the shooting, they received much help from the troops but apparently were ignored by the general of the Bolivian army, Hans Kundt. After it was edited in La Paz, General Kundt demanded that *La Campaña del Chaco* be suppressed until it had his personal approval. After a month of travel, Peñaranda and Camacho returned to Kundt's headquarters, where they were received by the general with the domineering coldness he exercised over his troops. Kundt demanded that the one scene with corpses be removed, suggesting the war was without casualties and covering for the horrible defeats the Bolivian troops were taking. His only public remark in response to the film was that it would have been better if the prestigious Paramount Company had made it (Susz 1990, 94).

Representatives of Paramount in Bolivia were actually denied access to the battlegrounds of the Chaco War. They requested permission from the minister of war to film, but exclusivity already had been granted to Peñaranda's project. Paramount bought a three-minute scene from Peñarada's film for $4,000. Screening it as a newsreel in the United States, Paramount titled the scene *The Battle of Viacha*. This scene was the only dramatized portion of the original documentary, consisting of a reconstruction of men preparing to leave for the Chaco from Viacha, an Altiplano town near La Paz and distant from the lowland theater of the war.

Announced as a sound film (though nonsynchronous and without dialogue) that would evoke "civic emotion" (Susz 1990, 97–98), *La Campaña del Chaco* debuted in La Paz in 1933, breaking attendance records in movie theaters, yet it was only exhibited for three days in the Teatro Municipal before being replaced by commercial Hollywood films. Responding to popular requests, the film returned to the Teatro Municipal screen for several weekend exhibitions. On the second weekend, *La Campaña del Chaco* was exhibited in a double feature with *Wara Wara*, which had been released earlier that year, in a program that connected the defense of the nation in the past and the present. In *La Campaña del Chaco,* the indigenous conscripts were valorized as the "brave combatants patenting the noble force in defense of the territorial patrimony" (Susz 1990, 96). Such scenes of Bolivian peasants and mestizos joining forces to defend their nation were valorized as a crucial moment in the emerging national imagination, where they were figured as allies against foreign forces, including the elite oligarchy that had not only invented and brutally lost the war and soldiers but was also tied to the transnational corporations behind the war.

Despite the success of *La Campaña del Chaco,* Peñaranda's production company recuperated little more, if any, than its original investment in the project even after exhibiting the film in other Bolivian cities, selling the Viacha scene to Paramount, selling rights for thirty days to the Fox Company, and, finally, selling all national exhibition rights to the film altogether. Further, Peñaranda and company eventually sold their rights and lost track of the film after 1933 (Susz 1990, 101). It was almost a decade before a new production made in Bolivia occupied space on commercial movie screens again. In the long decade following the Chaco films of the early 1930s and well into the post–World War II 1940s, movie screens were occupied by "foreign" films made in the United States, Europe, Mexico, and Argentina, and capital in the hands of the commercial bourgeoisie was directed toward the construction of new cinemas in central La Paz, thereby making the 1930s and 1940s the "silent era" of Bolivian cinema.

Suspended in the assemblages of filmmaking and political projects in Bolivia, filmmakers in the first half of the twentieth century struggled to work with available and accessible international traffic of cinematic materials and technologies, producing films that reflected their imagination of Bolivia as a modern twentieth-century nation-state. As social discourses in the press fashioned and tracked the emerging "national cinema" as a part of the twentieth-century national project itself, the accomplishments of new narrative films, such as sound, were seen as instances of Bolivia's increasing involvement in the world system of nation-states, though not on equal terms. If the multiple nationalities of films in circulation through La Paz provoked desires for the modern and national, Bolivian films configured romance and desire so that devotion could be directed toward the nation itself. As much as the national cinema was evidence of Bolivia's modernity, it also activated historical memory. The early cinema substantially envisioned a path between the nation's past and the future as film stock itself traveled in trajectories that registered selected performances and settings that could be sequenced as a narrative whole. Linking together strips of film that were exposed to the resilient archaeological ruins and archaic cultures, filmmakers celebrated these sites as the heritage of a distinctively Bolivian and sovereign national state. While the cinema was used to romanticize and popularize contemporary Indianness by portraying continuities with the past, however, the traveling film stock in the cameras of these filmmakers avoided indigenous uprisings in the present. With such exclusions, the cinematic past and present could be selectively edited together as a filmic sequence and connected in the social imaginary as a national narrative culminating in the fantasy of a national and cultural synthesis. This fusion into a mestizo national identity, as we will see in the next chapter, became conflated with political populism and conjured up a visible and potent revolutionary state.

[**4**] *Fantasies of Modernity:*
The Social Imaginaries
of Revolutionary Films

▶

Bolivia, the Movie (1958)

This scene takes place in 1958 at the early evening exhibition at the
Cinema Monje Campero, the large, magnificent new theater built just a
few years earlier on the beautifully manicured Prado in the center of La
Paz. Arriving at the theater, people from the city's expanding mestizo
middle classes enter the lobby. They approach the ticket windows with
money drawn from the new tin-based economy that has been boosted by
providing raw materials for the Allied arsenals of World War II. Outside
on the sidewalk, Aymara residents of the city take advantage of their con-
doned access to the city center in the six years since the revolution in 1952.
While they still would not comfortably enter this location in the socially
divided cityscape as patrons, they set up tables outside to sell the moviegoers candy and potato chips (after all, this is Bolivia). Above the theater
entrance is a large hand-painted banner still announcing "Hoy! Gran
Estreno!" (Today! A Great Debut!), displaying a scene from the night's
film, which has been playing here for a week, Terence Fisher's 1958 adaptation of Bram Stoker's *Dracula*, starring Christopher Lee.

When the lights dim, the audience quiets and directs its collective
attention toward Bolivia's largest movie screen. Before the feature, the
documentary fiction film *Los Primeros* (The First Ones, 1958, dir. Jorge
Ruiz) begins and, through a fictional story, explains how the development
of oil drilling in the tropical lowlands will connect landlocked Bolivia to
the world economy and pull the country out of its stubborn traditional
past and into industrial modernity. In a story that mixes documentary
and fiction, oil is discovered by state engineers near the community of
a lazy protagonist and his superstitious mother. An off-screen narrator

explains aerial and ground-level oil prospecting to viewers, which leads to scenes of powerful dynamite explosions and oil shooting skyward in a burst of opportunity and optimism. Heavy machine equipment, tractors, and helmeted men move on-screen in a spectacular sequence of Fordist images of a gleaming steel modernity under construction, all headed by the organizing center of the oil industry in the La Paz offices of the state-run company, the Yasimientos Petroliferos Fiscales de Bolivia (YFPB). While the film shows domestic amenities, such as electricity, and values like self-sufficiency and the hard work that the oil wells developed by the government have brought to the community, it ends with the implications of prosperity this form of progress promises for the whole nation by imagining national integration across regions and the potential of exporting oil abroad from the seacoast. A triumphant musical sequence follows oil pipelines and railroads that make their way from the lowland tropics, up and across the Altiplano, through the glacial Andes, and finally to the Pacific coast where massive ships await the Bolivian oil at cargo piers.

The final images of *Los Primeros* go beyond the cargo piers, with a musical crescendo, to the restless sea crashing over rocks at the seashore, resolving some of the nation's deepest concerns with the tension between tradition and modernity and the longing of Bolivians to recover their seacoast and fulfilling the fantasy of recuperating access to the world's stage by exporting oil wealth, leaving behind economic dependency, and restoring the dignity lost when the entire Bolivian Pacific coast was relinquished to Chile in the War of the Pacific in 1879. If this final scene uses familiar striking images of twentieth-century industrial modernity to point toward a prosperous national future, its hyperbole is built from the inherent selectivity of the movement in narrative and the fixations of fantasy. Indeed, the film defines modern progress by featuring visible infrastructures of circulation such as pipelines, communication networks, and transportation systems that were envisioned as exhibiting and consolidating the translocal reach of the nation-state in the international system.

Los Primeros was produced and financed by several organizations coordinated by the National Revolutionary Movement (MNR) government's Bolivian Cinematographic Institute (ICB). In fact, creating the ICB itself was one of the first actions taken by the MNR coalition of workers, peasants, and new bourgeoisie after forcefully taking over the state power from a mining oligarchy in 1952. One of the crucial cultural projects of the new bourgeois state was to define and solidify itself as a popular nation. The revolutionary imaginary coalesced around images of a state-led, market-mediated society, a culturally mixed mestizo nation, and a commonly educated and sovereign citizenry that would include indigenous peoples as voters and consumers and redefine them as "peasants" (though only those who were literate). Film also provided a temporal form through which the nation's destiny could be narrated; that is, the nation could be emplotted as a linear tale that would account for its traditional indigenous roots and diversity, on the one hand, but also point toward a prosperous future in the modern industrial and capitalist world. Alongside the emergence of official folklore parades, the cinema was not only the vehicle through which the discourses of modernity and the popular nation were circulated, but it was a sphere where the revolutionary filmmakers themselves framed their own desires for the future.

Exhibited in urban cinemas and in rural towns, dubbed in Aymara or Quechua, ICB films reflected the promises of modernizing the country's infrastructure. Films like *Los Primeros* ended with wish-images that envisioned the future before the eyes of viewers, as if they could be seduced out of backward traditions with fantasy scenes that took the images of industrial modernization to paroxysm. Seeing these films from 1958 more than forty years later, you could feel it—this was a country on the move. The train of serial images cast onto the screens and reflected back onto the faces of the audiences was freighted with the fantasies of an approaching prosperous industrial and modern national state, making it appear as if the cinema itself were the well-oiled vehicle in which Bolivians could ride into modernity itself, just around the bend (cf. Lowe and Lloyd 1997; López 2000a; Martín-Barbero 1993).[1] In fact, these films seemed to be moving ahead so fast that it looked like Bolivia was making up for lost time in order to catch up with the North.

The fantasy for modernity displayed in the ICB films seems to exceed the visual frame itself, grasping, sustaining, channeling, and directing attention toward the feature films that followed them. In fact, ICB films were typically shown in the city's theaters before the commercial features, which at that time were usually from Mexico and the United States. There, the advancing technological progress and consumerist lifestyles of modernity were being disseminated in films and projected larger than life so that they could be sought, bought, emulated, and achieved by audiences here. Moving along a linear narrative continuum from tradition to modernity that extended over the entire film program, these short documentary films functioned like seductive trailers or previews or even as preparation for the subsequent film and elusive lifestyle that was appearing on the horizon. Perhaps this is not immediately obvious in a sensational horror film like *Dracula*; yet the narratives, image quality, and diegetic world on the screen itself all indexed the capital of the North that films embodied. Produced with high-color film-image quality, elaborate sets, compelling professional acting, music, lighting, special effects, and masterful story-telling, *Dracula* exhibited capital in motion—precisely at the historical moment when the modernity of the nation-state depended on making a connection between national prosperity and participation in emerging technologies and consumer modernity.

▶

Revolutionary Imaginaries: Modernity as Dream and Nightmare

In early-twentieth-century Latin America, as Ana López suggests (2000a), modernity first appeared as a fantasy in the vehicle of cinematic machinery. As I have described in earlier chapters, access and participation in a variety of modern formations, outlooks, and ideologies, such as the international system of nation-states, emerging global trade and consumer cultures, and technological infrastructures for travel and communication, all were appearing in enticing images and cinematic machineries prior to comparable industrial and political transformations that had developed in the North along with the commercialization of cinema.[2] In mid-twentieth-century Bolivia, cinema provided such a medium with which revolutionary economic and political transformations could be imagined, enacted, and tested on-screen as well as in the very practice of filmmaking itself. For as much as cinema and televisual media have been analyzed as powerful ingredients in constituting national imaginaries, they must necessarily be seen as social practices (Ginsburg et al. 2002a).

Focusing on Bolivia around mid-twentieth century, this chapter explores the sharply divergent cinematic forms and practices that filmmakers used as equally distinct revolutionary projects to envision and transform Bolivia as a modern nation-state. Across Latin America, political filmmakers self-consciously combined social projects with their own filmmaking practices. On the margins of the film economy driven by commercial value, they often experimented with alternative production practices that challenged dominant industrial modes of film production and consumption. More broadly, they intended their practices to model the wider social transformations they were provoking and proposing in their films. As readers may well know, the term "revolutionary cinema" typically has applied to films made by leftist filmmakers in Latin America and beyond who used film in various ways to bring about a transformation in social consciousness or provoke social revolution in bourgeois states and against imperialism. One well-known Bolivian filmmaker I discuss here, Jorge Sanjinés, represented this classic mode of revolutionary filmmaking during the 1960s and 1970s. In this chapter, however, I widen the frame of the "revolutionary" to include the films that were connected with a social revolution in 1952, a project for a modern bourgeois nation-state. As I will show, the films funded by the state during the revolutionary regime (1952–64) represent the kinds of scenarios and narratives that filmmakers like Sanjinés would subsequently work against in his politically revolutionary films. Taken together, these two historical projects form a synthesis that represents a larger revolutionary imaginary containing connected yet dialectically opposite and equally vigorous revolutionary historical projects and visions. Let me explain further the revolutionary social imagination that encompasses both forms.

In the years surrounding Latin America's "second wave of modernization" (Philips 1998), which was prominently marked in Bolivia with the revolution in 1952, Bolivian filmmakers pursued fantasies of modernization in state-sponsored works that were saturated with images of industrial progress and tones of optimism that promised and prepared Bolivians for a future as a coherent mestizo nation within a prosperous bourgeois state that would fully participate in the consumer economy and the international system of nation-states. Soon thereafter, however, other filmmakers departed from this project and struggled to excavate imagery from beneath the sparkling visions of modernization in order to reveal present social cleavages, forms of popular subordination, and indigenous cultural realities and provoke an alternative scheme for a more socialist future, also underway elsewhere in the world. The heightened contrast between these two film movements dramatically shows how historical projects for Bolivian modernity were driven by highly charged dreams in the first scenario and profound nightmares in the second. Together, their films evoke the "dialectical images" seen in Walter Benjamin's writing (Buck-Morss 1989) in which heaven and hell, progress and ruin, and utopia and dystopia are the disparate frames with which we can view the ideological parameters and material traces of historical projects to define modernity. Yet the substantial connection between these dialectical images is the way they each imply and challenge each other's contrasting scenarios while also drawing on narratives of linear progress.

To describe these film movements within a framework that accounts for their stimulating and even hyperbolic allure as well as the contrasts they conjure up, I align Benjamin's dialectical optics with Slavoj Žižek's (1997) argument that fantasy functions as a framework that constitutes, organizes, and saturates the experience of the historical world. Rather than an illusory category that operates apart from real conditions or as a mask that conceals power relations, the fantasies in political representation are an actual social force that drives and shapes "a fictional reality" through scenes of desire and narrative plot forms (Aretxaga 2000). Žižek writes that fantasy takes the basic form of narrative because it organizes desires "to resolve some fundamental antagonism by rearranging its terms into a temporal succession" (1997, 10–11). At the screening of *Los Primeros* in La Paz just described, tradition and modernity were aligned into a single forward-moving historical narrative that perceptually transported its viewers to the seacoast and beyond it along a "circuit of desire" (Fischer 2003, 70) to the fantasies displayed in the subsequent film. As we will see, the two forms of revolutionary filmmaking discussed in this chapter emphatically rework social inequalities and cultural differences into their respective scenes of industrial progress and socialist revolution by utilizing temporality as a vehicle to emplot (and incite) radical social transformation and eliminate social conflict. In this regard, we will see how revolutionary films invent the future as well as the past, making particular ideological accounts of the nation-state possible and desirable.[3] At the same time, as Žižek describes, fantasies also imply, index, and even conceal the phantasmal horrors they also conjure up (1997, 6–7). It is this dual fabrication that inheres in fantasies that fittingly makes Benjamin's dialectical images of utopia and dystopia immanent to the wider "revolutionary" framework in which competing fantasies of modernity are at once the objectives and driving forces of social transformation. It is the disparity between the films produced following the social revolution and the succeeding socialist revolutionary films, in which each form reveals the mythic proportions and elements of the other, that synthesizes these dialectical forms within the imaginary of "revolutionary cinema."

As revolutionary filmmakers imagined competing futures by experimenting with their own filmmaking practices in order to actualize their visions, they used production practices to construct their ideologies and vice versa, seeking to use film as a concrete medium to close the circuit between their ideology and historical processes (Burton 1997). Beyond and within their texts, revolutionary filmmaking in Bolivia exploited film's capability to experientially convey knowledge about cultural difference, mediate social relationships, provoke political transformations, and imagine a potent national identity. By emphasizing the materiality of film and by conceptualizing filmmaking as a form of transcultural cinema (MacDougall 1998) that draws forces together and mediates differences, revolutionary filmmaking also entailed modes of consumption (Burton 1997) that mediated the experiential aspects of cultural, physical, intellectual, and emotional worlds between film subjects and viewers such that viewing itself was a form of experiencing them. What kinds of understandings, experiences, and social action have these transcultural films been intended to mirror and provoke in Bolivia? How were the transcultural and material qualities of filmmaking and film viewing exploited as mimetic practices and forms of experience in order to imagine and orient the formation of a modern nation-state? Finally, how did the sentiments and images of revolutionary film linger in the subsequent neoliberal political environment that has overturned much of the revolutionary models that prevailed at midcentury?

▶

A Cinematic Modernity: The Social Revolution (1952)

A year after the National Revolutionary Movement carried out the popular-nationalist revolution of 1952, the government created the Bolivian Cinematographic Institute (ICB) as part of its plans to modernize the state. As described earlier, one of the crucial cultural projects of the revolutionary state was to consolidate a popular nation of peasants and a mestizo bourgeoisie who had allied to carry out the revolution against a European-descended criollo oligarchy. Film became a principal vehicle in which regional cultural diversity could be visually displayed, celebrated, and tied together as a new popular nation. In the years preceding the formation of the ICB, Jorge Ruiz and several colleagues had become the center of a network of governmental and international organizations that reversed the long absence of filmmaking since the 1930s with a period of vibrant documentary activity. Ruiz, the principal filmmaker of this era, had learned and practiced principles of filmmaking from reading the magazine *American Cinematographer* while studying in Buenos Aires as a young man. Although Ruiz describes himself as "autodidactic," having received no direct training in Latin America, he recognizes the influences of Leo Seltzer, Richard Leacock, and Willard Van Dyke, filmmakers from the United States and England with whom he also later collaborated on projects for the United Nations and CBS in New York. He also had a relationship with the progressive British filmmaker John Grierson. Before joining the ICB, he had made several films with Bolivia Films, a company that Ruiz ran that was initially financed by Kenneth Wasson, a former North American staff member at the U.S. embassy. Ruiz also worked with Telecine, a film company opened for future president Gonzalo Sánchez de Losada by his father, himself a formerly exiled member of the MNR party and UN diplomat. During the first year of the revolution, Telecine and Bolivia Films contracted work from the United States embassy, the Alliance for Progress, United States Information Services (USIS), and then the ICB when it opened. The ICB funded hundreds of newsreels and documentaries about the revolutionary state. This was the only period in which Bolivian filmmakers were well funded and continuously occupied as the gears of the state and cinema fully enmeshed.

Ruiz explained to me that his filmmaking in indigenous communities was inspired by his years growing up in rural Luribay, where he also learned to speak Aymara. "My first friends were *campesinos* [peasants]. I developed a lot of affection for rural life then," Ruiz recalled.

> It's important to have a lot of respect for other cultures. First, establish a friendship with the *campesinos*—the people of the countryside—first the friendship and then see how they would express their world, and try to show that. But we never have had great difficulty.

He realized too that his personal approach had depended upon delicate exchanges:

> You cannot go and impose things. We brought them gifts, never money if possible, we always brought gifts for the school, we gave them notebooks, books. They liked it if we helped with sports. So we brought soccer equipment, shirts, balls. . . .

For Ruiz, another sign of his own success is that he was able to work within what are often portrayed as "closed and insular indigenous communities" where others may not have succeeded. He worked with the African Aymaras, who he says are "a very rebellious group." Additionally,

> We achieved a great friendship with the Kallawayas [indigenous healers], and they opened doors to us to things that are very secret . . . that many researchers have not found among the Kallawaya people. So the most important thing is to have that friendship.

One of Ruiz's main goals in making films about indigenous peoples in Bolivia was to save their cultures. He said to me:

> They are entering a very Westernized culture where they are gradually forgetting their culture. Every year there is less. So it's important. My point is that it is important to rescue them as soon as possible before they disappear totally.

Ruiz's award-winning *Vuelve Sebastiana* (Come Back Sebastiana), sponsored by the mayor's office in La Paz and made in 1953 at the height of the revolution, is about a young Chipaya woman who ventures into the forbidden territory of a neighboring Aymara community that had previously seized Chipaya land. *Vuelve Sebastiana* is formulated with urban nostalgia, in which people from the capital sympathize with the destruction of a rural past they claim as their own, and then turns to the fantasy of heroically rescuing the cultural ruins. This scene is particularly revealing of this nostalgia:

> [Wide shots of the Chipaya village] At one time, between the fall of Tiwanaku and the birth of the Inca Empire, lived a mysterious race distinct from the Quechuas and Aymaras and which few know of today. 2,000 years ago they were called the Ch'ullpa's. [Camera moves slowly into the dark entrance of a Ch'ullpa tomb] In the interior of the surviving ruins of their culture, human remains are found [shots of human skeletons]. Mummified Ch'ullpas that have defied eternity since the dawn of time. Asleep. As if frozen. Strange creatures of legends that tell us of remote times and disappeared peoples. Where does the past begin? Where does the future lie? [Match dissolve from skeleton in fetal position to a young Chipaya girl seated in a similar position]. Today, this is Sebastiana Lupi, a girl from the Chipaya tribe that lives in Charangas, Oruro, and proclaims to be authentic descendents of the Ch'ullpas. There are only a thousand. They suffer from hunger. Drought. Isolated . . .

This film constructs cultural otherness in a recognizable technique common to conventional documentaries: the other is a mystery and frozen in time. The other suffers from hunger and is isolated and struggles against the elements of an inhospitable environment. It is the off-screen narrator who is the authority on the Chipaya. Filmed without location sound, this is his story, not theirs.[4] In fact, the story itself was written in La Paz after the filming. (In the next moment of the film, in fact, the voice-over shifts from addressing and informing the audience to the voice of Sebastiana's grandfather, more directly embodying the paternal position of the off-screen voice.) This mode of address toward both the audience and Sebastiana from off-screen closes the gap between the exotic protagonist and urban middle-class spectators by creating parallel subject positions that are addressed by the voice of the film. The paternal voice speaks to both the urban mestizo and the rural Indian:

> [As Sebastiana leaves the village with the sheep] . . . Today you are thinking of going very far . . . there where it is said that the pastures are good. . . .But here the Chipaya territory ends. You shouldn't go further. Ahead is the domain of the Aymaras. Those Aymaras who submitted us to isolation . . .

When the narrator makes a more complex representation by mentioning that the Chipaya do not have wood and must buy it from the nearby Aymaras who have some control over them, he connects the "isolated" Chipayas to the present by way of the market. Because it is the Aymara-dominated marketplace that separates them from essential resources, "foreign assimilation" is understood as a threat.

In a mode of history that moves forward, the Chipaya are a sympathetic and fragile culture that has been left behind as the fossilized "ruins" of Western progress. If the appearance of Ruiz's film camera in the Chipaya community, which had not seen films before, is also a concrete sign of modernity, its capacity to record and pile up history as it happens, or "rescue" it, in Ruiz's own terms, produces the ruins as a ruin as it records them in a manner fascinatingly analogous to how the Ch'ullpa mummies represent imprints of some former social life. In this scene, it becomes difficult to determine whether the ruined and decaying cultures have provoked filmmaking or whether modern filmmaking itself is a key condition for the "ruins" as such. Do signs of the primitive depend on the modern, or do signs of the modern conjure up the primitive? This double-register is what makes the match dissolve from the ancient Ch'ullpa remains to Sebastiana in her "present" sensational. Sebastiana's historical and social connection to her ancestors is bound up in the physical resemblance between her momentary pose in the present and the mummy from the past and frozen in time. But it is the physical contact and material superimposition of two separate strips of film material itself that makes possible the very dissolve and the represented historical relationship created between them when printed as a single third strip of film. Guided by a sympathetic and paternal narrative voice and framed by its contemporaneous use of cinema as a modern form of recording the past by virtue of its contact with history as it happens, the film fossilizes Sebastiana and her community as vestiges of historical progress who themselves appear to be bound so closely with their own remote past that they are only knowable for their pastness.

If indigenous cultures like the Chipaya were seen as unchanged vestiges of antiquity and if the survival of some indigenous communities were seen as precarious, how were indigenous cultures both celebrated and seen as obstacles in narratives of cultural and economic progress? In other words, how to maintain contact with history safely so that the approaching future could also be measured and embraced? Consider again the match dissolve in *Vuelve Sebastiana* between her antique past and her present. Originating from separate contexts, and representing separate historical moments, a third single and connective narrative strip of film had to be produced to fill up the "empty historical time" between past and present, connecting them yet holding them apart while the scene moves forward. As if film were used to open up and then fill the very span for empty historical time to unfold cinematically, many of the ICB films assembled multiple histories and contexts within a common narrative and a contemporaneous national trajectory. Using this strategy of spatializing and temporalizing key sites along a cinematic and narrative continuum from traditional to modern, ICB films direct attention optimistically toward a modern future in the city, where indigenous culture can exist as folklore to celebrate its vigor, while they nostalgically locate indigenous culture and the past in the countryside.

The bearing of the temporal position of indigenous heritage on the film was clear when *Vuelve Sebastiana* was to be entered in a major film festival in Montevideo, Uruguay, in 1956. The Bolivian authorities in La Paz prohibited its entry, claiming that "a movie about Indians couldn't represent Bolivia in a foreign country." Fortunately, Bolivia's ambassador in Uruguay entered a copy of the film that had been previously given to him and it went on to win the first prize in the festival—in the Ethnography and Folklore category.

As were many of the films of the late 1950s, *Las Voces de la Tierra* (The Voices of the Earth) was produced jointly in 1956 by Bolivia Films and Telecine, both private companies, with money from the USIS, the municipal government of La Paz, and the ministry of foreign relations. The film's route from countryside to city tracks the nation's history of civilization and its urban mestizo destiny. Yet at the same time, this romantic connection between Andean landscapes and the spirituality of native culture was considered to be a source of energy for the mestizo nationalist movement by the influential writer and politician Franz Tamayo (see Sanjinés 2004, 61). The film opens with a young Aymara boy tossing stones into a small lake on the rural Altiplano. A paternal male voice-over explains how the young "Bolivian Indian . . . the son of the land" magically communicates with the voices of the landscape and the wind. The film explains that the same voices speak in the indigenous agricultural rituals and dancing at all of the year's important fiestas. After scenes of ritual festivals in the Altiplano, we see an artisan in El Alto, the city above La Paz, making the folklore masks that personify forms of evil. Then in the very center of La Paz, where indigenous peoples had been tacitly prohibited from entering prior to the revolution, richly costumed and masked dancers parade in the streets in a municipal folklore event, bringing rural Andean culture into the city. In the culmination, the folklore dancers enter an outdoor stadium where immigrant Aymaras and mestizos observe. "Dances are memories," explains the narrator, "links to the past." If the dances suggest the idea of time travel within the narrative of the national project, any contemporary meaning for the dancers themselves is erased.[5] In the final scene "indigenous culture" is permitted in the city as "folklore," the emblem of a distinctive national heritage under highly regulated and official circumstances.

The synthesis of the mestizo nation reached one of its few moments of closure in 1973 in the cinematic postcard images of *La Gran Herencia*

(Great Heritage, produced by Jorge Ruiz), one of the last films made as part of this revolutionary mode. Showing the cultural artifacts of indigenous culture throughout the territory of the state, it begins in the Andes, moves through the tropical regions, and makes a return to the Altiplano—the spatial/cultural origin space of the cinematically integrated mestizo nation. The historical past of cultural mixing *(mestizaje)* is collapsed into the visible artifacts of a timeless national heritage, highlighted in the images of godlike figures of an indigenous pantheon beautifully carved into the front of a Catholic church. With its circular movement through space in the linear time of the film itself, this film lassos "the permanent treasures of the country," as the opening titles indicate, and then reins them in. "We are the proprietors of the past," claims the anonymous male off-screen voice.

As political agency and authority are funneled into the mestizo urban capital in these films, they leave behind depoliticized rural space—peasants as young innocent children to be civilized. Strikingly, indigenous political struggles, with their particular multiethnic configurations and complex alliances, are a structured absence in most of the films made in revolutionary Bolivia. This absence suggests that the hazards of cultural difference can be explained and managed safely—a message important to a right-leaning middle-class cinema audience nervous about the revolutionary government that began with an alliance with a coalition of miners and indigenous peasants.

By 1958, Bolivia's initially left-leaning revolutionary government had swung to the right and was in the pocket of the U.S. government, which began to sponsor the ICB, headed by Jorge Ruiz himself at that point. Distributed in urban cinemas and in rural towns, dubbed in Aymara or Quechua, the films made by Telecine,[6] Bolivia Films, and the ICB during the 1950s and early 1960s used vision as the means to reflect the optimism and temporality of the modernist nationalist projects: integration of roadways connecting distinct geographical and cultural zones and the nation-state (*Un Poquito de Disversificacion Económica* [A Little Economic Diversification], 1955); Western education for campesinos (*Juanito Sabe Leer* [Little Juan Can Read], 1954); agricultural and industrial development (*Semillas de Progresso* [Seeds of Progress], 1956); and national optimism (*Bolivia Lo Puede* [Bolivia Can Do It], a series of films made between 1960 and 1961 and distributed in rural towns in Spanish, Aymara, and Quechua. In 1956, the Institute began to make documentaries and a feature-length film in 35mm that also promoted development. In 1962, Ruiz made his last film as chief of the ICB, *Las Montañas No Cambian* (The Mountains Do Not Change), which celebrated the ten years of social changes through the eyes of a campesino who reflects upon the social projects of the MNR through images of highways, tractors, agricultural equipment, and the integration of Bolivian ecological zones and ends with the suggestion of the emergence of a distinct "Bolivian" nation entering modernity. As the Bolivian government became further tied to U.S. development models, cinematic images of machinery and industry set in Bolivian landscapes were pervasive on movie screens.

If the nationalist revolution was anti-imperialist to start, U.S. involvement and funding later began to affect the revolutionary project by the late 1950s. Although U.S. government and development organizations channeled funds into cinema, they did not exercise strict control. As Jorge Ruiz told me,

> Actually, they gave us a lot of freedom. They only gave us the themes, such as "We want to make a film like this, how can you do it?" They made the proposal and we said, "It can be done this or that way." Almost always we agreed with them. They left us complete freedom. That was a great advantage. There was no rigid imposition.

As a self-labeled propagandist, Ruiz also describes his work as "cine social," a form of "social cinema" that he developed most extensively in the film *La Vertiente* (The Spring). After a conversation with a teacher in the tropical community of Rurrenabaque, Ruiz planned a film based on a real-life story of how the community constructed a pipeline for potable water, a story "very well related with the philosophy of rural community development," Ruiz recalled to me. Oscar Soria wrote a script and Ruiz and his team planned to produce the film as the first 35mm title, "a little more ambitious than a documentary, but in black and white to keep the costs down." Yet by the time the film went into production in 1958, other government projects had absorbed much of the state budget, leaving virtually none for the ICB and the project. The USIS called Ruiz and told him they were interested in sponsoring the project if it would show the water pipes labeled as donations by USAID. Ruiz recalled, "So I said, 'I can't because it changes the point. The idea was that sometimes Bolivians forget that they always have their hands out, wanting to live off of American aid, with the help of the government, and waiting for the government to do everything.'"

Ruiz turned to President Siles for help and received a loan from the Central Bank. Incorporating a romantic story of two protagonists, Ruiz then produced the film with people from Rurrenabaque who reenacted how they had constructed a water system to pipe fresh potable water from the mountainous slopes above the community. The film was the first 35mm feature-length (sixty-five minutes) sound film made in Bolivia and it was exhibited in La Paz in two theaters, but for only seven days. After that the U.S. embassy phoned Ruiz again: "'Now things are different. We would like to buy copies,' the embassy said. We sold them 110 copies of the film, then they distributed it all over the Third World. They made versions in English and other languages, like an educational film." The eventual worldwide distribution of two hundred prints of *La Vertiente* by the Alliance for Progress recuperated the film's production expenses to pay back the loan.

Ruiz explained to me that his films were "fought over" by the movie theaters, which showed them before commercial features. "I never had a problem distributing my films because I was in another field [social documentary] that had nothing to do with the commercial films . . . the public liked to see something from Bolivia." Ruiz and the ICB navigated their films into the dominant Hollywood and Mexican flows of films by inserting their documentaries before the commercial feature films, which had attracted audiences to the theaters. Further, despite U.S. funding during the 1950s and early 1960s, contract filmmaking was an opportunity for filmmakers in Bolivia to get crucial experience with cinema technology and to develop their own approaches, some of which had a major impact on subsequent filmmakers, for example, the idea of a collective protagonist introduced in *La Vertiente*.[7]

While the story of *La Vertiente* resolves a tension between principal protagonists, the hero of the film is clearly collective: the state government collaborating with a mobilized community. In fact, once government equipment arrives in the community of Rurrenabaque in the film, there is a twenty-minute sequence of machinery and groups of people working together as they build the pipes, bridges, and roadways through the forest and up mountain slopes, accompanied by upbeat music, in scenes reminiscent of the oil pipelines at the conclusion of *Los Primeros*.

▶
Popular Revolutionary Cinema and Political Mimesis

The images of a coherent modern mestizo nation that composed the films of the revolutionary 1950s were intended to keep tradition firmly in national territory while perceptually inserting urban middle-class audiences into the forward-moving flow of mythic industrial modernity. Inserted before the flow of feature films, the social documentaries served as advertisements for a prosperous future; yet it is fitting to note that the Spanish word used for advertising in Bolivia is *propaganda,* while the

Spanish verb *advertir* means "to warn." Thus, if many of the ICB's films pulled audiences into the inexorable currents of progress, then the socialist revolutionary films of the 1960s and 1970s depicted these currents as a tempest (cf. Buck Morss 1989) that left the indigenous, the poor, and the peasantry ruined in its wake.

The early 1960s were the final years of the social revolution in Bolivia. By 1966, after the popular-military Barrientos regime took over the government, the United States was financing much of Bolivia's economy, and ten oil projects were owned by U.S. multinationals. A young director named Jorge Sanjinés, who had studied philosophy in Chile and filmmaking in Cuba, was appointed to the ICB and soon began making films intended to expose the exploitation that the indigenous peasantry suffered in the dominant mestizo society and, by extension, from U.S. imperialism.[8] His first full-length film, *Ukamau* (This Is How It Is), for which he won an award at Cannes as Best Young Director, takes place on an island in Lake Titicaca and shows an indigenous man taking violent revenge on a mestizo man who had violated his wife, evidently indicating aspects of colonial violence at the heart of Bolivian society and the mestizo imaginary. The ICB was closed immediately by the Barrientos regime after the first public screening of *Ukamau;*[9] and the films that Sanjinés went on to make while in and out of exile were prohibited from exhibition in Bolivia until 1989. The films were outlawed not only because they opposed the government but because they suggested social solutions through popular revolutionary uprisings. Sanjinés's film *Blood of the Condor* (*Yawar Mallku* 1966) reveals how members of an indigenous community learn through reading coca leaves that the U.S. Peace Corps had been sterilizing community women, which precipitates a violent revolutionary showdown. Other films made by Sanjinés while in exile in Peru and Ecuador also opposed imperial U.S. interventions in peasant life.

Although their films were censored, Sanjinés and his film collective did widely distribute and screen their films secretly in Bolivia, Peru, and Ecuador among the rural indigenous and mining communities who were the subjects of the films. Sanjinés and the filmmaking collective, the Ukamau Group, quickly learned after screening *Blood of the Condor* that their cinematic techniques, such as the use of flashbacks and close-ups, did not depict time and space in a form that made sense to indigenous viewers. Sanjinés then sought to portray collective protagonists, to incorporate indigenous narrative forms, and to use "long takes" not only to make their films accessible to indigenous and popular audiences and subjects in their films but to counteract what they saw as the alienating qualities of the majority of "imperialist" individual-centered Hollywood films. "There is an essential point of departure for thinking about a cinema directed toward the Bolivian people: the majority of our people do not deal with one another in a manipulative way, as does the dominant Westernized majority, but rather through integrated and reciprocal cultural and mental structures" (Sanjinés 1986, 43).

Along with Sanjinés's approach to "peasant" aesthetics and participatory filmmaking, the group deployed a Marxist frame to depict the structures of domination and the solutions for a popular revolutionary movement. *Blood of the Condor* ends with a signature freeze-frame of a rifle held high in the air, but the revolutionary ending is perhaps most forceful in the film *The Courage of the People*. Produced in 1971 during a brief leftist regime in Bolivia with funding from Italian television, the film depicts a violent massacre carried out by the government several years earlier against peasant miners in the Altiplano town of Siglo XX. As a unique combination of testimonial, memory, and reenactment, the film was written and filmed with actual survivors of the massacre who play themselves (and the military soldiers) in the film.

The film begins with a daytime reenactment of a massacre on the open plains of the Altiplano. A large group of several hundred miners appears and moves toward a hillside where Bolivian soldiers await. This scene depicts "the people" as a collective protagonist upholding the Bolivian flag in the face of being shot down by a government that refuses to listen to their claims. The collective image and the shouts of resistance against imperialism and tin barons reveal how the most vulnerable and humiliated people are able to oppose their own oppression. Then, accompanied by engaging, rhythmic drum-beating, the film introduces a series of historical photographs of the people in the government, the military, and the mining industry who were responsible for a series of mining massacres in Bolivia throughout the twentieth century. Through testimonials by surviving miners and on-screen text, the film connects powerful political economic and military relationships between the Bolivian government, tin barons, and U.S. companies that exploit peasant miners. The Bolivian tin miners are a highly class-conscious working class, as June Nash's well-known book demonstrates (1979), but the film does little to elaborate the cultural terms in which they see their lives and with which they formulate Marxist forms of opposition. The main part of the film is the reconstruction of the massacre at Siglo XX itself; it was shot at night without using additional lighting and conveys very well the sense of incoherence and alarm as the town was taken over in the darkness, beginning at the radio station.[10] In contrast to the films of the 1950s, modernity itself (and not antiquity) is depicted with darkness and the production of ruins.

Filmed with the very people who were victims and witnesses of the original historical events, the film is centered on "recollection images" produced through a kind of Marxist divination that falsifies official history by cinematically moving backward to reveal particular memories and histories hidden from the image repertoire of official history (Marks 2000, 51). In handheld long takes that plunge into the darkness and dimly lit rooms of the mining town, viewers sense, see, and hear bodies being shot, tortured, and finally dumped into a mass grave. As Sanjinés recounts the production,

> Several times, members of the production crew looked dumbfounded at a performance that could not be halted. The camera itself was forced into the role of protagonist; it had to interact as yet another participant. . . . A large number of scenes had to be captured on the spot, very quickly, in order not to lose them, since, like reality itself, they could never be repeated.
>
> Those images had not been conjured up by some scriptwriter. . . . No, these images were created—or rather, remembered—by the people. They were situations created on the spot by people who, amid the turbulence and explosions, were reliving their past. (1986, 42)

By virtue of its exposure to them, this film produces visible fossilized traces of its subjects in a technique of recollection that resembles the rescue intended for the subjects of *Vuelve Sebastiana*. But here the technique is constructed as a critique of modern forces such as the mining industry that render the film subjects obsolete and expendable. Further, the images of mining families as active speakers and survivors themselves provoke action beyond sympathy and nostalgia. They call for a bodily response from viewers as the indexical images in this film traverse several registers at once: In one, survivors are bound bodily to and index the same particular events they reenact, transferring onto the surface of the film the powerful events they suffered; in the second degree, the viewer's bodies experience the violence vis-à-vis their experience of murky film images and the visualization of the survivors' brutalized and threatened bodies on the screen. The key provocative moment occurs when, as David MacDougall writes about transcultural cinema, "we achieve identification with others through *a synchrony with their bodies* made possible in large part by vision" (1998, 262; emphasis mine). In Sanjinés's account, a "psychic climate had been unleashed, and it would only be present once" (1986), although its social life would not end there.

The political potential of the energy enabled by the visual registration of memories that inhabit bodies is exploited at the film's revolutionary ending. As Suzanna Pick explains it, "Memory becomes in this way a resource to contest official histories and a site where an alternative future can be imagined" (1993, 103). The last scene returns and repeats the beginning in which the collective protagonist of miners, men, women, and their children is gathered again and shouting in protest as they march across the Altiplano toward the camera and viewers. The difference this time, in the context of the preceding massacre, is that this scene of the "people" is courageous, defiant, and potentially revolutionary. It is a scene whose excess should spill over like the light reflected from the screen onto the intended audiences of the masses of workers, peasants, and miners who occupy the same world as those on the screen, and its political urgency be taken up by them. "We came to the conclusion that not only should we *not* reject the power of affective excitement that film can produce in the viewer. . . . This kind of emotional involvement would not desert spectators when the curtain fell, but would follow them, prodding them toward self-analysis and criticism" (Sanjinés 1986, 42).

As a revolutionary film with an emphatic claim to realism and loaded with intense emotional energy and brutal scenes, *The Courage of the People* also strives to produce what Jane Gaines calls "political mimesis" in the bodies of spectators (1999). Her idea resembles MacDougall's idea of the transcultural: "This is about the relationship between bodies in two locations—on the screen and in the audience—and it is the starting point for the consideration of what the one body makes the other do" (90). Yet Gaines's concept pointedly foregrounds forms of political transformation in documentary. "This has to do with the production of affect in and through the conventionalized imagery of struggles: bloodied bodies, marching throngs, angry police" (92). If the cinema is a form of mimesis that takes its power from the conditions in the world it copies, Gaines argues, then it makes viewers want to take action *because of the conditions in the world of the audience*" (90; emphasis in original). That is, the power of political mimesis and revolutionary film does not inhere in the images of bodies themselves, though they are the medium, but in the affect and consciousness formed in an engagement in which the world of the footage—that is, the material, historical, and social forces in and beyond the frame of the film—corresponds with the world extending beyond the screen ahead of the film audience. And if what makes *Courage of the People* especially striking are these parallel registers of mimetic activity, as described above, then they widen into the contexts of viewing. When I saw this film at the Cinemateca Boliviana in La Paz in 1993, I observed many people in the theater displaying anger and shock but not surprise as the lights came up during the credits. Upon leaving the theater we all saw military tanks and armed guards that had been patrolling the streets for several weeks while the workers' strikes and protests were going on throughout the Center of the city. The film's history of a particular past scarred with political violence was extended to our popular memory.

As leftist politics in Bolivia shifted from an emphasis on class issues to cultural politics over the course of the 1980s (Albó 1987), from the oppositional strategy of revolution to ethnic movements for participation, and as Bolivian political ideologues themselves later began to drop the model of *mestizaje,* Sanjinés took on key issues of identity in an alternative cinematic form. *La Nación Clandestina* (The Clandestine Nation), made in 1989, attempts to portray the inherently plural sense of Bolivian identity as well as that of Aymaras who move to and from La Paz. The film's visual space and narrative move between city and countryside, past and present, with remarkable cinematography and editing. Multiple narratives from the present and past of the principal character, Sebastian Mamani/Maisman, are visually interwoven in the foreground and background of the same shot as the narrative of the film moves between them without any of the transitions or superimpositions (e.g., cuts or dissolves) that formed *Vuelve Sebastiana* or *Las Voces de la Tierra,* for example. These co-present layers depict the character's multiple identities and the conflicts between them as shifting but simultaneous layers in the very same physical space as the camera. Informed by rural Aymara conceptions of space-time, according to Sanjinés, the film challenges the linear modernist cinematic narratives of linear progress in Bolivia: Here, it is the future that is "behind" and unseen, while the past is knowable and visibly manifest in the present landscape where it coexists with the present. If the presence of the camera in Chipaya signified Sebastiana as a modern ruin, constructed in the binding of past and present in the superimposed strips of film that made the match dissolve, then the camera on the set of *La Nación Clandestina* deconstructs those very ruins. The film visualizes an alternative relationship between present and past as vividly coexistent in the same physical space. They appear simultaneously in front of the camera in the production of a single strip of film rather than by juxtaposing two to invent a third. Using these cinematic depictions of visual depth and narrative juxtaposition, Sanjinés tangles up the linearity of the discourse of national *mestizaje* as seen in cinematic space and heard in the political ideology earlier in the 1950s. This film uses a montage of imagery to reveal the cultural heterogeneity and realities hidden beneath the uniformity of the mestizo national project; here, they refuse to integrate or be narrated with unilinear temporality. *La Nación Clandestina* corresponds to a turn in Bolivian politics toward "neoliberal multiculturalism" (Hale 2005), a discourse in which political elites would describe national diversity with the term "pluri-multi."

Bolivian revolutionary filmmakers deployed mimetic realism not only to form ties of national affiliation but to provoke action and transformation in the worlds beyond the screen. Yet perhaps the only space in which revolutionary projects were most fully achieved in Bolivia was in cinema.[11] Perhaps this explains why Jorge Sanjinés indirectly included himself in a rare self-reflexive subtext about the socially transformative capabilities of his films in a more recent project. *Para recibir el canto de los pájaros* (To Hear the Singing of the Birds) was Sanjinés's belated (1995, due to financial obstacles) engagement with the 1992 Quincentenary. In it, he remarkably reflects on his own films' incomplete attempts to radically transform Bolivian society, as a team of awkward filmmakers appear throughout the film as colonizers in the encounter of the Spaniards and indigenous peoples.

In *Para recibir el canto de los pájaros,* Sanjinés went beyond questions of political economic domination and addressed lasting colonial structures of racism in contemporary Bolivia. He asked the actress Geraldine Chaplin to play a key role in the film as part of a strategy to place the film in wider international circuits of distribution and the "star system" that he had opposed two decades earlier.

> We invited Geraldine Chaplin to participate in the film for several reasons: We chose her because she amazingly corresponded with the character of the foreign person that she interprets. She is one of eight important persons, she plays a determining role in the story we tell but she is not the protagonist; and there is no individualized protagonist in the story. And we chose her because we knew of her committed attitude.
>
> She is not, despite her widespread fame, the Hollywood "starlet," the prude and greedy actress who demands a helicopter to bring her from her hotel to the film set. None of that. To the contrary, she gave us lessons in humility and sympathy. And to be sure, her extraordinary charisma and her enormous talent supported the film.
>
> We invited her because with her presence we wanted to overcome the barrier of isolation to which practically all of Latin American cinema is submitted and by which it cannot penetrate the global circuits of distribution, not even those of our continent.
>
> Now, Bolivian cinema, which is barely alive, must make this jump. Our internal circuit doesn't permit us to recuperate the cost of a full-length film, and we are obligated to design another strategy to survive and move ahead.
>
> What is important is that in this case, we did it without making the slightest concession in the script or in its contents.[12]

In 1993, Sanjinés explained that the state does not "organically" support cinema, even though as an industry it could provide jobs. A cinema law that had recently passed followed years of struggle and pressure. Still, he says, as filmmakers, "we cannot import virgin film, elementary material, without finding ourselves with troubles in customs, paying guarantees, and the same humiliations as always. . . . We have lost presence on our own screens, which are occupied and manipulated principally by the American transnationals."

Also working in circumstances very different from the busy days of the ICB when the state funded his work, Jorge Ruiz and his son Guillermo continued making documentaries, using photographic stills and video, which are more affordable, for clients like the European Economic Community. "They are not commercial. They are what feeds us and we get by day to day," Guillermo said when I talked to them in early 1993. "Now no one wants to invest in projects here. . . . We have mountains of ideas, but no one wants to finance them. . . . To finance them here is difficult, very difficult." While there are more possibilities of getting financing from Europe than from the United States, Guillermo explained,

> The Bolivian business people do not invest money if it is not a sure thing. And cinema is not a sure thing, at least in Bolivia. They know that in Bolivia it's difficult to recuperate the investment. You can recuperate half in the best of cases. So you need an external market. So you have to send to Europe or the United States. So this has discouraged many Bolivian business people from making projects that my father has had. So we're frustrated. Although there have been possibilities of coproduction, in the last minute they get inhibited.

When I called Guillermo and Jorge again after the June presidential election, Guillermo told me he would have to try to fit a visit into their suddenly busy schedule. Their longtime colleague from Telecine, Gonzalo Sánchez de Losada, had become president (his first term), Guillermo told me, and they would have work to last them until the end of the year. When I met with Jorge Ruiz again, he recalled to me,

> He [Sánchez de Losada] saw that cinema wasn't a business. And he told us frankly that "We are not going to go anywhere with cinema. In this country there are only two things that are worth dedicating oneself to, mining and politics." He was successful in mining and next he went into politics.[13]

While Sánchez de Losada personally carved out a unique circuit from film-making to state politics, Ruiz expressed uncertainty about whether he would improve the general situation for filmmakers.

The filmmaking of the revolutionary 1950s and 1960s exploited cinema's promise of time and space travel, converting movement across cultural boundaries into a temporal vector that was intended to produce a prosperous, industrial, and culturally coherent mestizo nation, a cinematic national space of community and communication, self-determination and dignity, all led by a paternal and omniscient off-screen narrator. In contrast to the gleaming images of modern progress, the revolutionary films of the 1960s and 1970s revealed the subterranean nightmare that political and economic structures of domination had buried beneath the mythic images of progress. These films featured the very national subjects who most suffered from "progress" and whom the films also hoped to lead toward revolutionary change. Yet a majority of the films of the 1950s through the 1970s interestingly share and combine classic forms of documentary realism with the almost predictable, if not familiar, utopian and dialectic terms of the modernist discourses they hypostatize.

Despite the unfinished historical projects with which they were associated and intended to orient, the revolutionary images and narratives from the midcentury revolutionary era have had new lives, resignified as potent images of neoliberal politics of state making and party politics in twenty-first-century neoliberal Bolivia. In addition to the widely circulated and discussed wish images of the seacoast, noted earlier in relation to the 2003 uprisings, for example, images of popular marches and uprisings continue to be resignified and reproduced in media form. In a remarkable twist, during the 2002 national elections, political consultants from the United States, including James Carville, helped the MNR party to design its populist television advertising in which their neo-Liberal candidate Gonzalo Sánchez de Losada ("Goni") and his running mate Carlos Mesa led a crowd of people across the Altiplano. This scene strikingly resembles the scenes of popular rebellion that bookended Jorge Sanjinés's anti-imperialist *Courage of the People*. As contemporary circumstances call for this kind of hybrid recycling, juxtaposition, and resignification of earlier fantasies, cultural imagery, and narratives, they implicitly conjure up and recall the incompleteness of the original revolutionary projects that the film movements discussed here had intended to bring about. As these transfigurations contest and destabilize the linear narratives embedded in the kinds of revolutionary films discussed in this chapter, they begin to disrupt the dialectic shaping the linear and progressive narratives of modernity (Moreiras 2001, 51) that dominated popular nationalist projects in the twentieth century.

III Popular Publics and the Televisual Public Sphere

[5] *Reality Affects: Cultural Strategies and the Televisual Public Sphere*

The revolutionary fantasies promised by the centralized Bolivian state quickly dissipated in the economic crises of the early 1980s, when the same, perhaps disillusioned, MNR party and the bourgeoisie that had carried out the revolution in 1952 abandoned their state-led models and populist ideologies of mestizo nationalism in 1985. Introducing drastic structural reforms, the MNR and subsequent governments sold shares in state enterprises to transnational corporations, praised free markets and consumerism, and reimagined the popular nation as fundamentally multi-cultural; all were transformations driven by their own neoliberal fantasies (Comaroff and Comaroff 2001). The state that had been conjured up in the 1950s staged its own disappearing act by seeking to attract and with-draw into private capital (as it was then called, "capitalization") and then reconfiguring as an austere yet potent defender of the free market while retaining its role as regulator of the price of currency. At the same time that the state was transfiguring, official discourses reimagined Bolivian populations as "pluri-multi-cultural," a new, visible civic society that os-tensibly would be empowered to take on and benefit from the streamlined economic and political reforms. Just as the revolution had done decades earlier, however, the neoliberal fantasies produced their own countervail-ing realities and desires. Among them were massive layoffs, the drug war, and, as I will describe in this chapter, a lingering nostalgia for the dreams of coherence and prosperity promised earlier in both modes of revolution-ary films that were discussed in the previous chapter.

During these social transformations of the 1980s, broadcast tele-vision entered the circuits of the social imaginary as a new public venue in which national problems and conflicts were delineated and debated in the flow of programming alongside commercial programs from the United States and Mexico (Rivadeneira Prada 1993). As this chapter will show, the possibilities and the crises entailed in the neoliberal reforms produced an intensification in fantasy as well as realism in the televisual public sphere. In such contexts of rapid and complex global structural transformations of the late twentieth century, Bill Nichols observed "a pervasive hunger for information about the historical world surrounding us. But our hunger is less for information in the raw, than for stories fashioned from it" (1994, ix). Among the urban popular classes in La Paz, if there was a profusion of realism circulating in a televisual public sphere that demanded narrative treatment, it was because the very terms of reality were up for grabs.

▶────────────────────────────────────

Crises in Representation and Reality

The beginning of the neoliberal era in 1985 itself promised to end a volatile period in which "reality was absurd," as a Bolivian mother of five children recalled in talking with me. Ending a difficult transition to democracy that followed seventeen years of left and right military rule that had jacked up the national debt, an elected left-wing populist coalition (the UDP) took control in 1982 and inflation shot to 12,000 percent. Reality had turned upside down for the poor and working classes who suddenly had stacks of money but nothing in the marketplace to buy. The subsequent MNR government quickly reversed reality again when it was elected in 1985. Then, as people remember, money was scarce but merchandise filled the stores and unofficial street markets along with thousands of recently laid-off workers as vendors. The MNR's "New Economic Plan" (NEP), identified with what is popularly known as "Decree 21060," reduced the soaring hyperinflation overnight with the introduction of new currency, the boliviano, which took its value from the dollar by removing nine zeros from the previous currency. The MNR then began to adopt structural adjustments under pressure for loan repayment by the International Monetary Fund that reduced the public budget and privatized vital public services. The NEP also saw the layoffs of tens of thousands of miners in the state-run tin mines and 150 small industrial plants that closed, following the collapse of the price of tin itself on the London Metal Exchange. Many laid-off workers migrated to valleys in the Chapare region and became involved in growing coca at the same time the area was militarized in the U.S. drug war. In La Paz and the highland city of El Alto, tens of thousands of people arrived from the countryside and mining towns, surviving on a daily basis in the higher "peripheral neighborhoods" in adobe shanties from which they descended as sidewalk and ambulant street vendors in El Alto and La Paz (Gill 2000). The unemployed stood in long lines in La Paz to collect a remuneration of about $30 a month. The new social crisis expanded if it did not create new classes of impoverished and culturally marginalized poor among the urban popular classes whose interests were not advocated successfully by the declining political left. Later, decentralized political reforms such as the "Law of Popular Participation" officially recognized cultural differences and political formations at the municipal level, but the official attention to "culture" only incorporated these differences into existing structures of economic inequality and political representation.

Earlier, during the military period of the 1960s and 1970s, the relation between the state and urban popular classes was one of direct control, institutionalized clientelism, and visible repression. Although officially sponsored citywide folklore events staged popular visibility, the central forums for mediating society and the state government were debilitated as the once powerful Bolivian Workers' Center (COB) was continuously repressed and political parties were abolished. In the electronic media, small resistant rural radio stations were closed and Bolivia's single black-and-white television station was operated by the de facto government. The return to representative democracy entered with a void in the sphere of public discourse. When an elected coalition of political parties eventually took control in 1982 with high popular expectations, their key task was, as Jorge Lazarte put it, "to legitimate themselves before the population, demonstrating that they could function as structures of mediation" (Lazarte 1993, 191). But in the several chaotic years of the UDP leading up to 1985, the traditional political classes and parties had lost popular credibility as mediators and advocates of popular concerns (Lazarte 1993).[1]

If Bolivia's once powerful leftist unions, which had aligned and co-governed with the MNR in the 1950s, were further crippled with the neoliberal layoffs, the authorization of commercial and color television broadcasting in the neoliberal decrees of 1985 only further protracted the perceived void between the state and the popular classes that appeared in the structures of representational democracy. The state had been operating a black-and-white television station in the La Paz area since the late 1960s, which was used for political purposes and for commercial programming taken from the United States, but few in the city's popular classes could afford televisions. Many families acquired their first sets in the mid-1980s when dozens of private and color television stations began operating in Bolivia; these stations were connected with elite families and political parties and their news programming made no claims of political impartiality in their reporting, like most newspapers in Latin America.

In the quickly emerging televisual culture, the urban popular classes and rural indigenous people were structurally absent or represented only in romanticized scenes or in news reports using an off-screen narration consolidated into a singular and directive voice. Often, this same relation of representation was echoed by men and women I met in the upper and middle classes in La Paz. One former military officer explained to me that the urban popular classes in the city had an innate "Aymara psychology that is cold and closed." Another woman rehearsing a part for a film as an Aymara mother told me that her character is "humble" and "inexpressive." Both held a common elitist conception that the popular classes were incapable of representing themselves.[2] This chapter discusses how a popular television program overturned this image and staged the emergence of a distinctly visible, vocal, and potent popular public, with a clear Andean orientation.[3]

▶ ───

Opening a Tribunal for "the People"

In the midst of these crises of social well-being and representation, the testimonial television program *The Open Tribunal of the People (The Tribunal)* opened space in the televisual public sphere to the urban popular classes on the RTP network (Popular Radio and Television). While RTP's commercial and news programming differed little from other channels, *The Open Tribunal* uniquely changed prime time, charging the airwaves with politically contentious and personal denunciations as well as the emotional and stark images of social conditions as told by the people who were suffering them the most.

Mario Condori is a middle-aged man from a popular neighborhood in La Paz whose parents moved to the city from the countryside in the 1950s. Mario frequently watched *The Tribunal* after *The Simpsons* (on another channel); he described the program to me by positioning it alongside other realist media in the televisual public sphere, namely, the news:

> Watching the show, you can learn the details of the lives of the people. You get another kind of news, not all about outside Bolivia that you get from the other stations. You see what happens in the home. We see ourselves on that channel. I feel a solidarity with the people. As you know, I come from a family that came here [to the city] from the countryside and so I feel solidarity with the people. They are situations that upset you. You never know what you are going to see.

In saying "You never know what you are going to see," Mario suggested how voyeurism, scandal, or even gossip surrounded the program.

Indeed, people often chatted with each other about cases they had seen the night before as if they were gossiping about people they knew. In his combination of realism and sensationalism, Mario also characterized both the emerging popular public sphere as well as the more formally political neopopulist projects that had appeared on the new democratic landscape in the late 1980s, including the UCS party led by the taciturn owner of the country's largest brewery, Max Fernandez. In Robert Albro's analysis (1997) of provincial politics at that time in Bolivia, he has shown how strategies of public image making and self-stylization extended from mass media to "face-to-face" instances of political production. *The Open Tribunal,* I will argue, operated by appearing to condense the potent scale of mass media into the intimacy of face-to-face contact.

Taped at midday and broadcast nightly, *The Open Tribunal of the People* was hosted by the well-known radio and television host and owner of the RTP network, Carlos Palenque. Rural-born Aymara residents in La Paz (cholos) and their urban-born families, many of whom were illiterate, postliterate, or monolingual Aymara or Quechua speakers converged at Palenque's television studios in the center of La Paz, where they sought to meet with Palenque personally to obtain his help. They sought help to obtain access to medical assistance; to charge spouses with domestic violence; to obtain legal assistance; to call for lost children and family members; to publicize lost, abandoned, or beaten children; to warn people about scams; and to denounce government policies. Occasionally they returned to thank Palenque for his previous assistance. After briefly interviewing his visitors on the air, Palenque directed them to his network's Social Wing, which provided social workers, lawyers, medical counselors, and a women's commission, all of whom were available to supply the urban downtrodden with the social aid otherwise lacking from the government. The program was as politically potent as it was socially therapeutic, for it opened discursive space and provided public visibility of immediate and direct social justice for the *gente humilde* (humble people) who had long suffered cultural and social marginalization in labyrinthine legal and political bureaucracies as well as from the modern representational systems of television and electoral democracy.

The Tribunal's visual and testimonial realism provided direct evidence of these many crises, and Palenque himself often ardently pointed to neoliberal policies as the cause. Appearing as an outsider to the political system, the former musician and radio host was seen and supported by the urban popular classes as a legitimate and moral leader who related to them in terms of *compadrazgo* (ritual coparenthood), which conveys familial solidarity and mutual respect between social unequals. When the government closed *The Open Tribunal* for a year in June 1988 following Palenque's telephone interview with a well-known drug trafficker who had implicated top government officials, all the electronic, cultural, and familial social bonds disseminated from the stage of *The Tribunal* were quickly consolidated. When the station stopped broadcasting, members of more than forty social organizations including workers' unions, neighborhood committees, and petty merchants marched to denounce the closure. A group of about sixty men and women supporters formed "Defense Committees" who saw the network as their own. One of its members demanded that the government "immediately return our media of communication whose closure signifies the irremediable loss of our only source of social help for our primary needs, for hunger, and misery that we must put up with."[4] Led by the Defense Committees, the dispersed and widespread support quickly coalesced into a social movement as supporters joined in marches through city neighborhoods. Under this popular pressure, the network was permitted to reopen in August. During an open-air celebration, *The Open Tribunal* publicly entered politics when Palenque accepted a proclamation that he run as candidate for president in the upcoming elections in May 1989. Rafael Archondo, a former member of the Defense Committees, recalled that Palenque and the committees wanted to convey the impression that the new political party was the direct creation of "the people," so they held a campaign for people to send in names for it. The Condepa party (Conscience of the Fatherland) was officially founded in Tiwanaku that September.[5] But Palenque and the Defense Committees were forced again to limit their political action to the Condepa party itself only two months later when the national supreme court reinstated the closure of the network until June. With that, the social movement was converted into party politics and *Tribunal* viewers became supporters of Condepa.

In the elections of May 1989, Condepa shocked political analysts when it obtained enough popular votes to put Palenque into the negotiations with the second- and third-place winners to decide Bolivia's president.[6] In the pact, Condepa obtained seats in the Bolivian congress and Palenque appointed his Aymara cohost Remedios Loza to one of them. Afterward, Condepa had particular success in regional municipal elections. In municipal elections after 1989, Condepa won the city government three times successively, including one in which Palenque's wife Monica Medina was elected mayor of La Paz. In the 1993 presidential elections Palenque obtained second place in La Paz and third overall.[7] As the June 1997 elections were closing in, many had believed it was Palenque's turn to win the presidency, but he unexpectedly died of a heart attack two months before the elections in the midst of a public scandal concerning the possible breakup of his marriage. After his death, the program and Condepa became embattled sites for popular authority: Palenque's cohost, Remedios Loza, and Monica Medina pulled apart the *The Tribunal* into two versions, Monica's in the RTP studios and Remedios's on a platform across the street. Both "Open Tribunals" each lost their legitimacy and then Condepa disintegrated over the course of several years. When Palenque died and the political infighting took over, people often commented that *The Tribunal* had become "too political," underscoring how Palenque's charisma had driven *The Tribunal* and Condepa. Indeed, many viewers had watched the program not so much to follow all the details of each case, in the way they might have watched a *telenovela,* but rather to witness Palenque steer each visitor toward an immediate resolution.

In my research at *The Tribunal*'s Social Wing, I learned that many of the cases ended up deferred and unresolved. *The Open Tribunal* seemed to duplicate the same official bureaucratic delays that the program itself contested on the air. In the formation of the Condepa party as well, Palenque had re-created the social barriers that the party ostensibly attempted to overturn as its leadership became organized along ethnic and class lines that contained the urban Aymaras who had backed the party in their own neighborhoods to gather voters.[8] These fundamental divides that organized the program and the party were reproduced when Palenque defined the social organization of *The Tribunal,* saying, "They are the participants in the media of communication, they are transmitters of messages, they feel they are part of our media."[9] Clearly, Palenque reproduced social divides in this statement, but across the line he drew, he objectified the protagonism of the participants and popularized indigenous symbolism to authenticate a scenario of popular self-representation in the public sphere. In fact, Palenque established *The Open Tribunal* as a stage for the democratic ideals of representation in the public sphere when, in the elections of 1989, he offered, "A new Bolivia of Indians and cholos . . . given direct access to participation in the decisions of the state."[10] If the Condepa party provided access to political structures, *The Tribunal* was an arena where a new popular nation was being staged.

This staging of a new social imaginary for the popular publics in Bolivia clearly appealed in its Andean tones. As Mario Condori described the critiques of the show, he suggested that the program's authority was tied to the indigenous identities among the city's popular classes: "There is a critique of the show, but that comes from people in the upper class. That is because Palenque positions himself with the popular classes, the people from the countryside, who they [the upper class] see as 'Indians,' 'peasants,' the popular classes."

For over ten years, *The Open Tribunal* was a decisive site for mediating popular politics during the neoliberal social crisis and the collapse of the earlier mestizo ideals of the revolutionary project. During that period, the growing urban "popular sectors," a heterogeneous, elusive, yet recognizable sector of urban poor and middle classes with varying Andean affiliations, entered political culture, popularizing indigenous imagery and practices for their political value to forge political alliances across social classes. How did *The Open Tribunal* achieve its popular hegemony and bring the popular classes into public visibility as social protagonists? What strategies of publicity produced and marked the Andean popular as a decisive citizenry?

▶ ───────────────────────────────────

Framing the Popular

The Open Tribunal of the People combined the testimonial realism of face-to-face communication between hosts and participants with location video images over their voices to connect the program's discourse with specific urban social spaces, an indexical practice that I discuss further in chapter 6. *The Tribunal* was conducted by Carlos Palenque along with several cohosts; when Palenque could not be present, one of them conducted the program. They included his wife Monica Medina (until they separated in August 1996); Remedios Loza, the Aymara woman who had become Condepa's first member of congress and who also replaced Palenque as Condepa's presidential candidate for the 1997 elections; and Adolfo Paco, a network head and TV broadcaster who was fired by Palenque's daughter Veronica after Palenque's death in 1997. As this core image of Condepa and *The Open Tribunal* family was broadcast to homes and televisions throughout La Paz, viewers became related and linked to the program as family members through an everyday idiom of ritual co-parenthood *(compadrazgo)*.

Palenque himself was usually referred to as "El Compadre" in a fatherly tone that evoked familial solidarity. As if he were able to stem social crises with his own melodic voice and hypnotic charisma, Palenque followed each interview by reframing the participants' often incoherent testimonies, thus providing for them and viewers a sympathetic and soothingly coherent understanding of larger social forces within a common frame that included viewers. Using testimonials from the poor and examples of the myriad problems brought to him as evidence, he frequently indicted government neoliberalism and corruption in his ardent demands for social justice. A crucial element of Palenque's treatment of the real-life cases took the form of his narratives and promises of direct aid, emphasizing its testimonial realism and social mediation, both of which were desired by participants and viewers. Palenque's charismatic presence in mediating social problems was always in high demand; this made direct social contact with him worth insisting upon even though the widely watched program was often a last resort for its participants. For viewers, the therapeutically soothing and musical voice of Carlos Palenque himself addressing each social crisis personally was as enjoyable as the possibility of seeing wider social problems resolved. It was well understood among RTP staff that on the days when Palenque was not present to conduct the program, the number of viewers and participants declined.

Palenque's commentaries at the beginning and end of each evening's program served as a larger frame through which the diverse realist images and testimonial voices of the entire program were channeled, broadcast, and interpreted (see chapter 6). One evening in August 1996, the night before I began fieldwork at *The Tribunal*,[11] Palenque closed the program by addressing the television audience directly:

Figure 17. In frequent discourses in which he directly addressed his viewing public, the television host and political leader Carlos Palenque reviewed individual cases and made ardent social commentaries by expanding the discursive frame wide enough to include the viewers.

You see the endless problems that happen. Here we show them as they are. We do not decorate them. We do not distort them. Just as they are. [Background music comes up.] Here the protagonist is you, who makes the demands to the authorities or brings up your problems. That is the philosophy of *The Tribunal*. God willing, in September we will complete twenty-eight years of being in daily contact with our people. With our family. Talking face-to-face and searching for solutions. Twenty-eight years of being intimately linked with the family and with our people. Maybe in a few years we will be able to say, "Mission complete." But no. There is still a long—very long—road to go.[12]

In these instructions for watching *The Tribunal*, Palenque makes the realist claim that the people's "endless problems" were aired undistorted in a directly accessible ("open") public forum. Then he plots the real-life social problems of the downtrodden within the linear narrative framework of an ongoing twenty-eight-year social project. *The Tribunal* is a "mission" tied together by "intimate" familial relations that will eventuate into an overall social change. Furthermore, although he was concluding the day's program and providing an ending, he also leaves it open-ended: "There is still a long road to go," as if their social project depended on continued social support in the form of votes and viewing. These framing discourses are crucial moments for defining and limiting the meanings of the potent testimonials and images seen in the program, placing them within the social fields that the program constructs and within which it embeds itself, such as the Condepa party and a reconfigured popular Bolivian nation.

In cases where Palenque's treatment would not be as concrete as sending a visitor directly to a social worker, lawyer, or medical clinic, he and his cohorts often made public demands that substituted a narrative treatment at a wider national scale instead of a concrete resolution to the case itself. Palenque's image of a popular nation could be heard in his comments at his crowded birthday celebration broadcast from the *Tribunal* set in 1994. He and his cohorts were recalling how his first radio station, Radio Metropolitana, went on the air, broadcasting in Aymara, when Palenque turned to a camera and to viewers to say:

From the first year we had in our eyes and hearts the native languages, which represent the power and force of *el hombre boliviano* [the Bolivian man]. We determined thirteen years ago to emphasize what is ours. And to emphasize the capacity of the Bolivian, to emphasize our traditions and our customs, our ancestry—the millenarian culture—cultures. [He quickly repeats "cultures" to stress the plural.] We always have admired Tiwanaku, what remains in Bolivian territory of the indigenous-American. This is why we rescue the languages. . . .

Aymara may be, for example, a more perfect and more complete language than Castellano [Spanish]. And Quechua is "sweet" with the conjugation of verbs. And the Aymara language too. That is to say that Bolivia is diversity. And our task is to unite it.

Reverberating in this address is the ideology of the Bolivian social revolution of 1952, which advocated the construction of a single, culturally mixed mestizo nation. In contrast with the models of a plurinational state that were being advanced by Palenque's contemporary neoliberal political elites, *The Open Tribunal* rescued mestizaje just as it was waning by addressing "diversity" with a paternal and folkloric stance toward culture that advocated and echoed the social project with which many urban Aymaras had aligned their hopes in 1952.

On the program, such stabilizing national narratives were assembled from the fragmented self-portrayals of the personal lives of visitors. One case concerned a woman whose cantina had been burned down as a response to rape committed by a young man who had been drinking there. Palenque provided the important service of publicizing the event and then enclosed her fragmented testimony by turning to viewers to say,

> What we can do here is simply repeat to the municipal and police authorities that they be careful with the operation of bars and cantinas. Everywhere there is so much anarchy in all the cities of the country. Here in La Paz . . . the neighbors decided to burn the cantinas. Why? Because some of the boys who left one of the cantinas raped a fifteen-year-old girl. We have to order ourselves. We have to bring order to the country.

More directly addressing the political scene in 1994, an older Aymara man came on the program to denounce the neoliberal government.

> Until when will we support this? The rich continue earning money. Democracy is killing us, passing laws against this country. Workers are dying of hunger. Children are now sleeping in the street. How will the mayor pay for the education and health? . . . The people are not in agreement with this! We do not agree! This is why I have come to protest. In the name of the construction workers—I am a construction worker . . .

Palenque interrupted the man and quickly set himself up as the people's solution:

> Very good, compadre. Your words are very reflective, compadre. We have to have patience because things are going to change. Really. [He turns to viewers and the frame switches to a close-up of Palenque.] Things will change for the better, not for worse as the present government is doing without consulting the people, turning their backs on the great majorities.

This visitor provided an image of fragmentation and social crisis for Palenque to treat. Palenque reconfigured the elements of such fragmented testimonies into linear narratives and then channeled them through the frame of national space. He imported the threats of anarchy and crisis into wider narratives in which he and the party were positioned as agents of resolution. By converting the people's "endless problems" into a single political project, Palenque maintained narrativity as "one, or even perhaps the, principal mediating link between nation and national subject,"[13] performing it through face-to-face encounters. In discussing the politics of publicness, Benjamin Lee has argued that "the voice of the people is ventriloquated by the voice of the narrator, and the homogeneous empty time of modernity is that of narrativity itself (1993, 14). Indeed, Palenque's discursive work expanded individual cases within his program to fill the progressive temporality of modernity with his project. Furthermore, the principles of cause and effect with which he configured the elements of his narratives (Abercrombie et al. 1992) compounded *The Tribunal*'s direct perceptual realism with narrative realism. But the narrative he evoked was driven by the fantasy of the primordial sentiment for a popular-nationalist project that might complete the promises of national synthesis of 1952. In this way, *The Tribunal* merged its gritty images of testimonial realism and charisma into fantastic, melodramatic, and charismatic narratives.

As much as *The Open Tribunal* promoted national coherence and cultural synthesis, its frame extended beyond that of the nation and began integrating the popular media available in transcontinental television programming.[14] For many years, the program was broadcast each weeknight at nine o'clock in a primetime slot between a *telenovela* and the RTP network's news. In April 1996, however, RTP chiefs dramatically altered their nightly programming. In its new format, *The Tribunal* appeared in four fifteen- to twenty-minute segments that alternated with fifteen-minute segments from the program *Ocurrió Así* (It Happened This Way), a Spanish-language program produced in Los Angeles with coverage of human-interest stories across Latin America. Then after eleven o'clock, segments from RTP's former weekly reality crime show *Telepolicial*[15] alternated with segments from the other two for the last hour. The network's decision to change the format was mainly a strategy to maintain their top ratings, as cohost and network executive Adolfo Paco told me then. Yet as Carlos Palenque described it to his television audiences in August of that year: "*The Open Tribunal* is the vertebrae of *Ocurrió Así. Ocurrió Así* appears *inside The Open Tribunal* and [Telepolicial] appears after eleven. *Take note*: The children should be going to bed at ten-thirty."

Here, Palenque converts the network's commercial strategy into terms of cultural incorporation and positions *The Open Tribunal* as the mediating window onto world news (which can be seen, of course, on any other channel). An Aymara man with his family in line at the TV studio told me that he liked to watch *Occurió Así* "because I cannot travel there [to the United States]. I can see in it that there are also poor people there. Problems with bureaucracy." *The Open Tribunal*'s intervention in commercial media offered the urban popular classes a hybrid space of engagement with transcontinental publics. The sense of the program's internal heterogeneity was sensationally heightened in new self-identifying titles before and after commercials. Made with images from the three programs alternating in a fast-paced visual sequence accompanied by vigorous music from a Ninja Turtles video game, the montage "mediates" (Martín-Barbero 1993) heterogeneous transnational social spaces within the compressed and regulated space and time of RTP's television programming. This change in programming resembles the shift in film distribution that began at the same time in Bolivia in the mid-1990s, as described in part I, in which the staggered distribution of single film copies from Hollywood declined with a rise in film debuts that were synchronized with U.S. debuts, juxtaposing national sentiments and continental affiliations among moviegoing publics. As with the cinema, the extent to which the new programming integrated *The Tribunal*'s viewing publics into an abstract, aggregated, and heterogeneous transnational "television audience" resided in the advertising rates obtained by the value added by its perceived transnational global synchronicity.

As the coordinating center of its "felt internationalism" (Acland 2003), *The Tribunal* offered a safe framework for transcontinental engagements without threatening the tethers of national affiliation and state institutions. Through *The Open Tribunal,* Condepa emerged as a new popular movement by expanding the frame of the popular beyond the national, "the traditional," and class-based populisms as earlier national popular movements had done (see chapters 3 and 4). While Carlos Palenque and his cohosts regularly informed viewers that *The Tribunal* did not limit itself to visitors from any single social sector, the program's mission was always stated to be "to defend the humble" and it had strong Andean structure of feeling. Resembling other popular movements at the time, such as the Unión Cívica Solidaridad (Albro 1997), Palenque and his cohosts strategically cast a wide net and left *The Tribunal* open to a cultural plurality that was matched by the Condepa party's ideological elusiveness in political discourse. Despite the fantasies of coherence that Palenque's treatments articulated, *The Tribunal*'s identification with the "popular" was driven by ambivalence if not plurality, thereby filling the indefinite category of "the popular" public with tacit imagery.

If the Latin American "popular" had once referred to a folkloric nostalgia for the "traditional" vestiges of a precapitalist past in the mestizo imaginary, yet corrupted in the hybrid contexts of urbanization, Néstor García Canclini has redefined the hybridity of contemporary culture "entering and exiting" modernity. In the global circuits of commerce and mass media, he argues, we see "the staging of the popular" in which the popular subjects appear simulated as modern historical agents. He asks, "Is the popular nothing more than the effect of certain acts of enunciation and staging?" (1995, 193). García Canclini argues that the immediacy of realist television, for example, provides scenes that give people the confidence of a sense of agency because they are made to feel as if they participate in a larger system that includes them. Can we define the popular classes envisioned in *The Open Tribunal* as agentive historical subjects rather than as the simulated effect of a ventriloquist's enunciation? Does the televisual circulation of popular classes mean their political disappearance? In order to address these questions, I turn to anthropological studies of culture and media in combination with Latin American studies of popular culture to develop a situated understanding of the multiplex representational practices and cultural strategies that informed, orchestrated, and surrounded *The Tribunal*'s media practices. I argue that it was by drawing on the tactical complexity of everyday and ritual life that urban popular classes shaped the terms of their media representation, access to social resources, and political participation.

Figure 18. The set of *The Open Tribunal of the People*. Regular cohost Adolfo Paco interviews a visitor while a woman and a child wait off-camera to speak with Paco next. The set featured a backlit outline of Bolivia and columns wrapped in Andean-style textiles.

Media Agency and the Appearance of the Andean Popular

Even as *The Open Tribunal* was a powerful space of social and political action in the Bolivian public sphere, the seeming contradictions between its charisma, paternal social authority, and delayed social aid raise questions about the force of mass media in the production of social authority, political action, and social identity. What are the vectors of its "media agency"? By this term I mean the historical forces, social relations, and cultural strategies that construct media texts and their meanings. The question of media agency corresponds to the crucial issues in the anthropology of mass media raised by Debra Spitulnik: "Where to locate the production of meaning and ideology in the mass communications process, and how to characterize processes of agency and interpretation?" (1993, 295).

At first glance it would be easy to see the "Palenque phenomenon" as having deceived and exploited the city's downtrodden for Palenque's own political and economic gain. Viewing Palenque as the owner of the commercial RTP network, which earned top advertising rates with *The Tribunal,* the program could be seen as exploiting social problems while providing only minimal solutions. Knowing that the program also boosted Palenque to become an influential national politician supports an inference that he exploited his participants by broadcasting public displays of his own generosity in order to obtain votes that would sustain his political party. This frame, which suggests exploitation or deception, may seem obvious because public media discourse in the United States generally has been ambiguous about the democratic potentials of mass media and suspicious about religious and populist figures who emerge in the media, especially when money is involved. If claims that charming appearances mystify the real exploitative relations of production going on "behind-the-scenes," then this top-down model of media power overlooks the agency of consumers and audiences. In a significant theoretical turn in media and cultural studies since the 1970s, the dominant top-down vectors of media agency were reversed by models that depicted consumers as active poachers on popular media and as tactical producers of cultural meaning who subvert dominant ideologies without leaving the frameworks of powerful capitalist systems, as argued by de Certeau (1984), for example. More recently, however, scholars have brought attention to how the neoliberal discourses of consumer sovereignty and pleasure are implied by highlighting the endless creativity of reception (Mattelart 1994; Morley 1993); inversely, others have argued against the romanticist conceptualizations of popular culture as exterior to power and naturally oppositional (e.g., Ang 1996). One critique asserted that studies of audiences and television in everyday life have turned up "banal" endless restatements about the pleasure, resistance, and creativity of audiences at the expense of contradiction (Morris 1990). In an essay on "radical contextualism" intended to push media analysis beyond the TV room and toward the texture of social contradictions involved in actual media practices of audiences, Ien Ang argues, "A more thoroughly cultural approach to reception, however, would not stop at this pseudo-intimate moment of direct contact of the text/audience encounter, but address the differentiated meanings and significance of specific reception patterns in articulating more general cultural negotiations and contestations" (1996, 137).

The expansion of media ethnography in anthropology brought the discipline's wide-ranging theories of cultural production to bear on the ethnographic study of media (e.g., Ginsburg, et al. 2002; Askew and Wilk 2002). With a wide frame for analyzing social and cultural production, anthropology has rejected the narrow perspectives of both the monolithic top-down models as well as their reversal in individualistic active audience studies. Cross-cultural studies of media audiences have demassified the uniform assumptions of individual subjectivity formed through the exhibition practices of global media (e.g., Hahn 1994; Larkin 1998–99) and the uniform transmission of intrinsic meanings implied by the ubiquitous scale of global media distribution (e.g., Michaels 1994). In chapters 1 and 2, I argued that media distribution itself is an uneven social terrain that poses the challenges to the presumed uniform desire for the dominant commercial media from the Unites States (see Himpele 1996a).

Anthropologists have also complicated studies of reception by employing "thick description" as a way to trace media signification throughout the multiplex cultural and political lives of audiences as well as back and forth across the production–consumption divide between viewers and authors of media texts (e.g., Abu-Lughod 2005). Jacqueline Urla's (1997) work on alternative radio in Spain sees the radio public acting not exclusively as a consumer of transmitted public media but as a participant or as a producer. Studies of commercial television talk shows in the United States (Carpignano et al. 1993; Nichols 1994; Shattuc 1997) analyze how this form of programming plays with the divides of production and consumption by converting home viewers and television audiences into performers and participants in a carnival-like exchange of positions. The anthropologists Barry Dornfeld (1998) and Tejaswini Ganti (2002) have examined how media production entails its own practices of consumption, further challenging presumed social categories as they have been located in the circuits of commerce and mediation.

Ethnographic work on the mass media has stimulated anthropologists to further explore the heterogeneity of practices of self-representation, effectively breaking apart the monolithic category of "producer" (Dickey 1997). Combing the terms of reception studies with the insights of the ethnography of media production, we can see how the social practices of media involve strategies and tactics of use, poaching, and resignification. The anthropology of media has not only problematized approaches of too-narrow ethnographic scope; it has pluralized the meanings and sites of agency in mediated social processes, and it has sought ethnographically to represent the complex links between media practices and hegemonic structures that have global range in order to trace the complexities of how subordinated peoples engage with contemporary political circumstances.

Similarly attempting to avoid limited ideological and romanticized models by promoting a pluralistic approach, Jesús Martín-Barbero argues for opening media analysis "to mediations—that is to say, to the institutions, the organizations and the subjects, to the diverse social temporalities and the multiplicities of cultural matrices from which media technologies constitute themselves" (1988). He emphasizes the global condition of mass media and argues that as media are incorporated into, or mediated by, local meanings and the daily practices of the popular classes in Latin America, they produce and activate rather than consume and suppress popular cultural practices (see also Rowe and Schelling 1991). Although he emphasizes reception, what is distinctive about Martín-Barbero's view is that mass media now entail crisscrossed loyalties and alliances that permeate the boundaries of states and subvert traditional class-based and party politics. He seeks to overthrow Manichaean models of media agency that are based in the sharp separation of producers and consumers and he focuses on "the thick texture of hegemony/subalternity, the interlacing of resistance and submission, and opposition and complicity." Martín-Barbero describes popular culture with multiple sites of media agency with a subtle sense of collusion in social engagements with media.

This interlaced image of mediation is especially suggestive of *testimonio* discourses in Latin America (see Gugelberger 1996). Testimonials are typically multiauthored, made in collaboration between subjects and their advocates who have access to the public sphere on the one hand, while on the other they also set up alliances between readers and authors in order to promote social causes (Larson 1995, 9). George Yúdice defines the *testimonio* as "emphasizing popular, oral discourse, in which the witness portrays his or her own experience as an agent (rather than a representative)." To be sure, as Javier Sanjinés writes, *The Tribunal* turned the *testimonio* form into a TV spectacle (1996). Yet I would maintain that agency is still its underlying currency and it is emphasized and exchanged with specific authenticating claims. How then, can we re-theorize "media agency" in the terms of this program in which particular practices objectify and orchestrate agency as they create and expand alliances across social classes?

In the next section of this chapter, I examine more closely the objectification, orchestration, and distribution of agency among the hosts, visitors, and viewers of *The Open Tribunal*. What cultural strategies were mobilized to produce the potent and affective relationships that resulted in the populist party Condepa? I will argue that *The Tribunal* was embedded in a wider historical complex of social and political strategies forged between political elites and peasant and popular classes in which they colluded to produce the social authority that *The Open Tribunal* and Condepa held as well as a wider and "interlaced" network of affiliations.

▶

Agency Play and Ritual Exchange: Collusion as a Mode of Production

The Tribunal broadcast a wide net across the heterogeneous and polyvalent shifting social classes in La Paz, rather than defining any essential features of its popular publics. If this underlying ambiguity funded *The Tribunal*'s capital category of "popular" as a value that took shape tacitly in the eyes and ears of its hosts and viewers, then the program's social discourse explicitly objectified agency as its underlying currency in the combination of testimonial and social discourse. How did interlocutors on *The Tribunal* objectify and orchestrate agency in order to create, authenticate, and expand social alliances through "popular" discursive practices?

Debra Spitulnik has pointed out that we have given little attention to linguistic forms in media, such as the culturally specific ways in which speakers "create the contexts for their interpretation, as well as the relationships of participants to the event of communication" as situated within broader social processes (1993, 297). In this perspective, a principal task of Palenque's discursive treatments was to provide viewers with instructions for how to view the program; he also formulated the social fields, or conditions, within which the heterogeneous cases would make sense. As Richard Bauman and Charles Briggs have pointed out, such acts of reframing, redefining, and recontextualizing texts are acts of control that entail social power (1990, 76) that turn back and objectify discourse itself.

Palenque's social authority was intimately connected to his oral competence and confidence in performing in the televisual public sphere, qualities that were put into relief against those of his cohost Adolfo Paco and the sometimes bold yet incoherent narratives given by many of the program's participants. Yet the authority of the program also derived from how he defined his participants' testimonials as genuine and undistorted in an "open" public space where he conferred protagonism on them. "Here the protagonist is you who makes the demands to the authorities or brings up your problems. That is the philosophy of *The Tribunal*," as he stated in the discourse quoted earlier with which he closed a broadcast in August 1996. He first attributed agency to "you" the viewers and participants as protagonists and then incorporated them into his larger social project using the collective, plural, but notably unspecified "we" as the subject. "Maybe in a few years we will be able to say 'Mission complete.'" This reversal and incorporation within the frame is organized by a grammar for locating and orchestrating the sites of agency in the public sphere.

Analyzing media agency from a dialogic and discursive perspective, the *Tribunal* turns on a fundamental ambiguity that Deborah Battaglia has called "agency play" in which "agency is invoked, ascribed, concealed, obfuscated, more or less strategically" (1997, 506). This approach to the discourses of agency breaks from what would otherwise be a reality-driven analysis that would seek to delimit agency to either pure instrumental manipulation or romanticized active audiences. I use the conceptual tool "agency play" to focus on the performances and exchanges that bring agency into being in moments of meditation and circulation (see Bennett 2005). That agency itself emerges as such from exchange would be no surprise for readers of Simmel (1900, 81–82), who turned to the dynamics of political dialogue in making his argument that exchange is a scene of objectification. In fact, public discourses surrounding *The Tribunal* often mirrored Palenque's conferral of protagonism just described, exchanging his participants' protagonism for an emphasis on Palenque's agentive role on the program, thereby making agency itself an object of public discourse and exchange.

Here are a couple of examples of such discursive play that I commonly heard from people in La Paz: "Who does anything for the poor? Palenque is the only one who does anything." "I watch to see him solve the problems." Another example of the ambivalence underlying these exchanges in the public discourses that surrounded the *Open Tribunal* is this evaluation of Palenque by Mario Condori, whom I quoted earlier:

> For the people, he is like a god. Like a god, I say. Maybe he is living luxuriously now, but he is doing [social] projects, maybe positioning himself for the future.
>
> The people are innocent. Too innocent, I would say. I don't know if what

Palenque says are his feelings. Maybe. But where are the people going to go? They go where they give you more, although it is a big "show." Where else can they go? The situation is terrible here. The situation here in Bolivia is terrible. Terrible. You see how the people have to live.

Mario's comments evoke the fundamental ambiguity in the play of media agency. He begins by depicting the popular classes as passive while Palenque is active (as a strategist, if not a manipulator), and then he exchanges the terms so that "the people" actively seek out Palenque as a social resource in the ongoing social crisis. He identifies *The Tribunal* as a social field in which "the people" may be critical of Palenque but they are also strategic and praise him in order to obtain social resources. In light of this last point raised by Mario, we might ask whether the participants on the program are self-consciously performing and positioning themselves any less than Palenque himself. After all, if we don't know "if what Palenque says are his feelings," why assume we can know whether participants are revealing their feelings?

During the taping in the studio, the initial moments of encounters between Palenque and the participants set up a scenario in which agency play was performed as a transaction in which interlocutors performed, conferred, and established social authority. In one very typical case in 1996, Palenque finished speaking with participants and turned to greet new participants waiting beside him. "Hello, welcome to *The Open Tribunal*. How can we serve you?" he offered.

The first of two men replied while offering a customary handshake to Palenque. "It is a pleasure to meet you, compadre. I have never had the opportunity to visit this prestigious channel," he said, and turned to address the viewing public, "that helps the popular classes, those who are poor."

"I understand there has been a problem in Colquiri," Palenque said, moving directly to the case. "What is this problem?"

Is this a scene of ritual subordination? Deception? In these typically ceremonial greetings, participants define their social sphere as occupied by ritual coparents ("compadres"), which reproduces and marks social status and exchanges social prestige for engagement and social assistance. From one point of view, Palenque has offered aid as well as social and public visibility for which the visitors cannot compensate. From another perspective, authority, prestige, and deference are conferred and advanced to Palenque in order to obligate him to supply a form of social aid and justice. Most greetings in the program repeat this overture and define the grammar for the interaction between multiple agents in the idiom of ritual kinship and the social obligations they entail.

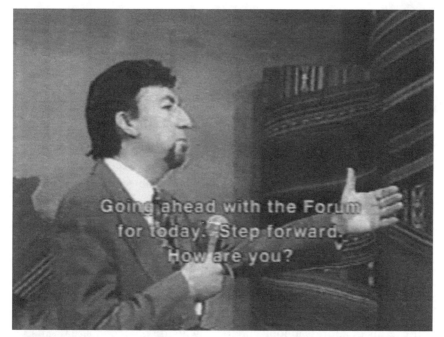

Figure 19. Palenque typically begins his interchange with guests by inviting them forward and offering assistance.

Figure 20. In greetings between Palenque and his guests, social prestige is exchanged for publicity and social assistance.

The orchestration of the plural social agents and their status relations in this televisual social field can also be discerned in the terms of address. In the first instance, when hosts and visitors frequently use the Spanish formal term for you—"usted"—it grammatically separates speakers as a sign of respect and of social distance. For native Aymara-speakers, however, the principal subject in conversation is not "I" but one's interlocutor, who is emphasized by frequently addressing him or her by name or title, which is also a sign of respect (Hardman 1988, 173). By prioritizing the other as a subject, there is no final individuation between interlocutors that would grammatically position either one as subject or object, or as active or passive. In this way, the sphere of interaction is linguistically defined as inherently dialogic and composed of plural agents (ibid.), though this does not by any means make the scene socially equal (cf. Mannheim and Tedlock 1995, 13). In fact, the frequent repetition of the titles "comadre" and "compadre" between Palenque and his interlocutors deliberately indexes the social hierarchy entailed in ritual coparenthood.

The everyday terms "comadre" and "compadre" are used as honorific terms of address among coparents who are related in ritual kin sponsorship, for example, of children in baptisms or weddings. In La Paz, people choose coparents who are "from a better economic situation" because they will help to sponsor more prestigious parties and provide contact with higher social circles that are otherwise out of reach. When Palenque is referred to respectfully and reciprocally as "El Compadre," it evokes familial solidarity and it marks the paternalism, authority, and social status held by ritual coparents. Yet the terms of coparenthood are used in everyday life to oblige people to provide a wide range of support including the mundane, such as the sponsorship of shorts for a weekend soccer team. Because it is socially and morally unacceptable to reject a request put in these terms, such obligations can be deployed to maneuver people, although such social tactics are rarely identified as such. This familiar and tacit "public secret" outlined the frame with which viewers saw *The Tribunal* and the procedures with which participants entered it. Orchestrating these interactions between social classes on *The Tribunal*, the obligations of ritual exchange in the moral sphere of coparenthood are part of a popular unspoken "cultural strategy" in which prestige is advanced through overtures of respect and deference in order to oblige and motivate social action. Roger Rasnake used the term "cultural strategy" to identify deference to vehicles of power, such as the state, which is seen as inherently erratic and dangerous. He defined the strategy as a cultural mode of contact with the wider world that "is perhaps not consciously chosen, or even verbally articulated, but a strategy nonetheless" (1988).

Further, as Javier Auyero argues in exploring the "habitual practical knowledge" that informs clientelism from the point of view of clients (1999, 305), such strategies of exchange are not seen as an all-or-nothing dichotomous power relationship.

It would be difficult to pin down specifically where these exchange relations were set into motion on *The Tribunal;* that is, whether it was Palenque's continuously advertised offers of visibility and assistance or his guests' advances of prestige. Perhaps a more interesting question is how these dynamics borrow from ongoing and deeper historical practices of transactions between peasantries and states in the Andes. In history, one finds striking echoes of these strategic alliances in the paternalist pacts struck between peasant Indians and political authorities that were organized by these exchanges of public respect for social aid or territorial autonomy within an implicit "moral economy" (Scott 1976).[16] Such patron-client relations frequently took the form of ritualized exchanges, affective relations, and fictive kinship between populist presidents and peasants. Tristan Platt (1982) has shown that during the late-nineteenth-century Liberal period in Bolivia it was when these pacts were violated that peasants rebelled, even though the transactions themselves were unequal since they marked and legitimated status.[17] The historical depth beneath *The Tribunal*'s social space suggests that the *Tribunal*'s opposition to the crises that followed the neoliberal decrees rendered the state as morally illegitimate for relinquishing the paternalist social responsibilities it had promised with the revolution and even with subsequent military governments.[18] In the neoliberal circumstances of increasing uncertainty that surrounded the *Tribunal,* as Libbet Crandon-Malamud showed, there was also a profusion of such "flexible" (rather than fictive) kin ties that formed social networks between urban employers seeking cheaper labor from the countryside and rural workers seeking work and access to urban social networks (1993). These historical instances illustrate that rather than engage in an all-or-nothing game, strategies of engagement and alliance are frequently adopted over those of exclusion in Bolivia (e.g., Albó 1997). The ritual exchange of prestige on *The Tribunal* also helps interpret those who saw Palenque's objectives as political power and social prestige rather than economic wealth. As one viewer said: "I am not sure about Palenque because maybe he does all that for the screen. The program is very manipulated. As mayor, Monica [Palenque's wife] has been doing many [public] projects and it will help him when he runs in the next election."

When some people said to me that his political aspirations would eventually allow him "to steal from the people as the political class always does," however, they were specifying how the cultural strategies of political prestige could be violated through crude economic motives. Although Palenque became wealthy in commercial television and radio, people nevertheless emphasized that he profited from RTP not to make himself prosperous but to make himself president and that he was the only one who did anything for the poor. To be sure, while many people believed that Palenque was the only hope the poor had, others combined trust with suspicion, arguing that his hypnotic performances were just strategic manipulations of the downtrodden.

> Yes, he helps the people. But who pays for it? He holds campaigns to obtain the money and he says, "Here we have this case of this sick young boy who needs medicine. Won't you send some money to help him? One hundred pesos or only one peso will be fine."
> Or he reunites a lost child with his mother only by making a "show" that makes him look like a savior. He says, "Señora it has been two weeks since you came on *The Open Tribunal* to find your little son and he still has not returned." The woman is crying and crying there next to Palenque. Then he says, "Mamita call for your son. Call for your son." She calls him and the child comes out from the next room. That's bad. He makes her feel bad for a longer time on TV so he can look like a savior.

These comments by Dionisia, an Aymara market woman, about the delay in reuniting parent and child on-screen, show she was critically aware of the staging of mediation in realist media; she is critical that the distressed must pay a cost for the production of the generous portrayals of Palenque.

Among its own employees as well as its visitors, as the next chapter will describe, *The Open Tribunal* sustained social crises, insecurities, and representational inequalities rather than cumulatively resolving them on the direct case-by-case basis that was promised through the images of direct and quick social action. Behind the scenes, visitors who had been given hope because their problem had been addressed often had to continually return and reestablish their contact with the RTP Social Wing and, by extension, the social network it sustained with Condepa. The deferrals and delays of the promising links to a quick solution built and expanded Condepa's social networks.

If this "popular" space in the media did not fully resolve problems as it appeared to do on television, was *The Open Tribunal* merely a simulation of a public sphere conjured up with the return to representative democracy? Despite its identification with marginalized popular sectors, the two hours of *The Tribunal* were a relatively small space of popular visibility and voice inserted into RTP's eighteen hours of daily commercial programming of local news and international entertainment. Its testimonial realism pointed to a space where the downtrodden in La Paz achieved visibility and voice in the mass media but did not entirely speak for themselves. It was a space in a social crisis where social justice and medical treatment were therapeutically promised, although the healing was often deferred. If Condepa's electoral successes in regional and national elections served as outlets for political complaints and neutralized popular opposition during the social crisis (Mayorga 1995), then *The Tribunal* also became one of the avenues through which the city's indigenous and popular classes could imagine achieving political participation. By popularizing indigeneity, *The Open Tribunal* sustained the promise of cultural visibility and political participation for the city's poor and indigenous by way of a network of mediated social relations and ritual interactions in which they exchanged positions by collusively defining and obligating each other as protagonists. Rather than being equipotent, emancipatory, or coercive, the implicit yet morally loaded cultural strategy of agency play between ritual coparents objectified and distributed media and historical agency among participants on *The Tribunal* while marking and reproducing their unequal social status.

Work by anthropologists who have examined the dialogic aspects of cultural processes has underscored how agency is in play, or emergent, in discursive forms that are intrinsically collusive (Mannheim and Tedlock 1995). As McDermott and Tylbor explain, "Collusion refers to how members of a social order must constantly help each other to posit a particular state of affairs. . . . Participation in social scenes requires that members play into each other's hands, pushing and pulling each other toward a strong sense of what is probable or possible" (1995, 219).

As Mannheim and Tedlock also have observed about such scenarios, "This interactional collusion is not socially neutral; rather it involves a carefully crafted set of social repositionings in which dominance hierarchies emerge" (1995, 13). The hierarchy that was crafted in the dialogues, exchanges, and obligations on *The Tribunal* produced appearances of hegemony that could be pulled off precisely because they were orchestrated in the public glare, even while audiences quietly knew its procedures. Furthermore, the lines of social hierarchy that were publicly produced, marked, and positioned demarcated "the popular" as a politically valuable object with which legitimate and strategic relationships could be forged. In this case, collusion was fundamental to the multiple "public subjectivities" (Lee 1993) and cultural strategies that the urban popular sectors performed to engage and participate in the very terms of commercial and political cultures that corresponded to their present circumstances. What the collusive

cultural strategies of the popular classes lost in purity was "gained in a capacity to take on the opacity and the complexity of life" (Martín-Barbero
1993, 464).

▶ ──

Conclusion: The Popular Public Sphere

Retaining much of the testimonial format that Palenque hosted for years
in his popular radio program *Radio Metropolitana, The Open Tribunal*
became a televisual space in which new Bolivia popular classes were vi-
sualized as historical protagonists through the social alliances that were
formed between Palenque, along with his cohosts, and their viewers and
participants.[19] The cultural strategy of exchanging protagonism and prestige by unequal agents on *The Open Tribunal* did not reduce to the ideology of reciprocity residing in the propositions of the public sphere and
free-market exchange. Yet how are we to define rationality in the public
sphere, asks Geoff Eley in describing Habermas's claims that rational and
symmetrical discursive exchange was a truly free market (1994). Indeed,
it was from the classic ideologies of Liberal economics that critiques were
leveled against *The Open Tribunal*. Bolivian critics writing about the
program argued that its melodramatic depiction of emotion and personal
stories prevented the "rational" articulation of social problems. They also
contrasted *The Tribunal* with the idealized model of the modern public
sphere as a speech situation in which rational discursive exchanges should
occur among equivalently positioned speakers.[20] *The Open Tribunal* was
modeled as series of exchanges, but the comadres and compadres in La
Paz were perhaps more realistic than the promoters of the Liberal model;
daily and ritual life reinforced how all exchanges in dialogue or in the
marketplace are not the same or equivalent and can be an ingredient in the
production of inequalities (Weiner 1992). In this instance, the inequalities
in exchange opened up productive possibilities that were seized by *The
Tribunal* and its publics.

  If it was the emotional images of self-representation in the public
sphere that antagonized the political elite, then it was also the presence
of the urban poor and indigenous in the hybrid popular public sphere
that disrupted their Liberal fantasy of a rationalized modern world.
One anxious Bolivian politician commented, "Condepa . . . wants to eat
ch'uno and *ch'arki* while we can see on the internet what is happening
in the whole world. They are not in the modernity that we are living."[21]
Against *The Tribunal*'s unorthodox, commercial, and melodramatic politics of recognition, the traditional political class expressed indignation

toward the hybrid "cholo populism" that had depreciated the national imaginary and the democracy they struggled to recuperate and control since the early 1980s in order to "modernize the state" (Rivera Cusicanqui 1993, 118). For them, it was not the imagined alterity of indigeneity that was put on display and inhabited the public sphere but the pronounced hybridity of the post-1952 bourgeois class in "Indian" clothing that was challenging the traditional political elites. This cultural hybridity supplied a jolting image for a twelve-year-old boy watching *The Open Tribunal* with his family in a popular neighborhood one evening. On seeing a well-to-do chola woman step up to a counter in a commercial for a bank, he exclaimed: "Hey, look! A modern chola!"

[**6**] *Indexical Binds:*
The Televisual Production
of Popular Publics

▶

The Demands of Trauma and Images

The traumatic texture and immediacy in many of the scenes on *The Open Tribunal of the People* make demands in several directions. In the case recounted here, the urgency of a young woman makes demands not only on the host, Carlos Palenque, for the aid he offers to her but also upon viewers for sympathy. Although her narrative is incomplete and calls for more detail, it is because of Palenque's haste to end the segment with her. In doing so, however, he opens an opportunity for himself to enter the story and to appear to respond immediately to her demands.

> HOST, CARLOS PALENQUE [CP]: *The Tribunal* continues. Good day, comadre [a medium two shot of Palenque and young woman widens to medium shot of them standing against *The Tribunal*'s set, with Andean textiles hanging on one wall and a window with a painted view of La Paz].
>
> YOUNG AYMARA WOMAN: [crying; the young *cholita,* about eighteen, has her baby wrapped in a striped aguayu on her back.] Buenos días, compadre. Buenas noches. I have come to denounce my boyfriend. [Cut to medium close-up of the young woman, microphone is visible in lower left corner.] He hit me and my son Sunday night. [Slow zoom in to her.] He and his mother kicked me out of his house with my son and now I am stuck in the street, compadre [crying; music softly plays in background]. I don't have any . . . I don't have any family and I am an orphan.
>
> CP: Where are you sleeping now, comadre?

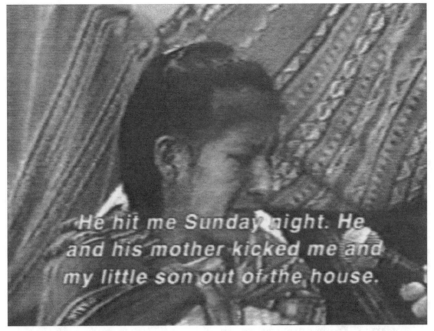

He hit me Sunday night. He and his mother kicked me and my little son out of the house.

Figure 21. A frame from *The Open Tribunal of the People* in 1996. The visceral immediacy of the needs of this young woman makes demands on Palenque for the aid he offers to her but also on viewers for sympathy.

WOMAN: [Slow zoom in to a close-up.] A woman has accompanied me here.

CP: You don't have any relatives, any family?

WOMAN: Here. No.

CP: Where are you from?

WOMAN: From the Loayza Province, Canton Hanch'allani [a rural area].

CP: From Loayza Province. What is your boyfriend's name, comadre? [Cut to two shot of Palenque and the young woman.]

WOMAN: [Cut to close-up of the young woman.] Ronaldo Luna Quispe. [Cut to a pencil drawing of policeman pointing gun at a young woman.] He works here for the police. With his gun he threatened to kill me. "I'll kill you like you kill a sheep!" he told me, compadre. [Cut to close-up of man in drawing.] Sunday night he beat me at one o'clock in the morning. He told me, "Go! Go! Get out of my house! [Cut to close-up of the young woman wiping her nose as she sobs.] There are a lot of girls waiting for me!" he told me. His mother didn't defend me. "My son has a lot of girlfriends that I can bring to the house. Get out of my house! You only come to feed yourself and fight with my son." I would like you all to help me, compadre. I don't have any family.

CP: How can we help you, comadre?

WOMAN: Now I left there and I am with the woman I was with before, when I was young, who I worked for before when I arrived from the countryside. I was a worker in her home. I was working as a domestic employee. That is when I met the man and I had my baby. When my baby was born, this woman, her name is Señora Demetria, she lives up in Alto Tejar, I had the baby in her house. I had no money [she pauses to wipe her nose and she continues sobbing] to go to the clinic. [Slow zoom out.]

CP: How long did you live with this man, comadre?

WOMAN: It is now four months, compadre.

CP: Now four months, comadre. And your green eye, did he hit you?

WOMAN: He kicked me and punched me.

CP: Okay. Comadre. Right now, the Women's Commission will talk to you, yeah?

WOMAN: Compadre, please, I would like . . . [Palenque cuts her off.]

CP: Right away . . .

WOMAN: . . . them to help me get my things from there.

CP: . . . For that. All of that. You talk to them.

[She turns and walks away, sniffling and wiping her nose.]

When Palenque's program went on his new television network, the *Tribunal* filled television screens with politically contentious denunciations as well as emotional images of new political economy as lived and told by people most severely marginalized and affected in it.

The gritty realism of *The Tribunal*'s testimonial dialogue and the stark visuals of the scene just described point to a wider global profusion of realist media consisting of indexical images and practices through which people are addressing their historical worlds (see Gaines and Renov 1999). Describing this realism in popular culture, Abercrombie, Lash, and Longhurst provocatively assert, "The *new* realist culture will be of a qualitatively more 'brute,' disharmonic nature than its predecessors. The new realist culture may indeed be cast in a mould that is . . . starkly *indexical* in coloration," and they advise us to "take realism seriously" (1992, 138).[1] As a social force, *The Tribunal* exploited the perceptual immediacy of television's indexical realism that coincides with "norms of rapid and easy customer satisfaction" (Feldman 1993, 90–91) in the expanding commercial arena. In other words, the perceived "liveness" of contemporary televisual realism offers an experience of direct perceptual access to and fast linkages between disparate persons, commodities, places, and events that are juxtaposed on the screen or assembled into a program like *The Open Tribunal*. If these desires for immediacy (see Houston 1984) were fulfilled for viewers who saw that Palenque solved cases directly and immediately, then his social aid took on the form of the perceptual immediacy of indexical realism itself. While the modern mass media have been analyzed as a technology of social communication (as a public sphere), Paolo Carpignano has argued conversely that we approach the public sphere as "a location where the material articulations, the technological mediations of social communication, take place" (1999, 177). This chapter will examine the materiality of *The Open Tribunal* in several respects, beginning with the urgent demands and the bodily presence of Palenque's interlocutors. I discuss how the bodily presence of interlocutors is materially registered, or embodied, in the physicality of indexical images as body and image each constitutes and circulates in the form of the other in the public sphere. Then I turn to the production of the broadcast in material terms. I discuss the relations of production as well as the material forms in which "the popular" was produced as a field of social affiliations. I explore the bonds forged between indexical imagery and the historical worlds it represents, as well as how the visual images of those worlds are physically aligned with an acoustic soundscape of discourses that coincides and binds them with their meanings.

In many instances, like the case described here, *The Tribunal*'s public depictions of social conditions resemble what Mark Seltzer called the "wound culture" that organizes the public sphere with heightened attention on "the exhibition and witnessing, the endlessly reproducible display, of wounded bodies and wounded minds in public" (1997, 3). Note that by putting social life in terms of "trauma," Seltzer connects both the material and the psychic. Thus what makes this scene and its demands especially potent (and "moving") is the televisual presence of the young woman—the materiality of her image and voice—and the highly charged emotions she presents. What is also striking about this scene is how Carlos Palenque was positioned not only as a mediator and healer but as a diagnostician of social conditions whose mediation in public could make her private pain "real" (Jackson 1994, 217). If "reality" is as traumatic as it was cast here, then it morally demands documentation and representation on the one hand, as well as forms of explanation and treatment on the other, that can appear to contain it.

The emergence of anthropological work organized around the study of trauma, violence, pain, and social suffering as phenomena of study and as categories for identifying sociality (e.g., "wound culture") has challenged the theoretical privilege of language over embodied experience (e.g., Csordas 1994, 11–12) by exploring their juxtaposition in situations of pain and trauma (e.g., Kleinman 1997). Much of this work illustrates how biomedical and therapeutic institutions work to employ coherent frames around bodily and psychic disorder (e.g., Mattingly 1998) or compel patients to repeat traumatic events until they develop narrative coherence in terms defined and measured by the medical institutions themselves (Young 1993). Using language that refers back to the same institutions, victims lack a form of signification other than narrative with which to understand, share, or convey their pain. In cases of torture, a similar paradox is carried out in interrogations of repeated questioning that deconstructs the victim's voice and converts it into the property and voice of the torturer's regime (Scarry 1985, 49). Elaine Scarry's provocative thesis is that physical pain shatters language and creates a thorny "double bind": "To have pain is to have *certainty*; to hear about pain is to have *doubt*" (13; emphasis in original). Pain's sheer interior intensity and material facticity provide absolute certainty of it for the victim, but because language is unavailable, Scarry writes, there is no means of objectifying, externalizing, and conveying the pain itself in public terms. As a result of this double bind, Scarry argues, an advocate is necessary to publicly validate and represent the victims' pain and the demands. I also agree with Jean Jackson's response to Scarry's thesis, however, in which Jackson argues that there is a language in pain that competes with everyday language (1994, 220), so that advocates could be seen as providing a publicly accessible language and venue in addition to validation itself. While the case of the young girl in the clip does not involve the kind of torture that Scarry discusses, she expressed her pain in a speech genre (Morris 1997) that embodied her felt distress and was recognizable to televisual viewers. Yet the palpable tension between a lack of sufficient and coherent language and the physicality of her experience does give rise to moral demands for treatment by an advocate, which is what she sought at *The Tribunal*. If her crisis demands both public representation and attention, how does television provide a possible vehicle for affirming, conveying, and even treating pain? Does her case, broadcast in the form of indexical images, embody the material that could subvert the double bind of pain and connect her with a community of those who have experienced and shared traumas like her own? As I argue here, *The Tribunal* and the Condepa party were built upon the perceptual and political implications of this possibility.

As a documentary and ethnographic filmmaker who also once worked in television news, I find this clip provocative because it aligns the strikingly similar structural circumstances shared between the issues in representing pain with the dilemmas and the debates on language and unstructured materiality in filmmaking. Consisting of indexical images that not only "point to" particular contexts but are physically bound (electronically in the case of video) to them through causal point-for-point correspondences (Nichols 1991), film and video do appear to provide material certainty. Yet the meanings of indexical images are not guaranteed by these material binds between language and referents. Their meanings are constructed along with the selection, exclusions, sequence of images, spoken narratives, and the sometimes contentious claims made about them *beyond* the frame.[2] Hence their double bind: The more analysis one provides in a film, through voice-over, for example, the more alternative readings are suppressed or effectively edited out by the voice-over narrative. How does one provide the valuable yet complicated anthropological account of context, history, social categories and their relations, and an analytic framing without closing off other possible interpretations, including those of subjects speaking in the images themselves?

The problem with the debate over what kind of knowledge is available in ethnographic film is that it has easily resolved into polarized positions that simplistically oppose text against image. For detractors of ethnographic film, it offers only "thin description" and supplementary illustrations for the rich contextualization and comparative aspects that textual analysis provides; others hold that its monocular field of view amounts to a detached, disengaged, and omniscient authorial point of view (see Crawford and Turton 1992). In his collection of essays *Transcultural Cinema,* the filmmaker David MacDougall (1998)[3] argues that since films are structured from their primary physical material, "raw footage," filmic ethnographic knowledge is more *unruly* than writing, which, he says, "channels data through the keyhole of language" (68). Thickly saturated with a density of possible meanings but with no intrinsic units, internal structure, or necessary "grammar," images are intensely particularizing and ethnographically specific. In Peter Crawford's words, they are semantically rich but syntactically weak; they emphasize sensuous experience over the more abstract codification of writing (1992, 70). Like writers, of course, filmmakers ultimately select what and whom to film, include, and exclude, to form something like a structure, but realist film images are understood to be uniquely made from the same "raw material" produced in the contexts they refer to; they thus index and retain both the particularity and the heterogeneity of their contexts (cf. Taylor 1996). MacDougall has argued that because indexical images are bound to their contexts, the plural and even subversive agencies of film subjects

and much of the contingent complexity of social life inextricably manifest themselves in the films; in short, they are physical "imprints" of the
very conditions and relationships of their production (156). Significantly,
MacDougall does not claim the materiality of images as a final authenticating claim; instead, he reminds us of their contingent social production.

If, because of their concreteness, images are "open" to multiple
frames, then, like trauma, images make similar immediate demands for
treatment. Sharing the double bind of subjective certainty and objective
doubt introduced by their particular materiality, or material particularity,
both *The Tribunal* and documentary film images are situated at the intersections of trauma and diagnosis and image and discourse. They force us
to ask: What kind of discourses respond to their demands to treat their unstructured density? Discursive "responses" to the demands made by images
may be a deceptive way of organizing their relation, however, since images
never exist outside of simultaneous discursive frames, though not necessarily in conscious language. The question is what linguistic strategies are
used to make images appear "raw"? How are new juxtapositions between
words and images forged to create new affiliations? What are the political
consequences of raw images of trauma circulating in the televisual public
sphere as they engage communities of sufferers with similar experiences
and their sympathizers (cf. Kleinman et al. 1997)?

In this chapter, I move via enthography beyond the debates about
images and language as forms of signification and toward, or among, their
materialities and the people who produce and experience these registers
of signification in social practices of (self)representation. To pursue these
questions ethnographically rather than reflexively, the avenue is wide open
to draw from ethnographic filmmaking techniques to do the ethnography
of media.[4] As a filmmaker and ethnographer, for example, I am situated
at the convergence of these positions, where a practical understanding of
the choices and limits entailed in media production techniques contributes
to an ethnography of media (cf. Ginsburg 1998, 176, 184), informing
my analysis of what the production of televisual traces of meaning are
doing in material, cultural, and social terms (cf. Carpignano 1999; Miller
1998). Here, I trace the electronic indexical binds of the *Tribunal* images
back to their contexts of production to understand their materiality, in
both senses, as a particular signifying form as well as a mode of social
production. Because *The Tribunal* was seen to expose and exploit the vulnerabilities of Bolivia's downtrodden, it met with a mixture of solidarity
and sensationalism among audiences in La Paz who both demanded and
denounced the program and its host. By studying the production of the
program, I examine how it was organized to manage indeterminacy,

plurality, and their potency of indexical imagery, and how meanings were fixed in images and sound and then channeled back into their social discourses and political projects. The question, as I will pursue it here, is how it made such volatile images stick to the social projects they were intended to refer to? How did the circulation of indexical binds operate as material for disseminating *The Tribunal*'s social bonds?

▶ ——————————————————————————————

Assembling the Case from K'ulta

An elderly Aymara woman from the Altiplano countryside accompanied by a young man had been waiting in line outside the yellow and white Spanish colonial style building of Radio Television Popular (RTP) in the center of La Paz for two hours before they and the thirty other waiting visitors were guided into the dim lobby. Though the lobby was quiet, the shocks of Bolivia's neoliberal reforms seemed to resound through people waiting to be attended by social workers. Among them, two sobbing women with bruised eyes rocked their infants held in bright, striped aguayu cloths on their backs. A well-dressed man in a suit and a briefcase whispered to a social worker. As they interviewed visitors, the program's coordinator and social workers were asking people to restate their problems, as if the repetition were a rehearsal or an interrogation in which they had to persist until something in particular was revealed. The coordinator and social workers told me separately that people who came to *The Tribunal* often "confuse their situations." I had asked them if they tried to have the participants relate their cases on the air in a chronological order, thinking that putting the details into a unilinear sequence of events would help to clarify the details of the case and put them into their cause-and-effect relations. I was surprised to hear that they did not seek such smooth narrative coherence nor coach the visitors. "We want them to get to the central conflict," the social workers explained to me. "The audience can comprehend this better." Did the producers of *The Tribunal* imagine that their audiences and participants had a common difficulty in clarifying complex social situations, or were they reserving the linearity and narrativity for Carlos Palenque and preparing the cases for him by compressing them into captivating and potent images of accessible singular social conflicts?

A half hour before the noon videotaping of *The Tribunal* would begin upstairs, the program coordinator, Raoul, a young man in his early thirties, greeted the elderly woman and young man. "Kunsmunta, señora?" He asked the woman in Aymara what she wanted and why she had come to *The Open Tribunal*. Replying in Aymara, she began to explain her case. Not understanding her well enough, Raoul interrupted her and asked if the young man was with her. The young man was her nephew, it turned out, and Raoul politely told him to explain the case. The nephew began reciting legal details of how his aunt was trying to recover land in her rural community. By the time the nephew finished his account, Raoul had already assessed the case: it was not dramatic enough to appear on the television program. He instructed them to visit RTP lawyers at the network's Social Wing, which is how cases excluded from the air were typically treated. The elderly woman did not accept the immediate attention, however. She began to cry and in Aymara again she insisted on meeting with Carlos Palenque on television. After acquiescing, the coordinator instructed the nephew, "I am going to ask that you appear with her to explain the situation. Besides, she could confuse things. You want to emphasize that the trustees took the land and that you are waiting fourteen years to have the conflict resolved."

▶ ───────────────────────────────────

"The Lady from K'ulta"

During the taping of *The Open Tribunal* in the studio, host Carlos Palenque finished speaking with a group of men and women visiting from a rural town and then turned to address one of the three studio cameras: "*The Tribunal* continues." He continued turning and in Aymara he greeted the elderly woman and her nephew who stepped forward to meet him.

"Kunsmunta, señora. Welcome, comadre. How are you? Do you come together?" Palenque began, and then held out the microphone for them to speak.

The young man began to explain her case, "Yes. We came together, compadre. We came with a complaint from San Juan de K'ulta, in the province near Patacamaya. Pardon, Señor Compadre, this grandmother has suffered. There was a robbery in 1981, the twentieth of July, where she was robbed of all her possessions, and the thief escaped and the grandmother put an embargo on her land and now the alleged owners show up. This man Carlos Mamani has been designated as the trustee, and his brother, Francisco Mamani also—he didn't have anything to do with it. No? And now this last lawsuit has lasted fourteen years and the judge of Sica Sica has excused himself for not judging in favor of the grandmother, and he has sent us to Coro Coro. I am her nephew that . . . not even her son helps her, the grandmother. She has one son and I am a distant nephew who is helping her because I feel for her. No? Then this time all went well with the auction, but now that the testimonies have appeared saying that they are the owners. They did the buying and selling after the embargo and I am asking for justice, that this gentleman, Augustin Coronel, who is the judge of Coro Coro, give her justice. And in this last lawsuit, the grandmother made an affidavit indicating that the ex-trustee, this Carlos Mamani, he stole this land fourteen years ago from the moment that he became trustee . . ."

Palenque interrupted and asked the nephew, "Is she alone?"

"Yes, she is. There is no one to help her. She comes here and only cries," the nephew explained. "I work here [in La Paz], so she asked me to help her. Please, what we are requesting is a lawyer. She has no resources and cannot do anything. Fourteen years of lawsuits that do not seem to end."

"Fourteen years and it does not end," Palenque observed sympathetically and addressed the woman directly: "What a holdup in justice! No, comadre?"

The woman responded in Aymara, saying, "There is no justice, compadre. Compadre, I am alone. This trustee Carlos Mamani is lying. He happily kicked me out with the document. The problem will not end."

Palenque responded to her in Aymara, "This is how it is, comadre," and then switched to Spanish, saying, "This is what he is telling us." He then motioned them to go off camera. "Talk with Comadre Remedios Loza, mamita. She will help you. A lawyer will orient you. Guide you. What a shame! Fourteen years!" As the man and woman walked off out of the camera frame with Remedios Loza, Palenque looked into a camera and addressed his television audience directly. "A humble woman from the countryside suffers the delay—the *famous* delay—of justice."

The details of this case are difficult to follow. Out of the disconnected narrative bits from the bureaucratic labyrinth the young man described, viewers in La Paz to whom I showed a tape of the two-and-a-half-minute segment could only draw out and determine its central conflict: that the old woman had been robbed and that she had been struggling in local courts for fourteen years to have her land returned to her. Although it is significant that we had to watch this episode five times to connect and straighten out the details of the case, this is only partly the point. Viewers who only watch once, of course, do not follow the minute details as closely as they watch to see Palenque's treatment of them.

With his commentary, Palenque filled in the gaps between the fragmented details of the testimony during the interview by finding an alternative point of wider interest and sympathy. In this case, as he typically did, Palenque interrupted the nephew to ask if the woman was living alone, thereby turning the complicated legal case into personal melodrama. What happened on the air, then, was much like what had been heard in line earlier. In the prescreening with social workers, the testimony was left in fragmented and urgent "narrative heaps,"[5] which created an imagistic density of meanings that were open to and demanded immediate attention. This set up for Palenque a case he treated with soothing affirmations and then accumulated the myriad details into a coherent causal explanation and a wider meaningful frame that reassuringly confirmed for the woman and for viewers the certainty of shared social problems—"a humble woman from the countryside suffering the delay, the *famous* delay of justice."

After the Aymara woman and her nephew walked out of the studio, they waited to speak to a lawyer, as Palenque had directed. After they had been waiting a few minutes in the studio's anteroom, Marianna, one of the social workers, stopped chatting with a coworker and approached them to ask, "What is your problem?"

"The compadre told us we can talk to a lawyer," the nephew said politely.

Marianna responded, "The lawyers are not working today. Why don't you come on Monday? Can I give you the address?" She took out a small slip of paper and wrote the address for the Social Wing of RTP, which is located in a small office down the street.

In deferring cases this way, RTP's Social Wing duplicated the same bureaucratic delays that *The Tribunal* itself contested on the air. Yet this constant attention from and toward the Social Wing resulting from these deferred resolutions materialized the social network that *The Tribunal* disseminated electronically. It is also important to remember that while in line earlier, the old woman from K'ulta insisted on presenting her case directly to Palenque, thereby delaying her own resolution. In doing so, she sought, as did many visitors and viewers, the mediation that Palenque provided in treating social problems.

▶

Producing Indexical Binds

If Palenque demonstrates how powerful frames of meaning are produced through the arrangement of sound and language, I want to move "off-screen" to the specifically televisual materialities and techniques of producing and editing the realism of *The Tribunal*'s indexical images. In the studio, three cameras faced the lighted stage; one camera in the middle would usually take wide shots of interlocutors during a case on stage and the close-ups of Palenque when he addressed viewers, while each of two cameras on alternate sides of the set shoot from behind the person closest to them and over their shoulder to the person opposite them and facing the camera. During the taping inside the studio, each of the three studio camera-men explained that they usually know what to focus on and receive very few instructions over the headsets from Jorge, the director in the control room; a tally light in their viewfinder indicates when their camera is live. Jorge's directing between these cameras in a series of shots and counter-shots can be an intense effort to pull together, live and on cue, material that is happening along a number of disparate circuits: to switch smoothly and expeditiously between cameras along with the discussion, as well to control the lights and bring in audio, including the microphones and back-ground music. But in the control room with a row of video monitors dis-playing the three cameras and their available shots, Jorge quietly switched back and forth among the three cameras in a series of shots as they were recorded onto a single videotape; he rarely gave instructions to the camera-men over their headsets and the sound and lights came in and out without a word from the others on the crew operating beside him in the control room. In contrast to the intensity inside the studio, the dramatically quiet and composed atmosphere here suggested that in the windowless "control room" the social disorder outside was being calmly managed.

In switching between cameras, Jorge was continuously presented with a virtually infinite mixture of possible shot sequences and durations. He explained to me that in deciding when to switch cameras he only "fol-lows what is happening," as if his cues for dissolves and cuts between angles and wide and close-up shots flowed directly and naturally from the social interaction in the studio, and in effect, from the dialogue led by his boss, Carlos Palenque. What does it mean in this context to "follow the action" with camera switching, given Jorge's variety of choices for the length and sequence of shots? His sequence of camera shots could be fur-ther viewed in two ways: one, using classic theories of montage and edit-ing, informed by structural theories of language, would argue that the se-quences of shot and countershot produced coherent narrative meaning out of the alternating chain of fragmented visual presences and absences; that is, by a flow of alternating negations, each shot produced the meanings of the surrounding shots in a syntagmatic chain. As Stephen Heath has said in this vein, "continuity is built on fragmentation . . . that can bind the spectator in the strong articulations of the unity it seeks to create" (1981, 43). Thus, just as Jorge was following direction from Palenque's dialogues, the switching back and forth among the three cameras also incorporated viewers as they created coherence from the narrative control offered by Palenque's discourse. A second manner of viewing the scene in the control room does not fully insert the viewer into the positions of the participants within the unfolding plot because the plot and significance of a case may not accumulate until it is given by Palenque at the end; thus, the live switching of the cameras during production (rather than in postproduction editing) also entails a fragmented form of monitoring and pursuit, as Jorge himself did as director, creating an event from multiple angles, heightening the sense of contingency and televisual "liveness." In this scenario, viewers are in a subordinate position alongside Jorge, following Palenque's direction for the scene's coherence. These two positions that live camera switching opens up in this context correspond to the mix of solidarity and sensationalism that viewers experience in watching *The Tribunal* (see chapter 5). What about the time-shifted discontinuities *The Tribunal* and television embodied by adding location video footage in postproduction?

Along with the testimonial realism and intimacy of face-to-face communication between Palenque and his participants and viewers were the pencil drawings added to dramatize cases. But for those cases where location video footage could be obtained, video footage was shot and electronically inserted over the interlocutors' voices and images to visually connect the television studio with the peripheral urban social spaces of the "popular" classes. For over thirteen years this location footage was gathered by Bernabe, an Aymara man living in La Paz who observed the studio taping each day, taking detailed notes before spending the afternoon driving around the metropolitan La Paz area to shoot video that matched the cases from the day's program. At times he would give advice to participants on what they would have to do to resolve their cases and then explain, even raise hopes about, what Palenque would do to help them. In doing so, Bernabe himself extended the social relations of *The Tribunal* throughout the city, frequently stopping to have lunch and discuss political strategies with comadres and compadres at their food stands in the popular markets. One day, while I was having lunch with him at a favorite food stand, a politically active comadre who owned the stand reminded us, "We formed Palenque, we taught him everything he knows. How to give, how to please, how to smile, and how to talk with us." In less friendly situations, Bernabe encountered rock-throwing accused perpetrators waiting for him at the scene of a case. "They know we are coming because they listened to the program on the radio today," he explained to me. Since the television taping had been broadcast live on the radio, he told me, he often had to dash in and escape with his footage like a thief.

In tracing the production process beyond the televisual frame on these routines, I accompanied *Tribunal* production staff and social workers some of whom came from the popular sectors of La Paz and expressed their approval of Palenque's authority and praised the accomplishments of *The Tribunal*'s social mission. I also heard occasional cracks in *The Tribunal*'s coherent discourse about itself, as the sphere of patron-client relations was subverted by discussions of low salaries and inadequate resources at the Social Wing. Many workers subtly described their work as if they had been obligated to provide their labor power to Palenque because their relationship was bound by a more sacred set of exchanges than those between capital and labor. "I do not think that Palenque should give away all of his money. That would be equally unfair," Bernabe told me. And his driver described his own second job and the vertical social control at RTP in which one could not talk to or challenge Palenque without being dismissed. It was clear that job security was as dependent on productivity as it was on deference to Palenque both as "El Jefe" (the boss) and as "El Compadre."

As *The Tribunal* was taping and airing in the studio in the next room, the head social worker, Maria, told me that many people insisted on staying in line to meet with Carlos Palenque on the program even though they could have gone directly for aid at the Social Wing. "They think that he can make the solutions happen," she said.

"What does he do?" I asked.

"Well, he sends them back to us—the social workers," she said with a smile. One social worker I spoke with had resigned because of insufficient pay. Felicia had become disillusioned because her initial supposition that resources to provide quick solutions for people would be directly attainable from Carlos Palenque proved unfounded. "One has to do many miracles on that job," she said, referring to the extra time and personal expenses for travel and support required to provide assistance to people and to make up for the inadequacies of the resources given to her by the RTP network. She also explained how she had been frustrated by not being able to shape the network's social policies, by job insecurity, long hours and low pay, and by the bureaucracy that slowed frequently inadequate social services. Felicia and her former coworkers at RTP were in a position similar to that of the people they ostensibly were aiding. Palenque seemed to appeal to their moral obligations to "the people" in order to convert the quantifiable exchanges between capital and labor into nonquantifiable exchanges between himself and subordinate compadres and comadres. Like the people they were helping, they had a stake in Palenque's economic and political prosperity and they tactically complied in the televisual production of the image of his social authority as seen within the TV frame.[6]

At the network building late one afternoon, an editor at RTP searched through location video Bernabe had brought back and in the station's video library looking for scenes to match the situations discussed on the day's opening discourses by the hosts and in the testimonials themselves. Selected video portions of a prerecorded tape, in this case the program on the tape from earlier in the day, are replaced with new ones while leaving the prerecorded audio tracks alongside them. To portray "poor people" as Palenque was discussing earlier that day, for example, the editor searched for images of people who he said appeared "lonely and in need of social relations, such as family, work." Video of people's homes and schools lacking in basic services, views of peripheral neighborhoods in the higher elevations in the city, and other familiar urban scenes were also edited in alongside the program's discourse to point to and define the popular urban social space that many referred to as "Palenque's people." In the broadcast, this process of "insert editing" heightened, embodied, and technologized indexical signification by using the indexical bind between images and referents to make meaningful and visible connections between the discourse on the program and the urban social space to which it referred.

These material indexical binds between images and referents operated as circuits of participation in "the Condepa family," so that the program's indexical binds would be converted into social bonds. One day in line with a group of people outside the studio, a man with his family who had been involved in a truck accident in El Alto told me that he watched the program almost every night. He said he was not concerned about going on camera because as a regular viewer he already felt that he was part of the program. With his arrival at the RTP studio that day, the previous electronic disseminations of social discourse and indexical imagery had completed a circuit along the indexical bind. As the broadcast circulated outward from the studio to its popular audiences, people recognized themselves as participants and returned to the studio itself as participants, closing the circuit between the popular public prefigured in the program's discourse and the social worlds it indexed, a cycle that would continuously repeat like the mutual exchanges of agency between Palenque and *The Tribunal*'s participants as described in chapter 5.

The "editing" of *The Tribunal* had begun earlier as cases were selected for broadcast. One evening on the broadcast, Palenque discussed for audiences why not all visitors to the RTP studios appear on television. He said, "When there are issues that are not worth the trouble to air on television, the social workers immediately try to resolve them in another way. When there is a very serious request, for example, among siblings, they will talk first with the social workers. The social workers make the first contact."

Figure 22. In the production of *The Open Tribunal of the People*, editing begins with the program's manager and social workers, who select guests with dramatic stories to meet with Palenque. Visitors who do not go on air with Palenque are directed to the Social Wing of the program for assistance.

Figure 23. After meeting with the hosts, visitors to *The Open Tribunal of the People* meet with a social worker and are given an appointment at the Social Wing, located in a small office down the street.

Figure 24. Cameraman Bernabe talking with visitors to *The Tribunal* while taking video footage that will be edited to accompany their case in the day's program taped earlier.

In emphasizing how some problems are treated with immediate assistance from a social worker, Palenque heightened the sense of direct contact with *The Tribunal* and its images of immediate solutions as seen by viewers who said that Palenque treated cases quickly, as if people walked out of the frame and immediately had their problem addressed if not resolved. *The Tribunal* was constructed around the potency of this immediacy, which may also be seen embodied in the program's compression of time and space and the edited juxtapositions of video and audio tracks. The intersecting processes of selecting and preparing the participants converging at the studio each morning, the videotaped intercutting scenes of testimonials, and the subsequent inserted location video over oral discourses are all modes of compressing spatially disjunctured and temporally asynchronous moments into a single case. As host, Palenque carefully decompressed the unstable heterogeneity of each case and channeled it through his framing narratives and discourses to the Social Wing and into the televisual public sphere. More broadly, as Palenque attempted to contain the potent compressed heterogeneity of the entire program in his opening and closing discourses for each broadcast, he attached meanings to each indexical image as it was disseminated in order to control its impact as it landed in the social field. We could say that the indexical function of Palenque's discourse itself took a simulated form of the insert editing just described: his framing discourses were additional audio tracks added to cases *after* the original scenes, but their effect was to forge self-evident simultaneous connections between his discourse and the events he referred to because his framing packaged them together, making them perceptibly synchronous as if they were a single event.[7]

▶

The Soundscape of the Public Sphere

Listening to Palenque speak as if he were able to stem the wider social crisis with his own voice, or to the urgency of the young woman in the first scene, calls attention to language as a potent and sensual medium involving competence in techniques of performativity. To complement the attention to language and exchange in chapter 5, this chapter has empha-sized the materiality of *The Open Tribunal,* and in both I am addressing the discussions about the public sphere that have largely been structural—emphasizing commodification in decisive zones of public debate, plotting the uneven positions and erasures of speakers who seek to access zones of public discourse, or revealing the heterogeneity of publics and forms of so-cial dialogue (e.g., Robbins 1993). In such analyses, one implicit and often concrete figure for the plurality of public sociality and the dynamics of dialogue is the vivid metaphor of "voice." Remarkably little has been said about what voices actually sound like in the acoustic space of the public sphere, however. I turn to the sounds of voices as crucial material for de-fining and limiting the meanings of the disjointed testimonials and potent images as well as audible instruments for enacting social roles in these acts of spoken exchange.

In chapter 5, I analyzed *The Tribunal*'s discourses and dialogues in public space to argue that they entailed collusive exchanges. Marking social inequality, the diffuse and tacit moral standards of ritual coparent-hood that were transacted between unequal subjects exchanged and dispersed agency between them, objectifying each other's uneven social agency in the exchange of voices. Yet what also emerged from the dis-cursive exchanges of "agency play" were the voices of interlocutors with discrete material textures. If their collusive dialogues succeeded, it was in no small part due to the televisual reproduction of their voices in the acoustic space of the TV studio. Blocking the busy traffic noise outside the studio and the building, the walls inside the TV studio absorbed and reduced the vocal sound reverberations produced on the set, which en-hanced the auditory presence of speakers so they stood out sharply in acoustic space. Palenque's soothing and melodic voice and coherence also stood in sharp relief against the distressed voices and the grammatically fragmented and incoherent narratives of the participants, performing their own recognizable tonalities of distress, outrage, humility, and respect. The alternating rhythm of distinct vocal textures between interlocutors conformed—because it materially indexed—the distinct agentive subjects who conversed and exchanged respect, aid, and protagonism with each other. These auditory contours were tangible material substance that subjects grasped, objectified, and carefully exchanged in the public sphere. Grasped by television viewers and radio listeners in the circulatory matrix of broadcasting, Palenque's voice therapeutically soothed both the participants' and his audience's traumatic sensorium, extending the controlled acoustic space within the studio to the urban soundscape beyond. While Carlos Palenque "gave voice to the people," audiences similarly objectified his voice and agency when they emphasized or exchanged his social protagonism over their own. In fact, if his voice was objectified in their exchanges, it was available as a primary ingredient in forming the commodity people sought in watching *The Tribunal,* just as participants who were offered aid before the taping insisted on talking to Palenque first.

But how were voices primary material for the construction of a popular public? After all, as Webb Keane's (1997) work on such "scenes of encounter" alerts us, this business of ritual exchange inherently runs the risk of failing. In chapter 5, I quoted one of Palenque's discourses directed to his viewers at the end of one evening's program, which is worth repeating:

> You see the endless problems that happen. Here we show them as they are. We do not decorate them. We do not distort them. Just as they are. [Background music comes up.] Here the protagonist is you, who makes the demands to the authorities or brings up your problems. That is the philosophy of the *Tribunal.* God willing, in September we will complete twenty-eight years of being in daily contact with our people. With our family. Talking face-to-face and searching for solutions. Twenty-eight years of being intimately linked with the family and with our people. Maybe in a few years we will be able to say, "Mission complete." But no. There is still a long—very long—road to go.

This sample of Palenque's entextualization of the program's indexical imagery of disorder and trauma in his characteristically earnest and optimistic voice was crucial to his success and is an example of Keane's dual point that while "futurity" is as much a feature of indexicality as causation is, it also entails or implicates human agency. Whether it was the conferral and exchange of protagonism that Palenque enacted in this framing or in the dialogic exchanges with participants, his objectified discourse turned attention back onto himself and the quality of his performance (Bauman and Briggs 1990, 73). To be sure, lifting stretches of linguistic dialogue out of interactional settings and making radically heterogeneous, indeterminate, and volatile indexical images commensurate with one's own project is an act of control (Bauman and Briggs 1990, 73, 75), but a delicate one if it publicly calls attention to the competency and personhood of the performer in an act of exchange (Beidelman 1989). The ambiguities in exposing, exchanging, and attributing agency I have described here and in chapter 5 all run the risk of failure, especially among a wide popular audience. Palenque's broadcast network and his political authority held great stakes in these exchanges, while for *The Tribunal*'s participants the program was often a last resort for real assistance. Yet Carlos Palenque made it look and sound easy—as if he were above the vulnerabilities of performance and exchange. If these scenes were dangerous and their indexical images do not guarantee their own meanings, how did Palenque's voice manage their indeterminacy, plurality, and potency? If the entextualization and exchange did not succeed alone, how did he use his voice to make his discourse adhere effectively to the indexical images that substantiated his own political projects?[8]

One possible adhesive was the background music. Mixed underneath the voices during live taping, soft folkloric Andean music was played from a record turntable in the control room. The music not only moved viewers toward sympathy, as Palenque's voice itself may have done, but in an unusual production practice, the music could be heard in the studio by Palenque and the others, as it cushioned Palenque's own risky performance of himself with his interlocutors. But beyond the background music, no doubt, Palenque was drawing on his own experience as a singer with the well-known music trio Los Caminantes in the 1960s, a career that ended when he needed a vocal operation and then turned to radio. His musical discourses sonically evoked and echoed the recorded soundscape of romantic ballads that were also most popular on the radio in the 1960s, featuring brief heartfelt and heartbroken spoken-word segments that emphasized abandonment and the collapse of certainty and caring.

The significance of Palenque's deep melodic voice was in how he evoked this musical style to saturate the historical present, reverberating across the soundscape just as the popular classes themselves felt abandoned or marginalized by the promises of the paternalist nation-state that had dominated the twentieth century. Conjuring up tones of romantic loss in his original music, his voice recuperated desire toward the fantasy he conducted of a prosperous popular nation-state, putting into sonic and visceral experience the romantic popular nationalism that emerged from the "foundational fictions" of Latin American literature (on Bolivia, see Abercrombie 2003). In order to make his social discourses conform to the *Tribunal*'s potent indexical imagery, Palenque's voice circulated overtones of romantic loss that were familiar to audiences on several levels, but they were also compelling because they resonated among "abject" (Ferguson 1999) viewers who already occupied a political world where their fantasies of prosperity had been withdrawn. If it was mediation that conjured Palenque's voice as earnest, direct, and authentic (Kittler 1999), then his deep, confident, and sympathetic voice resonated with the off-screen voice of the earlier ICB films from the 1950s (see chapter 4), sustaining the fantasy of the nation-state.[9] Palenque's voice on *The Tribunal* may have been the last articulation of the paternal voice of the revolutionary project for unifying a popular nation-state. When Palenque himself died unexpectedly in 1997, many viewers turned off the program when it became "too political." When the charisma, nostalgia and fantasy, performativity and ritualized exchanges dissolved, their absence did not divulge political machinations that were hidden and unknown; Palenque's absence revealed the public secret of collusion of which audiences were well aware. His absence subtracted the crucial elements of fantasy and charisma from their experience of populist politics.

▶
_____

Palenque's Double Bind

The social production of Condepa and its popular publics took material form as a televisual production directed by "El Compadre" Carlos Palenque, a program in which televisual indexical binds and social bonds were assembled and disseminated across the city's popular classes who would become affiliated as "Palenque's People."

In this chapter, I have explored the social practice of media on *The Open Tribunal* as a combination of material modes of signification—the visual, the oral, and written—to show how these orders and media of signification are assembled and juxtaposed in a potent concatenation. Situated at the intersection of social suffering, popular politics, and media technologies, *The Tribunal* exploited for all it was worth the double bind of certainty and doubt in conveying images and sounds of pain. In this double bind, *The Tribunal*'s production process carefully orchestrated the tensions between televisual image and narrative and between trauma and therapeutic discourse. Publicly exposing social wounds in order to treat them, *The*

Tribunal could treat cases with modern political and economic institutions of the political party Condepa and the network's Social Wing.

Indeed, from the point of view of participants, the offer to appear in the public sphere and even have one's problem addressed on commercial television was one popular strategy for engaging and maneuvering within the very same neoliberal circumstances of their problems. Yet this was a collusive strategy in which Palenque and participants precariously traded attention and prestige in ritualized exchanges that were not fully in either party's hands. The indexical binds that connected participants and their images to the television screens in the neighborhoods in which they lived were vehicles that conveyed and transmitted an understanding of their social suffering to others inhabiting the very same historical world who had experienced and shared the social crises. This relationship, described by Jane Gaines as "political mimesis," is one "between two bodies in two locations—on the screen and in the audience that is the starting point for the consideration of what one body makes the other body do" (1999, 90). Though the political movement that originated from *The Tribunal*'s popular realism successfully exploited this socially embodied knowledge, the hosts and the Condepa party always held the risk of being subverted by the accumulation of their own popular audiences if they were not treated properly. This, then, was Palenque's double bind: Because of the open-ended materiality of *The Tribunal*'s participants—the particularity of their embodied images and their urgent testimonials in which there was no necessary general framing or guaranteed meaning residing in them—Palenque had to say exactly what people wanted to hear.

Conclusion:
Popularizing Indigenism,
Indigenizing the Popular

▶

Screening Bolivia: Indigenism Meets Indigeneity

For many of the immigrants from Bolivia who had settled in the environs of Arlington, Virginia, tonight would be the first time they would see either documentary or fictional works produced by trained indigenous video makers from their home country. Two of the immigrant organizations that had formed among the concentration of Bolivians living in the area, Comité Pro-Bolivia and Alma Boliviana, were collaborating to present video screenings occasioned by the visit of the video makers to the United States. Just days earlier in March 2002, a trio of Bolivian video makers had arrived to launch a month-long video tour called "Ojo de Condor" (Eye of the Condor) that would travel to universities, cultural centers, and film festivals across North America to present and screen some of the recent films for which they were well known among indigenous video networks across the Americas. The touring video makers included Jesús Tapia (Aymara), a video maker as well as president and coordinator of CAIB (the Bolivian Indigenous Peoples' Audiovisual Council); Marcelina Cárdenas (Quechua), a video maker, journalist, and graduate student in Quechua linguistics; and Ivan Sanjinés, a nonindigenous video maker and coordinator of the Cinematography Education and Production Center (CEFREC), a video training and production center based in La Paz. Their tour had begun only the night before as part of the Environmental Film Festival held at the Museum of Art of the Smithsonian Institution, whose National Museum of the American Indian (NMAI) in New York was also the organizer and sponsor of the Ojo de Condor video tour. After their opening night on the National Mall in Washington, the trio and their hosts traveled across the Potomac River and spent the weekend in Arlington, giving several presentations to Bolivian immigrant associations.

At the conference center they rented for the event in Arlington, Pro-Bolivia and Alma Boliviana began the evening with a dinner of home-made Bolivian dishes and then moved the audience of middle- and working-class Bolivian families to a large meeting room decorated with Bolivian flags and other national icons. After her introduction, Marcelina Cárdenas, dressed in her Quechua-style dress and hat, introduced her video *Llanthupi Munakuy* (Loving Each Other in the Shadows). As these video makers would do throughout their tour, Cárdenas defined their collective work as a response to the proliferation of commercial mass media that had accompanied the neoliberal policies of the 1980s in Bolivia. The new television channels opened in the broadcast marketplace, she explained, carried cultural messages that were not only incompatible with the cultural realities and experiences of indigenous peoples but devalued them as well. In an effort to counteract the dominant media, indigenous video makers across the country had begun to take up video technologies "as an instrument and a weapon" to defend and recuperate their native cultures. They were producing documentaries as well as fictional dramatizations of historical legends intended not only to preserve culture but to empower rural communities with resources to determine their own futures in native cultural terms.

As her films would do in many venues on the U.S. tour, Cárdenas's forty-seven-minute short fiction film brought an entertaining blend of humor, mystery, and melodramatic tension to its audience in a story about a young man and woman in the rural countryside who fall in love and run away against their parents' wishes. After the screening, the audience in Arlington was struck by how well the film integrated the elements of ritual, symbolism, social status, and cultural principles with which they themselves were familiar. Unlike the questions that came up at the screening the previous night at the Smithsonian, in fact, members of this audience did not need to clarify narrative questions that relied on knowing the vital invisible cosmological forces made visible to viewers of the videos. Like some members in the audience the prior evening, however, and as others would do throughout the subsequent U.S. tour, some expressed surprise that indigenous peoples from Bolivia were now making enjoyable fictional short feature films of such high technical quality. They wanted to know where they could buy copies and the filmmakers obliged by selling copies at a table set up outside the salon to help fund their work. Bolivians in the United States often collect videos of significant folklore festivals and parades held in Bolivia and of such events produced locally and held in synchrony with the same events in Bolivia. Many people use such home-made and semiprofessional videos as souvenirs of events in which they have participated as well as a means of engaging with their own heritage, in the manner, perhaps, that these new videos were intended to serve in Bolivian rural communities.

In Arlington, the comments by people in the audience who spoke during Marcelina Cárdenas's Q & A after the film revealed their nostalgia for their native country to which they continue to feel deeply attached. "We are all Indians, Latinos, and Bolivians. We carry the distinct cultures of our people even though we are here in this country," said one woman as she stood to praise the filmmakers for enabling her to connect with multiple aspects of her identity and her earlier years in Bolivia. From the viewpoint of their own temporal and spatial distance from their home country, these videos evoked nostalgia among Bolivians living in the United States for an indigenous national heritage they perceived to be threatened, especially in the countryside where Cárdenas's video takes place. Another woman in the audience stood to commend the filmmakers and then asked in urgent tones concerning the ritual knowledge and practices that were factors in the story, "How can we prevent these practices from disappearing?" Marcelina sensed a contradiction here, as she would recall with me afterward. Responding with what already seemed evident to her, she explained to the audience, "This is why we are making these videos and distributing them on VHS among communities." That the video makers had framed their work as a project of cultural self-determination was belied by the woman's question. Surely motivated by respect, concern, and nostalgia for Bolivia's cultural specificity, the question drew from an image of native culture as a singular and static thing that was essentially vanishing into the past but could be rescued by a paternalist effort to save and preserve it for them.

In Arlington, the Bolivian audience's nostalgic views of indigenous cultures in terms of singularity, pastness, and fixity met face-to-face with Marcelina Cárdenas's effort to demonstrate a dynamic presence by pointing out that her new film, which had just been screened, was an effort to use video to uphold and circulate indigenous cultures and their ways of knowing. Furthermore, the very scene surrounding the screen at that moment enacted the very same point. Only feet away from Marcelina at the podium stood Jesús Tapia, who was videotaping the event, wearing his photographer's vest and holding an impressive Canon XL1 digital video camera with its uniquely prominent lens on his shoulder. Together, Tapia and Cárdenas challenged the view of the disappearance of their cultures with their own active presence; they demonstrated that indigenous cultures

Figure 25. After screening her film *Llanthupi Munakuy* (Loving Each Other in the Shadows, 2001), the filmmaker Marcelina Cárdenas *(at left)* listens as a member of the audience *(far right)* asks how to prevent indigenous cultures from disappearing. *At center,* the filmmaker Jesús Tapia videotapes the event, while Ivan Sanjinés observes.

endure yet not without change as they took the form of film. Not only did Cárdenas's response contrast with the static view of culture by pointing out their own work of cultural production with modern representational media but also her and Tapia's very attendance at the event in Arlington demonstrated their plurality and mobility, rather than fixity, as cultural subjects. Standing in front of the movie screen, on which their "cultures" had been projected in motion, Tapia and Cárdenas were visible evidence of active subjects of cultures in motion.

At that juncture, two circulating formulations and historical ideologies concerning indigenous peoples met head-on. The first was brought in with members of the audience who experienced the videos with a nostalgia for Bolivia that was rooted in the mestizo projects of populism that dominated national belonging and politics for much of the twentieth century. Underlying this ideology were accumulated images of the Andean image world produced by the intellectual movement of *indigenismo* (indigenism) among non-Indian mestizos who participated in and romanticized indigenous Andean rituals, music, dress, and divine entities, for example (Poole 1997). Defined by their "pastness" and fixed features, these practices could endure into the present only in depoliticized form, excluded from national politics but preserved in folkloric pageantry and commodity form as a sign of the collective national heritage (read: past) while the country moved forward, progressing and modernizing. It was from this vantage point that members in the Arlington audience sought to preserve the indigenous customs seen in Marcelina Cárdenas's film. Moreover, this position omitted from view the contemporary native peoples producing and reproducing culture in films about their own communities, despite the evidence to the contrary standing before them.

Thus, the second viewpoint arrived with the video makers themselves and in the media of their video works. In the "language of indigeneity" (Canessa 2006) these were intended to feature the "presentness" of active indigenous and political subjects representing themselves. Over the course of the 1990s, self-identified indigenous activists representing the *pueblos originarios* (original peoples) from Bolivia's highlands and lowlands began mobilizing jointly in social movements against government economic policies and for control over land, resources, and dignity. As these movements episodically dispersed and then coalesced into forces of national scale later in the decade, they demanded their political rights as full national citizens and the recognition of their present cultural differences that had been marginalized under the earlier homogenizing project of mestizaje. Emphasizing aspects of native cultural and political values as principles to mobilize international networks, indigenous-led movements were dramatically reshaping national politics in Bolivia at that moment. In the 2002 elections two months later, Bolivians were stunned when Gonzalo Sánchez de Losada only won a razor-thin victory over the Aymara social activist Evo Morales.

Like two proverbial ships passing at night, the traditional *indigenista* view of native culture carried in with members of the Bolivian-born families that night in Arlington eclipsed a view of these visiting video makers as part of the cultural transformations that were indigenizing national politics southward in Bolivia. During the same period, a nationwide indigenous video movement had developed to pursue projects of cultural self-representation. While indigenism had been popularized through diffusion in folkloric and commercial culture in Bolivia for most of the past century, indigenous activists and media makers were inverting that circuit, *indigenizing* popular culture and representational media, in effect, and using them to serve indigenous communities and their own cultural projects.

After their presentations in Arlington, the trio of filmmakers began their itinerary of screenings at the National Museum of the American Indian in New York and several universities along the East Coast and the Midwest, and then on to the Taos Talking Picture Film Festival in New Mexico, where they received the Taos Mountain Achievement Award. While Marcelina Cárdenas, Jesús Tapia, and Ivan Sanjinés appeared on the tour as the directors and producers of some of the works they screened, they explained to audiences how their work was shaped by complex modes of collective and community production that displaces individual authorship with larger goals of revealing collective knowledge and histories. In this final chapter, I discuss the emergence of a process I call "indigenizing the popular" in which indigenous video makers are transforming and intervening in the popular national project and popular culture as well as their systems of circulation. As I will show, indigenous video makers appropriate styles from commercial mass media yet they subvert the marketplace as a moral space for the accumulation of individual wealth. Further, just as indigeneity has emerged in international and local networks to indigenize the national project, these indigenous projects of self-representation draw from alliances that extend from well beyond the national frame. To foreground this contemporary process, I first examine the backdrop of earlier cinema history in Bolivia by reviewing several key instances of the popularization of indigeneity in Bolivian media worlds before turning to the indigenization of the popular.

▶ ──

Popularizing Indigenism

For most of the twentieth century, the social imaginary of the Bolivian nation-state was dominated by the "popularization" of the images of early-twentieth-century *indigenism,* the widespread intellectual movement that also circulated in from Peru to Mexico: Romantic and heroic images of native peoples as portrayed by indigenista non-Indian scholars and artists were appropriated and incorporated into political strategies and historical projects headed by criollo (white) elites and mestizo middle classes to imagine a homogeneous popular nation-state with roots in a common indigenous heritage. As political and economic capital concentrated in La Paz, and the city became the country's de facto capital, the expanding middle and working classes promoted mestizaje as an ideology of national origins. By valorizing their own mixture of indigenous ancestry and contemporary European culture, this ideology promoted the fusion of a strong and coherent new national subject known as "Bolivian man." This response to the "Indian question" secured political control among non-Indian mestizos by effectively co-opting indigenous political issues with a paternalist model that valorized their culture as national heritage. In the images of popular culture that circulate in national folklore and festivals as well as in commodity form, notably in tourism, film and television, and music, "Indians" have been romanticized for their spiritual connection with the land and their ritual practices, authentic plastic arts and clothing, and collective politics. Inserted into the circuits of popular culture and populist national politics, this indigenista imagery advanced an account of the specificity of the nation and its deep past.

Bolivia's cinematic history begins with the excavation of indigenous culture in order to romanticize it—quite literally in 1930 when the Vienna-born archaeologist-filmmaker Arturo Posnansky sought to save the memory of Tiwanaku as the nation's glorious precolonial past in *La Gloria de la Raza* (The Glory of the Race). In the same year, emerging mestizo political and middle classes sought to represent their status as legitimate Indians and modern nationals simultaneously (Abercrombie 1991), and they appeared camouflaged in Inca dress in *Wara Wara*, the film in which the violence of the colonial encounter became a "foundational fiction" (Sommer 1990), a national romance between film viewers and Wara, the Inca princess who defiantly resisted the temptations of imperialism. These films set up primordial origins for a uniquely culturally mixed nation by redefining the present as an outgrowth of an imagined past that no viewer could actually recollect.

The Chaco War (1929–33) against Paraguay was a crucial moment in the formation of mestizo popular nationalism. Indigenous peasant men had been conscripted and were valorized in popular films like Luis Bazoberry's *The Chaco Campaign* (1933) as combatants who had bravely defended and died for the nation and territorial sovereignty. The depictions of indigenous peoples as historical protagonists culminated in the revolution in 1952 in which alliances of peasants, workers, and middle classes toppled a white criollo oligarchy. Yet as the social documentaries produced by the revolutionary Bolivian Cinematographic Institute (ICB) were inserted into the circuits of commercial feature films in La Paz, they portrayed indigenous peoples as citizens and in folkloric imagery, as the heritage of a new synthesized (i.e., mestizo) Bolivian nation. *Las Voces de la Tierra* (The Voices of the Earth), directed by Jorge Ruiz in 1956, incorporated indigenous culture into a folkloric mestizo social imaginary that synthesized cultural differences into a new urban modern Bolivian citizen. Opening with a young Aymara boy tossing stones into a small lake on the rural Altiplano, a paternal male voice-over explains how the young "Bolivian Indian . . .the son of the land" magically communicates with the voices of the landscape and the wind. The film depicts indigenous Aymaras as the traditional unchanged descendents of the land itself whose survival and political participation depended on assimilating as "mestizos" in the Western city (appearing as a sign of modernity). Thus in the final scene "indigenous culture" is permitted in the city under highly regulated conditions as "folklore," the emblem of a distinctive national heritage.

Like the earlier archaeological films, these films superimposed the claim of Bolivian heritage onto, or beneath, the national territory so that the past, the landscape, and the national project were merged. In the same way, Ruiz's 1973 film *La Gran Herencia* (Great Heritage) took a route that encircled and tied together regional differences with postcard images of the country. If images of Indianness represented the national past, the revolution also sought to dissolve present indigenous traditions into European forms of modernity (i.e., civilization, capitalism, and Western political forms) with the promises of a popular and beneficent nation-state organized around class and the state ownership of wealth and industry. To orient this project, films produced by the state such as *Los Primeros* (The First Ones) offered fantasies of industrial modernity and prosperity by taking the narratives of linear progress and images of oil wealth to paroxysm.

The social revolutionary films produced in the 1960s and early 1970s attempted to expose the underside of revolutionary progress and its gleaming dreams of industrial modernity by recuperating politicized images of peasant miners. In *The Courage of the People* (1971), the filmed reenactment of a mining massacre by its survivors, Jorge Sanjinés and the Ukamau Group applied lessons they had learned earlier in producing and exhibiting films in indigenous communities (*Blood of the Condor,* Yawar Mallku, 1966), striving for a genuine popular aesthetic by employing collective protagonists and avoiding fragmentary close-ups and taking the miners' and their memories seriously in directing the film. While Sanjinés revealed the dreams of capitalist progress and later mestizaje as ideological fantasies, he drew from an alternative repertoire of socialist fantasies that placed indigenous peasants and miners at the vanguard of a popular revolution that would oppose foreign imperialist forces that were controlling the country. Yet when Sanjinés returned to the screen in 1989 with *La Nación Clandestina* (The Clandestine Nation, 1989), he sought to reveal Bolivia's unknown cultural multiplicity. With the film's remarkable cinematography and editing that are informed by Aymara conceptions of space-time, Sanjinés challenged the linear narratives of assimilation and signaled how official political ideologues and social movements were imminently about to drop mestizaje.

In 1985, the state government began a sudden and radical turn against the models of mestizo nationalism and the centralized state-led political economy that had been instituted with the national revolution in 1952. The bold neoliberal reforms of a New Economic Plan (NEP) expanded the sectors of impoverished and culturally marginalized Indian-cholos in highland cities such as La Paz. As the state decentralized and television was commercialized, the resulting social crisis was played out and resolved in fantasy on *The Open Tribunal of the People,* a testimonial television program guided by a charismatic host who became a leading populist political figure and Condepa party leader. While representing a popular public sphere where the poor Aymaras and Quechuas and urban cholos could speak, dialogue, and denounce, the program strikingly transformed the European ideals of the public sphere as a zone of symmetrical discourse and reciprocal social exchange into a sphere of open-ended transactions and marked hierarchy. If the neopopulist ethnic tones of *The Tribunal* succeeded the class-based populism of the revolutionary 1950s–70s, it reverberated with nostalgia for the unity and order promised by the earlier state-led national project. That is, the recuperation of the dreams for national synthesis and state-led prosperity promised in the revolution of 1952 reappeared at the very moment in which the paternalist state appeared to be abandoning the indigenous, the poor, and its own crisis.

The Tribunal also coincided with the emerging official recognition of Bolivia's fundamental cultural plurality. As the "Indian question" became a pressing political issue for established parties competing to govern the indigenous majorities in Bolivia, the selection of an Aymara vice-presidential candidate (the intellectual and politician Victor Hugo Cardenas) on the MNR's 1993 national campaign conspicuously heralded Indianness as a political value that some have called "the return of the Indian" (Albó 1991). While much of the public sector was being "capitalized" (opened to foreign markets and control), the state also began to institute pluralistic reforms that reworked its very constitution, in both senses of the term. The reforms affected legal structures and the definition of national identity itself by recognizing Bolivia's multiethnic population under the official banner of "pluri-multi" and by acknowledging indigenous majorities as "indigenous citizens" with full equal rights. Next, established land-title reforms were passed to legalize communal land claims; new political reforms, namely, the "Law of Popular Participation," recognized traditional indigenous authority structures, a system of responsibilities organized around the ayllu (political units of extended kin and some non-kin), giving them a formal means for participating in municipal budgets and in shaping their political futures.

These sweeping economic policies and major political reforms were at odds with each other, however. The economic reforms were tied to the World Bank and United States, whose aid was contingent on allowing military intervention in its war on drugs that entailed forms of discrimination and violent repression, of peasant coca growers, for example, who would soon obtain widespread popular support. The popular political reforms also provided little financial support for them to be carried out, and political participation ran into entrenched forms of ethnic and racial exclusions, as well as existing clientelist party politics (Ayo Saucedo 1999). These reforms extended the reach of dominant party politics into "civil society" and "new citizens" at the margins of the state, especially in the tropical lowlands, who became visible within the purview of a state apparatus that was said to be diminishing.

Despite the fact that reforms like Popular Participation were a tactic of what Charles Hale calls "neoliberal multiculturalism" (2005) that sustained existing political interests, their significance as "double-edged swords" cannot be underestimated for how they could be cunningly exploited by culturalist movements seeking to force the government to back up its official recognition of "pluri-multi" Bolivia (Albro 2005, 435). Furthermore, the failed promises of participatory citizenship and prosperity made with the constitutional reforms and neoliberal policies had created expectations for millions of indigenous Bolivians who had nevertheless a new or heightened sense of their citizenship (Yashar 1999). Like *The Open Tribunal,* the law of Popular Participation envisioned a plural public sphere and political space in which indigenous peoples and the downtrodden could envision themselves actively participating as citizens representing themselves and contributing a critical voice to community and national decisions (see chapters 5 and 6). As further promise, indigenous politicians and scholars were staking claims in the public sphere; a substantial number of seats in the Bolivian congress were held by self-identified Indians and urban cholos. Indigenous intellectuals and cultural activists created new cultural centers such as the Andean Oral History Workshop (THOA) from which they based their struggles to control and produce new representations about themselves and recuperate their histories (Orta 2001; Stephenson 2002). These new centers worked to publicize oral histories, recuperate indigenous political systems, and perform indigenous forms of knowledge hidden beneath the dominant public spheres of discourse.

In the dominant media, campaign ads on television produced for the MNR's 2002 election channeled the classic imagery of popular marches into electoral politics, using images strikingly similar to the optimistic scenes that began and ended Jorge Sanjinés's film *The Courage of the People.* Even before then, mounting popular protests had rejected the implementation of the "capitalization" of Bolivia's social infrastructure.

In the "Water War" in Cochabamba in 2000, scenes of popular protest with an indigenous face reappeared as urban mestizo and criollo organizers drew from romantic indigenist imagery to ally with marginalized urban and peasant communities (Canessa 2006) to mobilize against hikes in water rates by the Bechtel corporation, which had recently bought a controlling part of the city's water system.

▶

Indigenizing Popular Politics

As much as in Bolivia, "indigeneity" gained international prominence during the late 1980s and the 1990s among transnational organizations during the "UN Decade for Indigenous Peoples" (Brysk 2000; Canessa 2006; Hodgson 2002). Organized around shared indigenous issues such as land rights, natural resources, economic development, and political autonomy (Warren and Jackson 2002), new indigenous organizations conspicuously arose in Bolivia to claim their rights as citizens and to keep public attention on indigenous issues, perhaps most visibly in the accumulating support for the movement led by Evo Morales against policies and repressions against coca growers. The 1990s also saw dramatic joint mobilizations by lowland and highland indigenous peoples, setting a precedent for publicizing pan-national indigenous movements, although they were unsuccessful in cohering as a single, organized statewide movement. Disparate groups of indigenous social activists also established relationships with NGOs who not only filled in the proliferating gaps in services left open by the decentralizing state but had their own international linkages with grassroots organizations and donors (Arrelano-López and Petras 1994, 557; Gill 1997). Facilitated by such alliances with nonindigenous networks of environmental activists, social activists, legal experts, scholars, and technologies, as is characteristic of many indigenous movements across Latin America, indigenous movements also articulated with movements across the Americas, drawing force from sources beyond their states to produce culture and gain political leverage at home (Brysk 2000; Warren and Jackson 2002).

After the 2000 Water War, coalitions of social movements, unionized peasants, and workers based in the Andean valleys and highlands created new scenes of popular mobilization that filled the streets with massive blockades and brought the state to a standstill. These uprisings were distinctively led by indigenous organizations that were making demands for real changes in the existing political system. On the surface, these mobilizations were directed against the government's contracts with and the operations of transnational companies involved in developing and managing the water infrastructure in urban areas (Cochabamba in 2000 and El Alto) as well as the potential wealth from large reserves of natural gas beneath the ground. Yet beneath the surface were histories and memories of subordination and resistance (Stern 1987) in which foreign and nonindigenous elites have extracted wealth from Bolivian territory, leaving the indigenous and working classes only poorer. In the Gas War of October 2003, the surge of popular opposition against the government's arrangements for extracting and selling large gas reserves to transnational oil companies was headed by Indian movements with an epicenter in the sprawling immigrant city of El Alto above La Paz. Further, these movements were pushing for the nationalization of the country's vast natural gas reserves and to wrest control from the country's "transnational elite," who were viewed as a "foreign oligarchy" of recently arrived Eastern European immigrants. That this new immigrant oligarchy is centralized in the lowland plains of Eastern Bolivia, in Bolivia's wealthiest city of Santa Cruz, where political and economic leaders are seeking their own national reforms for more political and economic autonomy, was frequently emphasized by the social movements in the Andean highlands.

When the neoliberal state's "armed retreat" in El Alto (Gill 2000) left dozens of protesters dead and injured in a suppression by the military, President Gonzalo ("Goni") Sánchez de Losada was forced to resign and leave for Washington. His successor, Carlos Mesa, later stepped down in June 2005 in the midst of combative congressional sessions and ongoing street protests. The social tensions and the new pan-national alliances between regions, classes, and ethnic groups also intensified public debates about popular solidarity, territory and sovereignty, and plurality and national identity. As several video makers visiting New York for the First Nations First Features Film Festival at that time had told me a month earlier, "There is no Bolivia." Marcelina Cárdenas said, "No one wants to be a part of what is called Bolivia." If she was implicitly referring to the nation-state with a mestizo-criollo political identity, then indeed it seemed it was being abandoned in 2005. The MNR's own use of images of classic Bolivian populism that had served their 2002 campaign ads was turned against them in the scenes on the streets of new coalitions of indigenized popular movements.

Just as it was dozens of indigenous people who were injured and killed in the government's repression of massive protests in 2003, the protests themselves were led by activist leaders and peasant organizations who were drawing heavily on indigenous imagery and political ideals. Unlike earlier Indianist social movements and political parties such as the

Kataristas and even the contemporary separationist solutions posed by the Aymara militant and congressman Felipe Quispe, the foremost demands among the protestors in 2003 were not exclusively indigenous. Rather, they made their objections on behalf of "all the Bolivian people" who shared the experience and the crisis of neoliberal reforms and contracts that had favored transnational corporations and nonindigenous Bolivian elites. Some argued for a sweeping return to an indigenous form of ayllu democracy and its forms of exchange and cultural values, a claim that was once limited to highland Indianist movements (Choque and Mamani 2001; Pacheco Balanza 1992; Rivera Cusicanqui 1990). With the 2003 uprisings, popular opposition emerged with a striking new form: indigenized popular movements that combined native imagery and political ideals with populist images and claims about the nation. Uniting indigenous and class politics and redefining the popular national project with images of a new Bolivian public that was visibly indigenous and poor at once (Postero 2005), the former coca union leader Evo Morales assembled the MAS party as a new form of indigenous populism.[1] Images of the coca leaf symbolized this amalgamation as a potent sign of national defiance against Washington's drug war and its economic influence and simultaneously the leaf's significance in native rituals and popular consumption. If, as Robert Albro has written, "Indigenous identity has become part of an articulatory language of popular solidarity" (2000, 450), then Bolivian "indigeneity" represents a multivocal, globalized, and multisector national public.

By the end of 2005, the indigenization of the populist profile of Bolivia culminated in the majority election of Evo Morales as the first indigenous president, having grown up in an Aymara community before becoming a coca-grower union leader. In a spectacular ritual ceremony on the eve of his inauguration before tens of thousands of indigenous spectators at the pre-Inca archaeological site of Tiwanaku, Morales was lauded as "Supreme Leader of the Aymara," demonstrating that performances of indigeneity had moved to the center of Bolivia's national political scene. While past indigenist forms of popular nationalism varyingly sought to incorporate the poor and indigenous sectors into existing political structures, thereby maintaining political and economic disparities, the Morales regime is seeking to carry out the structural reforms that would realize scenes of representation and participation in the public sphere that had been envisioned on *The Open Tribunal of the People*. After the inauguration, a constitutional assembly began to meet, ostensibly to restructure the state along cultural lines in order to defend and exercise the rights of indigenous citizens who will participate in crucial national decisions.

Armed with a self-awareness of their culturally distinct political and moral systems, and a historical consciousness that departs from indigenist accounts (Abercrombie 1998; Stern 1987), the political movements that are reshaping Bolivian politics are also asserted as culturalist projects in the anthropological senses of referring to cosmological and social consciousness (Turner 1991, n.d.). Although some Bolivians have said they perceive more "Cubanization" and "Venezuelization" in the new regime than "indigenization," new popular and indigenous social movements in Bolivia have claimed and indigenized the national project once it officially politically decentralized and culturally multiplied.

▶

Indigenizing Popular Media

A corresponding process in media and popular culture in Bolivia has similarly overturned the classic populist indigenist structures of representation that dominated the circuits of twentieth-century media worlds. At the intersection of state reforms and internationally connected cultural activists that gave the category of "indigenous" new political prominence and value, indigenous video makers in Bolivia insist on participating in public culture on their own terms. As I have described, cinema, music, tourism, and television incorporated Bolivian indigenism into the commercial circuits of popular culture in which the term "indigenous" connoted the national past. In contrast, indigenous media now represents the creation of new possibilities for video and storytelling that are grounded in indigenous cultural projects and ways of knowing. In fictional films, for example, Bolivian video makers use video as a powerful form to make perceptible the copresence of visible and invisible forces and forms—a representational practice that draws on knowledge that has puzzled some unaware U.S. film festival audiences and academics. Among the films shown in CEFREC's U.S. 2002 tour, filmmakers screened *Cursed Gold*, a film about a young man in search of gold whose greed must confront the figures of a young Quechua woman and a mysterious old man; *Whispers of Death* is about a man who is penalized with the disappearance of his spouse after he doubts the existence of souls and the spirit world; and the aforementioned *Loving Each Other in the Shadows* was an audience favorite. As if they simultaneously sought invisibility and visibility for themselves, Bolivian video makers seek to have their works enter film festivals and circuits of distribution alongside nonindigenous works without necessarily being marked as indigenous. Yet by visibly entering the modern public sphere as they continue to gain time on television in Bolivia, video makers also see themselves engaged in a process through which they are pursuing and performing their collective rights and distinctive cultural autonomy.

In what I call *the indigenization of popular media,* emerging centers for indigenous video projects have appropriated forms of popular culture and recycled them in projects of indigenous cultural self-determination. As small community video centers began appearing in urban and rural communities across Bolivia in the Andean highlands, valleys, and the tropical lowlands during the early 1990s, their activities intersected at joint video festivals and workshops, such as those held by CEFREC (the Cinematography Education and Production Center). CEFREC was founded in 1989 by Ivan Sanjinés, who is nonindigenous and the son of the filmmaker Jorge Sanjinés. At a CEFREC workshop in 1996, shared efforts coalesced into an independent national plan that brought together CEFREC and the new Bolivian Indigenous Peoples' Audiovisual Council (CAIB), headed by Jesús Tapia. Several overarching indigenous confederations also back the national plan, the Bolivian Rural Workers Sole Syndicate (CSUTCB), the Indigenous Peoples of Bolivia Confederation (CIDOB), and the Bolivian Settlers Syndicate Confederation (CSCB), all of which have historically been at the forefront of indigenous and peasant politics in the country. As Ivan Sanjinés recounted to me, they joined forces at CEFREC to promote indigenous self-determination by organizing, guiding, and facilitating film and video scripting, production, and distribution. Based in La Paz, CEFREC has provided facilities and training in La Paz for video makers across Bolivia since 1991. The center has been involved in producing over 100 films in documentary form and, perhaps most remarkably, short fictional features using state-of-the-art digital video equipment whose technical quality and storytelling have impressed North American audiences. Yet the high image quality of this work, much of which is shot in DVCAM, a broadcast format, is part of the strategy of indigenization; its high standards mean that they are suitable for TV broadcast and cannot be kept off the air for "technical reasons."

Participants at CEFREC and CAIB come from a variety of backgrounds. Marcelina Cárdenas came to CEFREC in 1997 as a student in Quechua linguistics from a community near the city of Potosí, where she organized woman's activities and was elected by her community to train as a "popular reporter" with Loyola Cultural Action. Jesús Tapia was born in an Aymara community on the Altiplano near La Paz but moved north to tropical Alto Beni when he was thirteen; he came to CEFREC as a farmer and educator involved in various agrarian and educational organizations. The center's workshops offer instruction from acclaimed lighting directors, cinematographers, and scriptwriters, including experts who visit from Cuba. Forming networks of media makers across the hemisphere, with their own definitions of national identity and political circumstances, their own historical cultures and subjugated knowledges, indigenous video makers began appropriating media technologies to represent their identities, strengthen their cultures, and demonstrate their capacity for self-representation.

▶ ───

Circuits of Indigeneity

CEFREC represents a node in widely dispersed and mobile networks of collaboration that extend to indigenous media organizations in Brazil, Ecuador, and Mexico, for example, which are affiliated through the Latin American Council of Indigenous Peoples' Film and Video (CLACPI), created in 1985 in Mexico City but housed in various countries, recently at CEFREC in La Paz. Rather than forming a unitary social movement, the media organizations and video centers across Latin America are also shaped like indigenous movements that pursue divergent goals embedded in their particular histories and political strategies (Warren and Jackson 2002). The dispersed hemispheric networks among these indigenous media organizations become visible and engaged communities of sociality in their workshops and at the Indigenous Peoples' Film and Video Festivals, events which have been held annually in Mexico, Bolivia, Guatemala, Brazil, Mexico, and Chile. The network of centers that are allied in CLACPI struggle for indigenous self-representation that extends beyond the transcontinental media centers themselves. Other significant and productive native media events have included the Native American Film and Video Festivals held in New York (organized by the Smithsonian's National Museum of the American Indian's Film and Video Center), which gathers indigenous media makers across the Americas including the United States and Canada. The recent First Nations/First Features Film Festival, held in 2005 at the Museum of Modern Art in New York and organized by a number of cultural centers (MOMA, NMAI, the Center for Media, Culture and History at New York University), was the first of its kind to showcase indigenously directed feature films and video makers from around the globe.[2] Such events provide "off-screen" opportunities for new alliances and discussions of common and divergent concerns as well as for filmmakers to buy equipment and meet with potential distributors for their works. The remarkable number of supporting media and cultural centers that converge from across the Americas at these festivals forms the circuits of a "transnational advocacy network" (Appadurai 2000) that operates across the boundaries of nation-states in a mobile and global manner that has characterized industrialized Hollywood and Latin American filmmaking (Miller et al. 2005; Noriega 2000) as well as artisanal "interstitial" filmmaking (Naficy 2001, 46). As locations within these networks, the personnel at CEFREC and CAIB select and assemble the transcontinental resources from national and international supporters, filmmakers, and instructors who all become connected and concentrated in the practices of video making and its products.

The interplay of these disparate elements has raised questions about the label "indigenous video" on the one hand and about the status of the videos themselves as culturally marked objects on the other. That televisual media could entail cultural empowerment or political leverage has run up against the primitivist idea that there are contradictions between the commodity form, media technology, and cultural authenticity (see Katz 1977), a reaction that started debates about indigenous media in the 1990s. At issue for the critics of indigenous media was that the links between nonindigenous subjects, institutions, and "Western" technologies in indigenous media projects could not empower indigenous peoples without also consuming them as exotic, or that these multiple ingredients and participants intrude upon and corrupt (i.e., "Westernize") native cultures.

Advancing beyond the debate (see, for example, Faris 1992; Ginsburg 1994, 1997; Turner 1992, 2002; Weiner 1997), I argue that Faye Ginsburg's definition of indigenous media captures best how people involved in indigenous media making view and organize their own activities. She writes,

> The term indigenous media comprehends the complex nature of the phenomena it signifies. The first word—"indigenous"—respects the understandings of those Aboriginal producers who identify themselves as "First Nations" or "Fourth World People." These categories index the political circumstances shared by indigenous people around the globe. Whatever their cultural differences, such groups all struggle against a legacy of disenfranchisement of their lands, societies, and cultures by colonizing European societies, such as Australia, the United States, Canada, and most of Latin America. The second word—"media"—whether referring to satellites or VCRs, evokes the huge institutional structures of the television and film industries that tend to overwhelm the local cultural specificities of small-scale societies while privileging commercial interests that demand large audiences as a measure of success. While the institutional dimensions of media— especially television—shadow their intersection with the lives of indigenous people, they do not determine the outcome. (1993, 558)

Against views that resemble indigenism, Ginsburg's explanation relies on a formulation of indigeneity that sees indigenous producers as active cultural subjects who are engaged with the multiplicity of the present. An internally heterogeneous term, therefore, indigenous video refers to instances in which the nation-state initiates and funds the very category of "indigenous video," as in Mexico (Wortham 2004), or opens up an infrastructure for production or circulation, as in Canada, Australia, and New Zealand (Ginsburg 1994). Indigenous media makers have used film and video to confront mass media stereotypes and to make political claims (Singer 1991; Weatherford 1990), but this could entail a "primitivist perplex" in which indigenous peoples exploit for themselves the powerful stereotypes about their differences (Prins 2002). Given the web of social and cultural connections and historical intricacies, the way to move beyond the debate is not the primitivism that boxes in indigenous cultural activists but an avenue that enacts forms of support (Ginsburg 1997) and explores their wide-ranging engagements.

Debates about indigenous media ought to be about specifying the complicated circumstances and the political significance of the cultural practices that indigenous video makers appropriate, transform, combine, and assemble into objectified forms of "culture" (Turner n.d., 1991). What are the culturally vitalizing uses of representational media? What productive connections and alliances do indigenous media makers and proximate and distant nonindigenous institutions, agencies, communications networks, and public supporters forge? While indigenous and other minority cultural producers work against circumstances of subordination, they connect, as all cultural producers do, with the material resources and the alliances available in their political present. As Terence Turner argues, "The purpose of such temporal and spatial connections for indigenous groups like the Kayapo has not been to insulate themselves from contact or engagement with the outside world, but to engage more effectively with their ambient national and global systems, to draw upon their power to control their own resources and determine the social and cultural terms of their own lives" (2002b, 245). In my analysis of the work of video makers from Bolivia, filmmaking mediates the coordination of multiple engagements with media and cultural institutions, which are the visible means and ends of indigenous media.

The Bolivian video makers are well aware of the complexity of indigenous media and the critiques among some scholars and audiences. In my interview with Ivan Sanjinés and Jesús Tapia in Taos in 2002 (Himpele 2004), they addressed responses to the questions they had been receiving from their audiences along their tour in the United States. Ivan Sanjinés explained that audiences sometimes cast impossibly rigid and monochromatic frameworks onto their works, seeking an impossibly alien and purely indigenous video form:

> They didn't seem to be aware that indigenous peoples could make this kind of film. They said, "In this film, the camera is positioned like this. . . . Had the Indians seen films beforehand in order to be able to make that shot?" That's what someone said! "Do you watch films from Hollywood in the workshops? How can you make these?" But, in reality, you can appropriate anything. Appropriation is not only about the object that you film. You do give it your own sense. You won't discover something that has already been discovered. Cinema has emerged over a long time, so we use the forms that are there. The question is, what sense do you give it?

Sanjinés displaces the emphasis on a purely indigenous moment in their videos with the significance of their appropriation of media technologies, genres, funding, and professionals. This practice, as Sanjinés frequently described CEFREC itself, is a *process*. While I am calling this process "indigenization" to refer to the cultural projects and political struggles that give video making specific meaning, I believe that Sanjinés's point is that if the category "indigenous video" is to have meaning, it must refer "off screen" (Ginsburg 2003) to the coordinated assembly of a variety of technologies, resources, social organizations, and cultural principles and imagery into representational media, all of which extend beyond the completed videotape itself. Sanjinés is, as it were, very concerned with getting audiences to let go of their fixed colonially derived schemes and think "outside the box."

As CEFREC actually packages videotapes in their boxes, they similarly announce their videos as necessarily heterogeneous through their labels and credits, which extensively index the very conditions for their production. In other words, video organizations package their products to exceed the frames of the film text and even the category "indigenous" itself by visibly indexing the multiple sources of funding and technical expertise that filmmakers assemble in their videos. The film credits are included on the back covers of the tapes and recognize the involvement of several prominent nonindigenous cinematographers and editors as well as other digital video specialists and production facilities in Bolivia. On the front cover, the icons and the acronyms of CEFREC and CAIB appear alongside that of the International Cooperation Agency of Spain, one of the principal funders of the center's work, and Mujarik Gabe, a Basque NGO. At the beginning of programs, the tapes credit the auspices of the three national indigenous political confederations mentioned earlier. Within Sanjinés's marked emphasis on process, the videotapes can be seen as inherently compound objects that are precipitated from the complex integration of video production practices and networked organizations, which are further tied to and assembled from elements of contemporary struggles for indigenous self-determination. Extending how the category of "indigenous media" might serve as "metaculture" (Urban 2001) that propels the circulation of video makers and their works during the wider international political shift in which "indigeneity" has obtained valuable political currency, I suggest that we conceive of the combined practice of production and labeling the videos as a form of "packaging." Packaging in the sense I use the term here does not refer to deceptive misrepresentation, although the term should connote a sense of intention. I use the term to refer to the coordinated assembly of the multiple resources into a media form as well as the strategy of self-representation that indexes these elements. In this way, the film credits and covers on the cassette boxes are themselves significant performances that assert self-determination because they index the work of indigenous directors as the coordinating figures of a multiplex process, with all its constraints, that extends beyond the box.

During the U.S. tours in 2002, Jesús Tapia demonstrated this point about self-determination when he redirected audience claims and questions about the cultural purity of the video makers' tapes. He stressed to audiences that the fundamental point is that native peoples are responsible

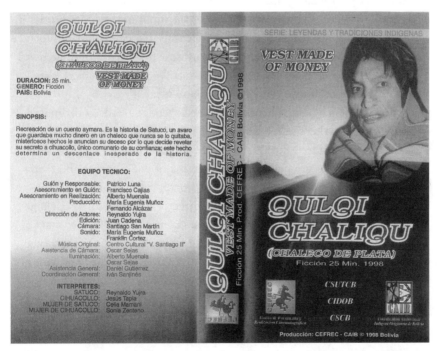

Figure 26. Packaging indigenous media: the videocassette box cover for *Qulqi Chaliqu* (Luna, 1998).

for producing excellent fictional and documentary works that are based in their own cultures, and that their works are capable of participating in nonindigenous film festivals (e.g., the Taos Talking Pictures Film Festival, the Arizona International Film Festival) and engaging a variety of audiences, two points that some audiences notably reacted to with astonishment or even had difficulty accepting. During the Ojo de Condor tour, Jesús himself could sometimes be seen at the front of the theaters videotaping the question and answer sessions with audiences along the tour; he was not only documenting the events but also performing the role of videographer as he had done in Arlington.

Often, Tapia and Marcelina Cárdenas explained to their audiences that "producer" and "author" are inaccurate titles since as individuals they do not produce culture but, rather, they communicate culture. They prefer to use the title "social communicator" to indicate that they are responsible for researching film topics and writing stories among the communities in which they work and for coordinating the video crew and finding ways of appropriating the capacities and genres available in representational media. Rather than claiming the image of authenticity, framed by audience desires for purity, originality, and individual subjectivity, however, Tapia and Cárdenas frequently described the value of their work in terms of collectivity with the word "integral." As Cárdenas explained to me, "integral" indicates that the work involves the input of the communities in which they work and to whom they are accountable. She told her audience in Arlington, "We have another manner of directing. We cannot demand that our 'brothers and sisters' follow a script. We give them ideas, they give us some input, and we incorporate these ideas."

"Integral" is also a value that can be extended to the coordinated work of media makers and organizations that are involved in the process of making a video. In this usage, the video center CEFREC itself resembles a video: a moment in the packaging of wider forces and forms in which Sanjinés and video makers coordinate, manage, and assemble activities and resources, much like a video director assembles and packages resources and scenes drawn from disparate contexts into a film, whose form also circulates beyond the moment of its production. On their own travels and tours representing CEFREC and CAIB, Sanjinés and video makers connect with an international network of indigenous media organizations in Mexico, Canada, the United States, Ecuador, and Brazil, as well as with important funders, such as those from Spain and supporting cultural institutions such as the NMAI and MOMA. Forging these kinds of alliances for the purposes of producing, distributing, and supporting their work was a crucial task for them when they visited the United States.

Their videos mediate connections between their own communities and transnational publics. Just as the images and discourses of indigeneity that have propelled popular protests and politics in Bolivia (and elsewhere) are linked to global elements, indigenous videos are "mediating objects" (Ginsburg 1994, 6) that connect native communities with transnational networks of diverse filmmakers, cultural institutions and publics.

Videos such as Marcelina Cárdenas's *Loving Each Other in the Shadows* (Llanthupi Munakuy, 2001) represent a production that contains and indigenizes popular forms of humor, narrative suspense, and romance that are prevalent in popular mass media, yet the stories also value specialized knowledge and ritual prognostications that are linked to ways of seeing visible traces of larger cosmological forces in dreams and symbols in such a way that the visible and invisible and the material and supernatural are extensions of each other. In many of the videos, viewers have access to seeing both worlds on one plane, but cultural knowledge is needed to understand what is and what is not visible for protagonists. Thus, in many of these videos a form of subjugated knowledge regarding visibility is itself made visible. Similarly, Marcelina Cárdenas's idea of "integration" and the packaging of CEFREC videos widens our field of view, making visible the wider circuits of coordinated social processes "off screen" from which their videos precipitate. If audience desires or critics' demands for pure indigeneity require fixed and limited attention to the purity of selected formal ingredients of a film or the authenticity of the original site of production or use, then these are desires that stem from the field of view of commodity fetishism in which the videos would appear to be self-propelled objects in the marketplace. Yet the Bolivian video makers direct our attention outside the box to the media worlds beyond, to the location of videos in social matrices of production or exhibition, and their struggles to produce new cultural possibilities. That is, they direct us to imagine the videos as mobile and mediating elements that may move in and out of a generalizable status as a commodity, but without occluding how filmmakers manage the flows of circulation to assemble their video works since this process is clearly indexed on the surface of the video tape case itself. What is of value in this regime, then, is the expansion of indigenous worlds via the circulation of their media.

The tensions between these overlapping regimes of value are clear in Patricio Luna's *Vest Made of Money* (Qulqi Chaliku, 1998). The film revolves around the high stakes of fixating upon and impeding circulatory material for the main character, Satuco, who secretly stores his money inside his vest that he never removes; by hiding and withholding money from circulation he risks the well-being of his own household and community.

By incorporating money inside his vest, the lines between wealth, corporeality, and well-being are blurred as his wealth becomes a part of him. This incorporation of wealth is an ostentatious aspect of urban Aymara (cholo/a) culture, where for men gaining weight with age and marriage are signs of well-being. Among chola women it is difficult to perceive where their bodies stop and their clothing begins; layers of expensive shirts and heavy skirts bulge with the money and jewelry they guard underneath. As a sign of prosperity that both fattens and sustains their status, wealth is embodied in the cultural sign of fat, which is considered to be a life force (Crandon-Malamud 1991). Like blood might be in other economic metaphors,[3] this excess value is understood as circulatory material that is in motion. In the moral terms of ritual exchange, surplus wealth is redistributed in the form of food, beer, and sponsorship at festivals and parades that feature excess consumption, and it is put in motion and flaunted in collective dancing in parades and festivals such as the Gran Poder in La Paz (Himpele 2003). Satuco, however, inverts this moral scheme by withdrawing his wealth from circulation, concealing it, and taking it with him to his grave. Indeed, he becomes immobilized and falls ill while walking and eventually dies; and his community is threatened by disgrace, disabling winds, and cold after his trusted friend Cihuacollo unearths and robs Satuco's money. If Satuco's vest of money foregrounds the hazards of concealed individual accumulation, it is also a critique of how commodity fetishism dangerously misapprehends moments in circulatory processes as autonomous material things. The film demonstrates the collective high stakes in sustaining the circulation of wealth and making visible the circulatory networks in which objects are enmeshed.

Vest Made of Money is a fascinating story taken from community legends by Luna, and it, too, contains the "embedded aesthetics" (Ginsburg 1994) of circulation in indigenous media. In other words, the video displays the values of integration and circulatory processes that organize the work of the indigenous media makers by openly exhibiting the translocal social networks that are coordinated in each project as a form of cultural production and self-determination.

If the video eventuates from the coordination, integration, and packaging of indigenous media, then how does CEFREC consider the commodity market? Ivan Sanjinés explained to me:

> We also need to change the logic of the market somehow. So what we have done is change what the markets of production and distribution dictate. And what we are trying to do is seek comparable markets and alliances—the ones that are submerged, not the ones that are very visible because the visible ones are the ones that rule the market and the forces of supply and demand. Our

economy runs on our internal strength, which you cannot see, so what we have done here is to show that and to look for alliances.

Sanjinés is alluding to the nonquantifiable activity that projects demand as well as forms of circulation and exchange that are neither closed-ended nor accumulative. Through the networks it sustains, CEFREC has kept profit maximization as a motive for circulation in check while dealing with the problem of money as a generalized measure and medium of exchange that funds their media productions. During the Ojo de Condor tour the video makers sold copies of their work to eager audience members, but they could not keep enough copies on hand and frequently ran out, hoping to sell typical tourist art instead. They were surprised and delighted to encounter this demand, for, as they explained to me, they need dollars to produce their works but they live in an economy of boliviano-pesos, a currency which had slipped down to almost one-seventh the value of the dollar. But the question of what to do with the money from sales of videos, since the tapes are community property, actually slowed sales as a source of funding further work. After 2002, CEFREC limited the sale of their videos to other indigenous video makers, academics, and social activists with whom they have ongoing relationships; these reciprocal obligations have helped to produce and extend social networks that are alternatives to the self-interested drive for accumulation in commodity capitalism. At the same time, however, CEFREC has begun to obtain small time slots on the state's television channel for the broadcast of their works, effectively indigenizing that popular medium. Yet in his engagement with the marketplace, Sanjinés suggests that commodification can be transformed with alternative practices of circulation and exchange that unite and extend, rather than atomize and diminish, human creative activity.

One principal force that *Vest Made of Money* keeps beyond the frame is the Bolivian state itself. Like many of the fictional works produced at the Center, *Vest* re-creates a community legend that does not visibly make the state a protagonist. Does it mimic the fantasy of invisibility that the decentralizing neoliberal state has been staging for itself? Does this represent the ways in which transcontinental networks of indigenous cultural activists have eclipsed the nation-state's tactics for engaging with difference (Turner n.d)? Or does the absence represent the state as an unseen and capricious force (Platt 1993; Rasnake 1988)? In *Vest Made of Money*, I suggest the form in which the state shapes the videos behind the scenes is exposed with Satuco's bundles of cash. This fatal substance of Satuco's fantasies inhabits the inside of his vest just as money is an intimate element of filmmaking, as Deleuze had described money as the internalized condition of the cinema (1989, 77). *Vest Made of Money* suggests how video makers work in the shadows of the state, an unseen force that regulates money as well as access to circulatory infrastructures, such as the state's own broadcast channel or sources for acquiring video equipment. The state is also a control center for capital, regulating the appearance and the value of currency, though not freely, and setting import taxes and awarding travel visas, thereby shaping the cost of the necessary importation of the equipment for video production as well as the mobility of the filmmakers themselves.

It remains to be seen how indigenous works will circulate after Bolivia's recent agreement to buy 5 percent of Telesur, the regional satellite television network founded in Venezuela and jointly owned with Argentina, Cuba, and Uruguay. Given the relevance of states as gatekeepers in transnational media worlds, indigenous movements still aim at states as targets of their claims (Warren and Jackson 2002).[4] Before Ivan Sanjinés and Jesús Tapia returned to Bolivia, we joked in Taos about how they would carry their large Taos Mountain Award trophy back home in its form as a carved eagle. Jesús joked that he would tie it on his back and carry it like the cargo carried by poor peasant porters in the markets in La Paz. When they arrived at customs in La Paz laden with the ostentatious sign of their tour and success in the United States, they were detained by customs and told to pay a large import tax on it before they could take it further. The video makers declined, and the eagle sat at the airport for about six months before the hosts of their U.S. tour, the National Museum of the American Indian in New York, helped to negotiate the release of the trophy for $50.[5]

▶

Closed Circuits

This book has traced the intertwined representational histories of indigenous popular publics suspended within the circulatory systems of Bolivian media worlds. The preceding chapters examined the divergent styles and projects of filmmaking, video making, and popular television that have mediated two historical processes, the popularization of indigenism and the indigenization of the popular, as they have been enmeshed in the indigenization of metropolitan La Paz and the Bolivian national profile. In this concluding chapter, I have traced mediations of indigeneity that invert the popularization of indigenism that dominated the twentieth century, perhaps first broadcast nationwide on *The Open Tribunal* as a public sphere where Bolivia's indigenous and poor citizens in La Paz were seen as political participants representing themselves in the present, which then was made more apparent in the work of indigenous video makers who are reappropriating elements from the circuits of mass media and popular culture in order to serve indigenous cultural projects. In these forms of appropriation, however, the inversion I have charted here and over the course of the book should not be understood as a unilinear progression along which history has moved from the formulations of indigenism to indigeneity. To elaborate on this concluding point, I return to the video screenings in Arlington described at the outset of this chapter.

The screenings presented by traveling video makers from CEFREC to the Bolivians living in Arlington in 2002 represent the concurrence of divergent formulations of indigenous identity; that is, classic indigenist views circulate along with the contemporary images of indigeneity. No doubt indigenous video makers are self-conscious about such imagery, as Ivan Sanjinés and Jesús Tapia told me at a lunch together in Taos: "People have the idea that indigenous peoples are untouched, in an idyllic world, that they are all good and taking care of the environment and smiling all day." At that point, Jesús Tapia chuckled in agreement.

This awareness suggests that the 2002 Arlington screening did not represent a clean disjuncture between circulating formulations of Indianness. It would be misleading to limit interpretation of the contending views in Arlington as an oppositional confrontation or as interlocutors talking past each other, as if from totally disparate discursive universes. In fact, if indigeneity involves images of new indigenous publics as insiders in Bolivian politics, this formulation has relied on the self-conscious appropriation of the scenes of the romantic indigenism that had accumulated internationally in the Andean image world, first in photography (Poole 1997) and then in film (see chapters 3 and 4).

As strikingly formulated in the 1954 film *Las Voces de la Tierra* (Voices of the Earth) and other films described elsewhere in this book, for example, among the most potent yet primitivist icons of Western indigenism are the naturalized attachment of native people to the land and their image as defenders of the environment, national identity, and territory. In Bolivia, such images continue to be disseminated in the discourses of indigenous politics, social activists, and intellectuals as well as by recent non-Indian protesters, as Andrew Canessa describes (2006, 253). As a strategy to attract and engage with international networks, press, and environmental and human rights organizations, indigeneity also appropriates and employs dominant images already circulating in media worlds. Though these images of domesticated "hyperreal Indians" (Ramos 1994) may look similar on the surface, they may not neatly correspond to indigenous cosmologies as lived (as Terence Turner also has shown for Amazonian Kayapo political leaders).[6] It should be no surprise, therefore, that the first screening on the 2002 video tour was at the Smithsonian's Environmental Film Festival, and that some basic elements of the story were perplexing for many in the audience, as their questions revealed afterward. Indigenous video makers, too, have explicitly produced extraordinary idyllic scenes of the countryside. Marcelina Cárdenas explained to me that this scenery is intended to challenge the images in the dominant mass media in which indigenous people are depicted as impoverished, passively tied to their harsh landscapes, and stripped of culture. She added that the picturesque scenery also demonstrates their own capacity to assemble the resources to produce and distribute beautiful images of their cultures and landscapes.

With Marcelina Cárdenas's account in mind, we see that what occurred at the screenings in Arlington was a connection between two circuits of popularized indigenous imagery and indigenized popular imagery, effectively creating a momentary short circuit between these moving image worlds. Indigenous video is indeed produced and packaged as such a junction box: a calculated recycling of romantic imagery crossed with contemporary storytelling with which video makers assert control over the circulation of Indianness in the circuits of popular politics and culture that have been the avenues for capturing the national imagination. As a technique of empowerment, this "indigenized indigenism" now propels these key vehicles traveling in Bolivian media worlds.

Figure 27. Production still from the opening scene of *Llanthupi Munakuy*. This scene is set at a festival in a rural community, providing a scenario of encounter, alliance, and tension, which are also reflected in indigenous video making.

Notes

Preface

1. Many of the names of film distributors and their companies, theater owners and managers, and the production staff and social workers at *The Open Tribunal* have been changed.

Introduction

1. The Andean devil is also known by some anthropologists to be the symbol produced by peasant miners' collective resistance against and negotiation with the extraction and accumulation of capital from underground. See Nash (1979) and an analysis based on hers in Taussig (1987).
2. "Cinematic" here refers to its etymological roots indicating motion and serial imagery. With its focus on moving images, this book does not touch upon the fascinating history of radio in Bolivia. Radio has been a vital link among metropolitan and rural regions that have cultural and technological breaches in social communication and high rates of illiteracy and lost literacy. Alongside festivals, then, radio has been a principal media of translocal mediation among cities and the many rural communities where there are no telephone lines. With the low cost of battery-powered transistor receivers and transmitters, radio has been an important alternative to the commercial monopoly of mass communication in cities and in the rural regions. Radio has been integral to the revitalization of Andean cultures and political projects; urban radio stations make announcements of rural community festivals and rehearsals for urban parades and they play indigenous and folklore music. Radio "Nacional" factored in the citywide growth of the Gran Poder in the 1970s by calling for dance groups and announcing their rehearsals each morning and it also supported the formation of the powerful Association of Folklore Groups (Archondo 1991, 83). On radio in Bolivia, see Robert Huesca (1995) and Alfonso Gumucio Dagron and Lupe Cajías on the miners' radio stations (1989) and Luis Ramiro Beltran on grassroots forms of democratic communication through radio (1993).
3. When describing projects made in both film and video, I use the terms "film" and "filmmaking" to refer to film-style production; typically this is a single camera shooting footage out of sequence that is intended for postproduction editing. Television-style production, as analyzed in part III of this book, refers to a studio configuration of multiple cameras, among which shots are selected during live action as a program is recorded to tape or broadcast. In this case, *The Tribunal* is shot "live to tape," that is, recorded first and then broadcast later after some editing (see chapter 6).
4. This book's approach to circulation takes its point of departure from work by anthropologists who have given careful attention to the practices and paths of cultural traffic. While our present understanding of circulation has grown out of an extensive ethnographic literature that has foregrounded exchange and the sources of social values, it has its roots in Malinowski's ethnography of the circulation of shells and amulets in the Kula rings in the Trobriand Islands (1922), in Marcel Mauss's and Lévi-Strauss's accounts of social relations constituted through exchange, and in Pierre Bourdieu's interest in the strategic timing of exchange. Alongside this anthropological work, Georg Simmel also shifted the question of value toward moments of exchange and away from production (1900, 409), as had been argued by Karl Marx. Marx had viewed bourgeois society as a complex totality of circulation where value was produced in the

antagonism between wage-labor and capital; the spatial movement of commodities from sites of production to the market enhanced their fetishism (Schivelbush 1989, 40–41). Seeking the conditions for this view, Simmel identified the money form itself as the condition of value and of the commodification of labor, having an objectifying effect in which commodities in circulation appear as things in the moment of interchange between money and commodity. In the melding of the anthropological literature on the sociology of exchange with Simmel's account of value, attention on circulation itself has become focused in ideas such as "the social biography of things" (Kopytoff 1986) and Arjun Appadurai's argument that categories of commodity and gift define forms of exchange that characterize specific "regimes of value" (1986). By foregrounding exchangeability, the mode of studying circulation that has emerged is concerned with tracking the shifting values of cultural forms as they move in and out of categories, across diverse contexts, and through the unstable borderlands and the contingencies of classifications such as art, commodity, modern, and authentic (e.g., Marcus and Myers 1995; Spyer 1998). The transformation of meanings is also the emphasis in the "circuits of culture" approach in culture studies following Stuart Hall (1993, 1980) and in recent studies of global community chains (see Hughes and Reimer 2004). In the present emphasis, however, exchange is the privileged moment where meanings and values are objectified, while circulation refers to the delivery of cultural forms to zones where the activity of classifying and reclassifying the significance of things and the objectification of their value happens. Unless we explore the materiality, spatiality, and temporality of mobility as well as the motion that cultural objects internalize, then circulation only manifests social and cultural differences when cultural traffic reaches the sites of exchange, reception, use, or criticism.

Eiss (2002, 292–93) has pointed out that limiting theoretical emphasis to the sphere of exchange effectively isolates objects from the material systems of circulation within which they have been produced and out of which they have precipitated as products. To approach these matrices, however, I want to begin with the social discourse surrounding the paths of circulation. In her own work on the kula in the Trobriands, Annette Weiner noted: "What is most strategic about kula action is the routes that shells follow. . . . If high-ranking shells are diverted from one path to another, the shells' names are changed and their former histories lost" (1992, 140). Similarly, Appadurai (1986, 18–22) discussed the importance of the *keda* (road, route, path, or track) of kula objects as competitive arenas in which traders achieve power and reputation by manipulating the very definitions of the paths and then strategically diverting circulating valuables among them in order to augment their own status. To show how social value entails shifting the social categories of the paths themselves, Appadurai also suggests a method: "For that we have to follow the things themselves, for their meanings are inscribed in the forms, their uses, their trajectories . . . even though from a theoretical point of view human actors enliven things with significance, from a methodological point of view it is the things-in-motion that illuminate their human and social context. . . . This methodological fetishism, returning our attention to the things themselves, is in part a corrective to the tendency to excessively sociologize transactions in things, a tendency we owe to Mauss" (5). If Appadurai's processual view of objects in motion shares Kopytoff's interest in the "biographical" phases of things in motion, his "methodological fetishism" suggests we examine the stories that things tell as they visit different locations. I adopt this approach here to illuminate the contours of the pathways of films circulating in La Paz and reveal the motives and selectivity that drive films in circulation. Yet things themselves do not tell their whole story, Appadurai also wrote; as the distance of the journeys of commodities grows, "culturally formed mythologies about commodity flow are likely to emerge" (1986, 48). Appadurai more recently has argued further for the importance of the materiality of "the thing itself" (2006), while other anthropologists also have established how the materiality of things bears on the possibility of their exchange, the routes in which they may circulate, and the processes of becoming objectified in fixed form (Myers 2001b; Keane 1997; Weiner 1992; Thomas 1991). While chapter 1 explores the stories related to circulating films and their publics, chapter 2 emphasizes the materiality of their circulatory systems. Part III considers circulation and exchange as social performance (see Graeber 2001; Keane 1997).

5. This book detours around a significant chapter of filmmaking in the 1970s in Bolivian cinema described by the sources mentioned here. During a period of dictatorships, most significantly under General Hugo Banzer (1971–78), filmmakers like CUNY-trained Antonio Eguino and the Italian immigrant Paolo Agazzi produced realist narrative films that were intended to portray the circumstances of life in Bolivia, raising questions for analysis rather than proposing revolutionary solutions, which Eguino had done in his work on the revolutionary films of Jorge Sanjinés, who was in exile during much of the 1970s. Among their important works, Eguino's film *Chuquiago* (1977) highlights four different social sectors in La Paz through the four characters from each and was the most well-known film in the city during my research there. Paolo Agazzi's film *Mi Socio* (*My Partner*, 1982) similarly explored regional differences in a tale about

a truck driver and his young companion on a trip across the country. Both Eguino and Agazzi would go on to work in televisual media and coproduce films with European funding in films strategically "denationalized" (Hjort 2005) and intended to circulate widely. Furthermore, this book does not discuss the recent films produced in Bolivia as coproductions with Mexican and European filmmakers and funding.

6. Lee and LiPuma (2002) are especially interested in tracking how circulation constitutes capital as a subject and the market as a collective agent in the social imaginary of contemporary finance capitalism.

7. For a vivid ethnographic account of the built social space of movie theaters in Nigeria, see Larkin (2002, 1998–1999).

8. For a discussion concerning media ethnography along these lines, see the essay by David Morely in the collection edited by Crawford and Hafsteinson (1996), which generally pursues a critique of media ethnography along the lines raised by earlier textual critiques of ethnography. Allison Griffiths's piece in the collection goes farthest in turning toward her actual field relations.

9. Charting the appearance of a decisive political majority from these sectors of La Paz, mobilized around indigeneity, this book addresses the elusive multiplicity among the urban cholo/a Aymaras and Quechuas that Barragán describes as a "Third Republic" (1993). Bouysse-Cassagne and Saignes (1993) have recognized this sector as "the forgotten actor of history," and Abercrombie (1996) has shown that such plural indigenous social spaces have been present since the sixteenth century in the Andes.

1. Film Distribution as Media

1. Here, I allude to the social or urban imaginary entailed in the reflexive modernization that accompanies late-twentieth-century forms of uncertainty and risk (Beck, Giddens, and Lash 1994; see also Ong and Collier 2005; Gaonkar 2002). According to these authors, the calculations and deliberations of experts and management involve a second order feedback system in which society becomes an object and problem for itself.

2. Complex social spaces such as cities pose particularly difficult epistemological and representational problems. As Patricia Yaeger writes, geographic space is multidimensional and moves out in every direction at once, making it difficult to render in linear narrative form (1996, 4). It is temporality, she adds, that provides "a comforting seriality" that enables narrative. Yaeger also points out that spatial narratives obtain their order, as Hayden White has described for historiography, from inherited plots or supreme cultural myths about social order. In the context of Latin American cities, Néstor García Canclini similarly suggests narrative paths as a way of organizing the disordered "multicultural" spaces of the modern city (2001, 82).

3. As Appadurai also more recently put it, "The apparent stabilities that we see are, under close examination, usually our devices for handling objects characterized by motion" (2000, 5; see also Graeber 2001, 50). Therefore the theater buildings themselves are in motion, even if in slow motion. Deleuze and Guattari write, "We are misled by considering any complicated machine as a single thing" (1983, 285). Because every entity is assembled by connecting flows, they write, "there is no need to distinguish between producing and its product" (7). Karl Marx identified progressive motion inside the commodity form as internalized labor itself: "That which in the labourer appeared as movement, now appears in the product as a fixed quality without motion. The blacksmith forges and the product is a forging" (1978, 347). In the case of a theater as a "building," we could ask if the term "building" best denotes its existence as a process that happens (a verb in progressive form) or its appearance as a fixed thing (a noun).

4. As these narratives about film traffic and chronotopes (theater locations) are reiterated, each location itself conjures up the encompassing field of circulation, including the other locations and the publics within it. Put differently, circulation is made of a succession of film appearances that conjure up the publics who attend as well as the contrasting publics who are absent.

5. The relationship between money and objectification offered by Simmel and others supplies a lead to understanding how publics appear as stable entities that travel. If we view the box office as a scene of exchange of tokens of quantitative value, money for tickets, then this is a key moment in which the moviegoing public and the film screening itself are objectified and specified as measurable, discrete, and stable exchangeable entities. Yet if we consider that the ticket and access are exchanged against money, the commodity sold represents no "thing"; the filmed commodity refers to an event that is inhabited, rented, or used, for a discrete period. As John Kelly explains in a discussion of commodified labor in Fiji, in a modern capitalist imaginary, money enables the material and immaterial world to be measured according to a single quantifiable scale of value, objectifying and stabilizing the world and creative action into discrete things that units of money can buy (1992, 103). When circulating films and mobile

publics converge at the box office, they make real their status as discrete things in the moment of monetary exchange that has enabled the possibility of suspending the flows of circulation to carve out events and things. The same point has also been made by Daniel Miller, who argues, "'The term objectification, however, always implies that form is part of a larger process of becoming'" (in Myers 2001a, 21). Nicholas Thomas also makes a similar point succinctly in showing that in the context of exchange, "Objects are not what they were made to be, but what they have become" (1991). Although there is no physical exchange beyond these tokens of value at the box office, the cinema and moviegoing public are not a "peculiar" commodity form, as some might argue (e.g., Chanan 1997). Like filmed commodities, material things have social lives as compounds of material and organic processes; their components eventually disintegrate or are transfigured into other forms (see Bennett 2004). The emergence of intellectual property as a commodity form of capital (on media, see Wang 2003) actually reveals that the ownership of commodified property does not guarantee the permanence or the unity of "things." Following Simmel, if payment is a condition of the imagination of things as discrete objects, payment also provides access and usufruct just as rent does temporarily, which is what occurs at the theater box office. Further, as Fred Myers has shown, ownership represents certain rights of control over duplication and dissemination that rent does not (2004). He quotes a key insight from Marilyn Strathern, which intersects with several elements regarding the relationship between property ownership and the ephemerality and heterogeneity of objects, that is relevant for thinking about the business of film distribution and exhibition: "'Ownership,' she has written, 'gathers things momentarily to a point by locating them in the owner, halting endless dissemination, effecting an identity'" (in Myers 2004, 14). The regulations over the profitable exchange and dissemination of filmed commodities are not only an abstract framework; they entail setting spatial and temporal trajectories, boundaries, and locations in a material infrastructure. On the trade and circulation of rights over filmed commodities and their piracy, see Wang (2003). Michael Chanan argues that the cinema represents a "peculiar" commodity form because there is no physical exchange (1997). Yet if we begin an analysis of the commodity form with circulation, then the cinema, suspended in webs of circulation, represents the social life of the commodity form very well.

6. During and after the hyperinflationary early 1980s, half of the twelve distributors in Bolivia closed, as did several cinemas near the Center. López, ZW, and other independents were consolidated from other companies in the aftermath of that period.

7. Clint Wilson and Félix Gutíerrez observe an end to the "melting pot" ideology in a world of identity politics and advanced communication technologies. They argue, "The audience of masses was essential to the media because advertisers demanded that they attract a large and somewhat undifferentiated audience. . . . But now with audience segmentation, the approach of the media to their audience is the opposite. The media now look for differences and ways to reinforce them" (1985, 231).

8. On the city as event, see Harvey (1989), and Goldstein (2004). In a view similar to my own, García Canclini imagines the megacity of Mexico City as a video clip composed of a montage of discontinuous shots (2001, 83-86).

2. Assembling the Cinemascape

1. While the cinema is defined by and draws attention to its own its own movement (i.e., elements of its own machinery as well as the movement of film; Charney and Schwartz 1995), its material components are also mobile elements assembled from disparate sources (Winston 1996) even on a seemingly small scale, as both Schivelbush (1986, 63) and Jonnes (2004) describe in Edison's worldwide search for a suitable fiber he could use as a filament for lightbulbs. To be sure, it is this assemblage of mobile elements that shaped debates on the historical origins of the cinema, as Andre Bazín has sought to explain, "how it was that the invention took so long to emerge, since all the prerequisites had been assembled" (1967, 19). This is not the place to resolve the question of whether it was a matter of vivid imagination or viable investment. It is worth noting, however, Brian Winston's view on the issue with his attention to wider social conditions—the arrival of urban mass audiences to a new theater industry that would serve as stable venue for the cinema (1996). Similarly, part I of this book analyzes this element of specific movie-going publics as a key historical ingredient in the assembly of the cinema.

2. The social ranking of theaters was not a Bolivian invention, of course. By 1916 a "class system" had developed among theaters in U.S. cities. Distributors made more money by debuting films exclusively at more prestigious theaters for higher prices and then staggering the release dates at smaller, cheaper theaters. Both prestigious and lower-rank exhibitors would not lower their prices to compete within their ranks because it would lower the standard of the theater "in the eyes of the distributors" (Donaghue 1987, 13).

3. Audiences preferred to read subtitles while hearing the voices of the English- speaking stars to which they had become accustomed (King 1990, 32; Usabel 1982, 83).

4. As the star system successfully attracted audiences on the basis of the names of famous actors and directors, Hollywood began to "import" the best European actors and directors under the guise of making products to appeal to international audiences and expand its markets. Peter Stead argues that this is a reminder that "Hollywood was never as monolithic and stereotyped as critics would argue. Hollywood advanced on a broad front and one that inevitably allowed diversity" (1989, 41). Yet the Bolivian film scholar Luis Espinal saw this diversity as an attempt to "ruin rival cinemas" (1982, 77, 79).

5. In 1941 the U.S. Coordinator of Inter-American Affairs (CIAA) opened a Motion Pictures Division. Director John Hay Whitney met with MPPA executives and Disney to collaborate on making and distributing films to "'further the national defense and strengthen the bonds between the nations of the Western Hemisphere.'" During the campaign, the CIAA blanketed Latin America with propaganda films made and distributed with an annual budget that reached $20 million (Usabel 1982, 162).

6. By the early 1990s, Bolivia accounted for 10 percent of the television stations in Latin America and the Caribbean (Rivadeneira Prada 1991, 16), but only 9 percent of rural areas and 37 percent of urban zones had electricity. In a dramatic ratio, 57 television stations were communicating with only 1.3 million people (11, 17).

7. In the United States we typically think of mass media and popular culture as the same, while in Latin America this has not been the case; popular culture has been considered subordinate and even subversive of the commercialized mass culture. Martín-Barbero's history of mediation also marks how the opening of regional and transcontinental trade agreements is merging the "pop culture" industries of the North with popular cultures in Latin America (1993). Thus Latin American popular culture and media increasingly refer to the genres, styles, and institutions of commercial television, film, and media that are widely disseminated in global circuits of distribution (see also García Canclini 1995).

8. Moreover, films from Europe and even elsewhere in Latin America are almost exclusively shown at the Cinemateca Boliviana, a semiprivate national film archive and "art" film theater originally endowed by a group of mining philanthropists in 1976. The Cinemateca also houses a national film /video archive and offers Hollywood films (about 24 percent of their exhibitions, according to Susz [personal communication, August 4, 1993]) in order to raise money, yet like a museum they arrange and recontextualize films in thematic series. Many of the non-Hollywood films offered are French films furnished by the Alianza Francesa, or Argentine or Spanish films contributed by embassies to help raise money for the Cinemateca. These are usually attended by visiting tourists, high school and local university students, and people of the professional middle classes.

9. If the rhetoric of circulation has been called up to overcome earlier emphases on capitalist production and consumption, some social theory has also been moving beyond Foucault's interest in surveillance, containment, and disciplinary societies and toward an interest in "societies of control" of circulation in terms of space, time, production, and money (e.g., de Certeau 1984; Deleuze and Guattari 1983; Hardt 1998; Harvey 1985).

10. "Criminalizing" video piracy was difficult and controversial for filmmakers and theater owners who pressured the Congress for a "Cinema Law" to ban the thousands of contraband videotapes and the hundreds of unofficial video clubs and street vendors who sell them. The pirated video trade, they argued, took tax money from the state that could be used to support national productions. The first version of the cinema law left Bolivia as "'the only country with legalized piracy,'" according to activists who later won their fight for an amendment.

11. Following Gracia Clark (1988, 5–6), I prefer to use the term "official market" rather than "informal market," which implies disorder and a deceptively clear opposition to the official "formal order." (The official markets have their own disorders and informal practices.)

12. On behalf of the major distributors, the MPAA is also actively shaping the legal terms for controlling the worldwide flow of copyrights. On the continuously shifting and complex legal environment concerning the distribution of international copyrights and the MPAA, see Wang (2003).

3. The Visible Nation

1. Thus, in an article examining "national cinema/s," Stephen Crofts (1993) outlines seven positions that filmmakers have taken in relation to Hollywood: European–Model Art cinema; Third cinema; Third World and European Commercial cinemas; Ignoring Hollywood; Imitating Hollywood; Totalitarian cinemas; Regional/Ethnic cinemas.

2. Of course, the mythologies of national cinemas also apply to those about Hollywood as "global

cinema," an internally differentiated and conflicted location whose circulation is culturally uneven.

3. The Movimineto Nationalista Revolucionario (or Nationalist Revolutionary Movement), for example, was traditionally composed of journalists who formed a nationalist and populist political awareness in the Bolivian middle classes (del Granado 1989). See also *Nacionalismo y Coloniaje* by the MNR ideologue Carlos Montenegro (1944), which includes a history of the press in Bolivia but is itself a clear manifesto for a middle-class nation-state.

4. In most cases, the earliest films made in Bolivia have been lost, but some of them have been reconstructed with research by filmmakers, witnesses, newspaper reviews, scripts, found negatives, and, in some cases, still photos that are archived in the Cinemateca Boliviana.

5. Named the Motion Pictures Patent Company, the Trust was Edison's response to violations against his patents. In the Trust, "all individual patents were pooled. Edison received royalties on all of the films. . . . If a distributor handled films of other companies, he would not be granted any of the Trust's films. For the privilege of renting licensed films, an exhibitor had to pay two dollars a week. Edison was the prime recipient of the royalties and his net profits soared to more than $1 million a year. In an attempt to enforce its regulations, the Trust filed hundreds of lawsuits and even hired private detectives to search for patent violators. . . . The Trust's failure to control the business spurred them into distribution themselves. In 1910 they created the General Film Company and bought out fifty-seven exchanges across the country. Exchanges that were granted licenses had to agree to buy films only from the Trust. The Trust aimed to drive other exchanges out of business by eliminating their supply of films, price-cutting, and other forms of intimidation" (Donaghue 1987, 10). Donaghue goes on to describe how William Fox's company and other independents also organized themselves to challenge the Trust's monopoly by producing, distributing, and owning theaters themselves. In this competitive scenario, Wall Street banks entered as power brokers, selling public stocks that funded the industrial expansion of cinema into multiple-reel narrative-style films (Cook 1990, 47). In 1917 the Trust was legally disassembled.

6. Ana López (2000b) has written more broadly about the significance of the mobility of early Latin American filmmakers.

7. This film was also lost; recovered photos and the original play have been used by film scholars in Bolivia to reconstruct the narrative.

8. The opposition set up in public discourse on cinema in Bolivia between the incipient national cinema as an authentic art against the profane business of commercial Hollywood cinema does not mean that national cinema escapes the condition of money. One of the fundamental circulatory conditions of filmmaking is capital, a medium, like the cinema, whose essential feature is mobility. As Gilles Deleuze wrote, "The cinema as art itself lives in a direct relation with a permanent plot *[complot],* an international conspiracy which conditions it from within, as the most intimate and most indispensable enemy. This conspiracy is that of money; what defines industrial art is not mechanical reproduction but the internalized relation with money" (1989, 77; see also Beller 2006). Indeed, scholars have productively explored connections between state financing and the industrialization of cinema (in Brazil, see, for example, Johnson 1987; for Venezuela, see Simis 2002), but this is only part of the story. Although money may underlie forms of circulation connecting the state and industrial cinema, neither commodity capitalism nor the state determined the styles and social projects that have been pursued with cinematic technologies, as evidenced by the wide literature on political films, alternative media, the New Latin American Cinema and "Third Cinema." In Bolivia, too, the internalized condition of money did not determine the plurality of social uses of cinema and television. Further, filmmakers have either been forced or have chosen to pursue their cultural and political projects by moving their work in, out of, and around the commercial circuits of exchange and commodity status.

9. Interview in *El Diario,* March 25, 1925. *Corazón Aymara* was adapted for theater from *La Huerta* (The Garden), written by Angel Salas.

10. Posnansky had claimed that Tiwanaku was evidence of the Aymara master-race who had constructed the site but that their superiority had Aryan origins in Atlantis, which was accessible through Lake Titicaca. After the defeat of Nazi Germany in World War II, Posnansky withdrew this claim (see Richards 2005).

11. Subsequently in the 1950s, Carlos Ponce Sangines began to carry out excavations and reconstructions at Tiwanaku to build evidence of the nation's glorious past. He wrote, "The archaeologist of indigenous ancestry must then decipher the profound roots of the people and the very foundations of the nation. In sum, the archaeologist can by no means hide away and engage with his discipline as though it were cold and detached" (in Condori 1989, 47). Elsewhere, in a book intended for a wider literate Bolivian public, Ponce Sanginés goes to some lengths to

demonstrate how the absolute chronology of "our country" is being reconstructed by means of carbon 14 dating. He provides a rather lengthy explanation and includes charts of test results and a photo of radiocarbon equipment. Like the cinema, modern technologies were a condition for producing the lineal history that the state needed in order to telescope itself into the precolonial past.

12. Free indigenous communities in the highland Altiplano had directly fought in a mestizo-led revolution in 1899 that sought to wrest and liberate Bolivian markets from a small elite. Yet as the hacienda (latifundia) system subsequently expanded, Indians were displaced to the city as the mestizos bought up community lands. When Indian communities in the Altiplano surrounding La Paz rose up fighting for their lands, governments responded with repression against those who had made their revolution possible. Indian participation in the Liberal Revolution, as Tristan Platt (1987) describes, combined with their struggles to reestablish a native Andean model of statecraft that would redistribute the agricultural surplus of their ayllu lands. On the formation of mestizo and indigenous categories in relation to commercialization, see Harris (1995).

13. See Susz (1990) for an excellent account and reconstruction of this film and others related to the Chaco War.

4. Fantasies of Modernity

1. I first viewed this film on television in 1996, and it appealed to Bolivians then in many of the same terms, which indicates the endurance of the fantasy the film had portrayed. The triumphant images of pipelines leading to the seacoast at the end of Los Primeros in 1958 would be one of the most enduring images that oriented the uprisings of October 2003. Now, after the "gas wars" of that year, the film may be an active fantasy, but people are well aware that a film like Los Primeros makes the control of the country's hydrocarbon wealth look much more than a little complicated politically.

2. I would not argue that the introduction of Western-style modernity in its cinematic fantasy forms reverses the history of modernity in the North as in Fredric Jameson's well-known periodization in which image and aesthetic production only recently has surpassed and oriented material and structural configurations. Similarly, David Harvey has written that the condition of postmodernity "is dominated by fiction, fantasy, the immaterial (particularly of money), fictitious capital, images, ephemerality" (1989, 339). Anna Tsing (2005) gives a fascinating account of how imagination and fantasy dramatically attract capital in contemporary globalization, but the phenomenon is not necessarily contemporary. I would argue that the emergence of colonial capitalism in the West was primed by such fantasies of pleasure and luxury as they were perceived to exist to the East. See Marshall Sahlins (1994) on England's trade with China, for example; see also Marco Polo's Travels for a primary text that vividly imagined the wealth of China for Europe prior to Columbus's voyages.

3. The state's relation to image and fantasy is a key issue here. Gareth Williams (2002) also traces the shifting visibilities and concealments of the popular nation-state in Latin America under neoliberal conditions. Fernando Coronil has examined the sleight of hand involved in the production and appearance of a dazzling Venezuelan state and shows how the state's selective exclusions from public view as well its fantasies of progress have been elements of its existence (1997). In this book, I seek to contribute to the emerging anthropological argument that the production of fantasy is an ingredient for the organization of statecraft, however, rather than the effect or mask of networks and alliances that are somewhat more real (Gupta 1995; Coronil 1997; Ferguson 1999; Aretxaga 2000; Grant 2001; Askew 2002; Navaro-Yashin 2002). Further, I show that the networks and institutions that are organized within the frame of the state are also symbolic fields (Herzfeld 1992) and performative "imaginary networks of political power" (Bartra 1992). Such intrinsic connections between the forces and forms of the symbolic and the institutional do not only cast the state in the model of an assemblage (see DeLanda 2006), but this raises the possibility of understanding the state not as a "thing" but as a filmlike happening that is produced and directed in the tensions between mobility and stabilization. To indulge this view, more could be made to join the two ideas that money (as capital) is a condition for cinema (see chapter 3, note 8; Deleuze 1989, 77; and Beller 2006) and that the circulation of money sustains the apparatus of the state (Deleuze and Guattari 1983, 197). The state's internalized and privileged relation with money makes the circulation of its currency coextensive with the state's regime of value. As Robert Foster describes how new currency issued in Papua New Guinea in 1975 displayed the contours of its source, the state, "the money was understood as a synthesis of elements drawn from different locations within the borders of the territorial state, thereby expressing the unity of the nation as a whole and the parity of

its constituent parts" (1998, 71). As its currency registers and embodies the heterogeneous locations through which it moves within and beyond its territory, the state comes to resemble a movie consolidated from the disparate paths through which its film stock travels. This congruence between the "national cinema" and the state occurs in this chapter and chapter 3 of this book. In their connection, the state is not only a coproducer of fantasy and signifying practices by sponsoring filmmaking but acts as an editor by limiting filmmakers' access to capital and material resources.

4. In order to provide ethnographic knowledge on the indigenous people of Santa Ana de Chipaya, a community that had not yet seen cinema, Ruiz collaborated with the protagonists and based his work on the writings of the Swiss anthropologist Alfred Metraux, whose work in South America emphasized "lost cultures." *Vuelve Sebastiana* was financed by Bolivia Films in 1953 and was shot by a team consisting of Ruiz, his friend Augusto Roca, and their driver with the collaboration of the people from Santa Ana. Before they began to shoot, the filmmakers spent a week learning about the community, showing its members how the camera functioned, and organizing the production. Afterward, the story line based on the footage was written by Ramiro Beltran, then a member of one of the film's sponsors from the mayor's office of La Paz.

5. Elsewhere (Himpele 2003) I show how, for dancers, folklore parades are part of the production of social status and an indigenized bourgeois modernity. Abercrombie also describes the ties of religious and national affiliation that are established in the parades by the dancers (1991).

6. Before it closed, President Siles forced Telecine to turn to aerial photography for North American petroleum prospectors. Gonzalo Sánchez de Losada and the writer Oscar Soria also had researched and wrote a script for *Gringo Smith*, a film about two fugitives from the United States who escape to Bolivia. Sánchez de Losada brought the script to the United States and a producer offered him $15,000 for it, which he rejected. Several years later, and perhaps not by coincidence, the film *Butch Cassidy and the Sundance Kid* appeared in the United States.

7. Jorge Ruiz and others from Bolivia Films and Telecine were drawn into a virtual transnational industry of filmmaking financed by the agencies of the United States. Outside Bolivia, Ruiz was contracted to make an anti-malaria film in Ecuador for USAID (*Los Que Nunca Fueron* [Those That Never Were], 1954), which was also the first sound film made in that country. In the early 1960s, Ruiz and the writer Ramiro Beltran were hired again to make a film about the agrarian reform in Guatemala (*Los Ximul*). After he left his position as head of the ICB in 1963, Ruiz continued to make socially committed documentaries in Ecuador and Peru. In Ecuador, Ruiz made a series of training films for the police, which were financed by USAID, as was a film he later made in Peru to promote the Peruvian Air Force, which had been discredited after its massacre of guerrillas and peasants. Before the Banzer dictatorship, Ruiz returned to Bolivia briefly in the early 1970s to work with Proinca Films, a company opened and owned by Mario Mercado, then a wealthy mine owner and the mayor of La Paz. Their first project was to buy the footage of the failed film *Detras de los Andes* (Behind the Andes) and remake it into *Mina Alaska* (Alaska Mine), an adventure narrative. Proinca went on to make other commercial films based on local landscapes, music, and folklore (e.g., *Volver* [Return]; *Patria Linda* [Beautiful Country], 1972) and some documentary-style films such as *La Gran Herencia*, discussed earlier.

8. On Jorge Sanjinés in the context of Latin America cinema during this period, see Armes (1987); Burton (1991); King (1990); Pick (1993); see also Sanjinés (1986) and a collection of his writing (1979).

9. After the IBC was permanently closed, the USAID created the Center Audiovisual at which Hugo Roncal was the principal filmmaker. Roncal was also the only filmmaker to shoot footage of Che Guevara when he was assassinated in Bolivia. Within minutes, the CIA took his film and it was immediately distributed around the world by the USIS.

10. Operating since the 1940s, highly politicized, sometimes clandestine, radio stations of mining unions frequently have been the first targets of military repressions in mining towns. As scholars and activists explore possible grassroots or horizontal modes of communication in everyday life for "theories of practice helpful to the aims of participatory media," as Robert Huesca puts it, the Bolivian tin miners' radio is an exemplary model of "participatory and alternative media . . . emphasizing the possibilities for change and . . . practice [that] has preceded communication theory" (Huesca 1995, 101). See also Dagron and Cajías on the miners' radio stations (1989) and Beltran on grassroots forms of democratic communication (1993).

11. Sanjinés's self-critical subtext about the transformative capabilities of revolutionary film raises the provocative and complicated questions that Jane Gaines also poses at the outset of her essay (1999) asking how documentary film can be exploited to produce social change given its particularistic capacities for mimesis and using the material vehicle of indexical signs.

12. Interview in *Hoy,* April 25, 1993.

13. Gonzalo Sánchez de Losada was the president ousted from his second term in office during the "gas wars" in October 2003 in Bolivia.

5. Reality Affects

1. Despite the struggle to return to representative democracy in the early 1980s, popular participation in elections was decreasing (Lazarte 1993).
2. To complicate the situation, people in the popular sectors said that they did not watch locally produced Bolivian television and cinema "because it is depressing," "they are only about poverty, only poverty," or "they are about Indians," confirming the elite assumption that people in the popular sectors "have no voice."
3. Just as I argue that film circulation brings publics into visibility, my work on *The Tribunal* does not seek the impact of mass media upon preexistent "people." Here I follow ideas about social class developed by E. P. Thompson, who used class as a historical rather than economic or structural category, and pursue the ways in which the popular classes eventuate "as something which in fact happens (and can be shown to have happened) in human relationships" (Thompson 1966 [1963], 9; see also Rowe and Schelling 1991, 10). This view is also adopted in Mark Liechty's (2002) processual account of the Katmandu middle class as well as in Purnima Mankekar's use of "social formation" in her ethnography of lower-middle-class television viewers in India (1999, 361n18).
4. Denouncement first published on June 28, 1988; in Archondo (1991, 183).
5. Indigenous groups opposed Condepa's appropriation of this site where the prominent archaeological ruins of the ancient Tiwanaku are located.
6. Palenque got 12.3 percent of the votes nationally. In Bolivia, when no presidential candidate receives 50 percent or more of the popular vote, newly elected members of parliament use and combine their votes to elect a president in exchange for political offices. This process has resulted in unexpected coalitional alliances.
7. Condepa had 14.3 percent of the total vote. The winning MNR (led by Sánchez de Losada) had 35.6 percent.
8. This ethnic incorporation was also evidenced in the ruptures created when the Condepa party was formed. Once the party was formed, the men and women from the cholo immigrant neighborhood Defense Committees were displaced from party leadership by Palenque's friends, associates, and others with political experience looking to situate themselves in the new political landscape. Politicos from the right (such as Banzer's ADN party) and a group of leftist intellectuals (the October Group, who had also successfully named Condepa) were incorporated into the party to organize and direct its activities and to assemble a uniform political discourse. Meanwhile original members worked in their neighborhoods to obtain supporters. By the elections of June 1989, however, many of the original members of the Defense Committees had renounced their affiliation with Condepa. In his last argument with one original member of the Defense Committee just before he resigned, Palenque told him, "You are understood as material from the neighborhood and not for administering the country" (Archondo 1991, 216). In this divisive statement, Palenque drew an ethnic line that contained members of the Defense Committee in their popular neighborhoods even as Condepa incorporated indigenous culture symbolically. Condepa's ties with its urban indigenous base also displaced the party's own self-identified Aymara founding members. When Julio Mantilla joined the party as a successful mayoral candidate who would also assist Condepa in the use of indigenous symbolism, he was virtually unknown by most of the original party members. Later, when Mantilla resigned from the party, he and Palenque argued across two television channels about who spoke Aymara better. In the 1993 national campaign, Palenque and Condepa staged a spectacle that portrayed him and his supporters as fulfilling the promise of Tupac Katari, the indigenous rebel leader who was quartered in the rebellion in 1781 and famously vowed, "I will return and I will be millions."
9. Quoted by Rafael Archondo (1991).
10. *Ultima Hora*, June 30, 1989, in Rivera Cusicanqui (1993).
11. For an analysis of the tensions surrounding my own access and positioning at the *Tribunal* as an ethnographer in a business of realist representation similar to Palenque's, see Himpele 2002.
12. Palenque's reference to twenty-eight years of work includes the years of his work on radio before *The Open Tribunal* first aired on television.
13. Anderson 1983; Bhabha 1990; Jameson 1986; Larson 1995.
14. Another RTP program hosted for years by Palenque's cohost Adolfo Paco was his live Saturday afternoon variety program *Sabados Populares* (Popular Saturdays), attended by cholo families in the Cinema Mexico movie theater near the Center of La Paz. The point of the program, Paco explained to me, was to address the mixed cultural interests of the popular classes. So in dance contests it was not unusual to see a Bolivian folklore dance character break dancing. It was also not unusual to see urban Aymara men and women as contestants stacking Monopol paint cans as high as possible for a half hour as Paco sang "Monopol Monopol" repeatedly.

15. *Telepolicial* depicted scenes from violent and dramatic crimes. This show was produced by RTP but not hosted by Palenque. Subverting Palenque's authority and popularity, one older Aymara woman who watched *The Open Tribunal* nightly said that she preferred *Telepolicial* because Palenque was not there "to interfere" and it gave her information about the increasing crime in the city.

16. My use of Scott's work on patron-client relationships takes into account Susan Gal's insightful critique of his subsequent work (Scott 1990) that his approach naturalizes both domination and resistance by relying on a unitary and hydraulic view of subjectivity. In Gal's words, "There is no room in this scheme for cultural or ideological mediation of emotion, for counter-discourse, or for the contradictions of mixed beliefs" (1995, 414). I think we can retain Scott's insights about how agency is performed and legitimated in the moral sphere of patron-client relations, but clearly we have to avoid reductive oppositions between "domination and resistance as *The Tribunal* shows." This dualism, I imagine, led Scott from the moral sphere of patron-client relations to concerns with arts of resistance in which "thick" masks of deference are performed to disguise hidden dissent.
    Also worth citing here are the striking ritual courtesies exchanged between viewers (as guests) and hosts that mark them as socially unequal on an Iranian exile television program (Naficy 1993, 109–11).

17. Platt shows how the tributary Bolivian state received tribute from *ayllu* communities in exchange for respecting community autonomy over its agricultural terrain. The republican state established itself as the actual proprietor of communal lands, granting access to ayllu communities and considering the tribute as the "rent" that communities paid to the state for the use of the land. This colonial relation also allowed for the "paternal generosity" that the state adopted toward ayllu communities. Yet it also maintained what Platt calls a "complex network of obligations and counter-obligations which based the relations between the state and communities in the Andean ideology. For the community even the paternal aspect of the State was correct and just, whenever it fulfilled its traditional role of protector, which included the obligation to accept its prestations" (1982, 100–101). This relationship was ruptured and violated during the Liberal Revolution of the late nineteenth century in which an agrarian reform law instituted market relations that entailed an individualizing and "civilizing" assault on the autonomy of ayllus and community autonomy. As I will argue, the present neoliberal circumstance violated a similar pact.

18. Especially vivid is the 1945 Indian Congress in La Paz held by President Villarroel and attended by over 1,000 Aymara and Quechua leaders as described by Jorge Dandler and Juan Torrico A. (1987, 352). Perhaps as a forecast of the exchange of protagonism and the promises of redemption often heard in *The Tribunal*'s populist discourses, one of the indigenous leaders publicly credited Villarroel as the authority who had made possible the National Indigenous Congress in the first place: "the indigenous people are assembled thanks to President Villarroel. . . . and that everything makes one think that the hour of redemption has arrived for the indigenous people" (252). The unprecedented Congress ended with a festival at which Villarroel and the peasant leaders celebrated. As Dandler and Torrico A. suggest, "An intense relationship was forged between Villorroel and the peasants who believed in him" (356); participants in the Congress recall that "we all loved him like a father" (366).

19. Radio also has historically been a widespread media of participatory communication practices in Bolivia, especially among tin miners and the Catholic Church (Dagron and Cajias 1989; Huesca 1995).

20. See Archondo (1991) and Sanjinés (1992).

21. *Ch'uno* and *ch'arki* are preparations of freeze-dried potato and meat typically prepared in the countryside and common in the menu of urban popular classes.

6. Indexical Binds

1. The contrast that Abercrombie et al. (1992) draw with indexical realism is with how popular cultures have long employed fantasy images to evoke the anxiety and scandal among urban underclasses of modernizing European and American cities. Nevertheless, melodramatic narratives, such as those on *The Open Tribunal* that evoke fear, violence, and mystery through sensational imagery, have a long history in urban media for attracting viewers in highly competitive media markets (Nichols 1994, 49, 53) and for attempting to culturally assimilate rural peasantries (Martín-Barbero 1993). One distinction I am drawing here between television and cinema is that the extended circulatory matrix of "live" television offers the promise of making television and real-life events coextensive (see Houston 1984 and Williams 1999).

2. In an eloquent discussion of the video of the beating of Rodney King by Los Angeles police,

Nichols (1991) argues that the court case depended on producing a hegemonic interpretation or framing of the images. On framing documentary, see also Nichols 1994; Platinga 1991; and Eitzen 1995.

3. MacDougall argues convincingly against linguistic analyses of the pictorial and yet he is not interested in establishing the ethnographic superiority of images. Instead he explores the analytic qualities of text and the revelatory properties of film and their respective capacities for performing anthropological knowledge.

4. This issue was particularly acute for me in the films I have made. *Incidents of Travel in Chichén Itzá* (Himpele and Castañeda 1997) concerns the orchestration of power and space as thousands of spiritualists and tourists, state agencies, and Maya vendors annually converge at the reconstructed archaeological spectacle of Chichén Itzá. The film embodies aspects of the event itself: the mobility of tourism, the contending narratives that claim to represent Mayas, the shifting identities of participants, and the collusion among different social groups who produce and consume images of a pure Maya antiquity. The multi-sited sequence of ethnographic encounters or "incidents" that constitute and direct this film is evidence of the contingent, improvisational, and experimental nature of ethnographic film. Although such incidents and plural authors are typically edited out of documentary film to exert narrative coherence and control, *Incidents* turned out to be a film about such dynamics, among other things.

5. The term is from Edward Branigan (1992).

6. Interestingly, workers were even more guarded after Palenque's death because their futures and incomes as employees had become more precarious.

7. This enlargement of the social field through television seems to run counter to arguments that new forms of communication and media are "shrinking the world" or compressing it. Perhaps so from a perceptual perspective, as noted above, but in terms of social processes, we can associate it with the social compression, expansion, and engagement of societies.

8. As Webb Keane argues, "the radical indeterminacy of meaning as a matter of principle encounters constraints in practice. For instance, over the course of conversational interaction, the full range of possibilities is continually narrowed down and confined—a matter not of linguistic structure, in the Saussurean sense, but of social and political relations and the centripetal forces they involve" (2003, 412). Here, I follow Keane as he shifts attention away from textual models and toward the materiality of things and the give-and-take of specific social and historical contexts and extends his analysis toward the processes in which the materiality and objectification of voices are ingredients of popular politics and the commodification of things.

9. Yael Navaro-Yashin similarly describes the persistence of the state as fantasy in contemporary Turkey (2002).

Conclusion

1. It would be short-sighted to view the indigenist and popular movements of the early twentieth century as the only historical strategies pursued until the emergence of contemporary indigenization. While typically class and ethnicity alternately have framed competing political strategies among Indianist movements (Albó 1987), fusions of class and ethnic movements have occurred in revolutionary episodes in Bolivia, such as in 1899 and 1952 (Hylton and Thompson 2005). Indigenous movements across the Andes, too, have sought to appropriate national projects and indigenize systems of self-governance (Mallon 1983; Stern 1987). No doubt the historical memories of such indigenous populism, nationalism, and insurrectionary projects inspire contemporary movements (Thompson 2002) as well as the shifting alliances and populist images that continue to mobilize contemporary Bolivian politics.

2. For details about this festival, see www.firstnationsfirstfeatures.org. Many of the films that have been screened at these festivals are available for viewing at the NMAI Film and Video Center in New York.

3. Indeed, the mythological Andean vampire figure of the Pishtaco (Quechua) or Kharisiri (Aymara) steals fat rather than blood (Wachtel 1994; Weismantel 2001). This figure leaves a small scar on the victim's side and is considered to be a white gringo who uses the fat to grease industrial machinery or to make soap.

4. Under pressure from filmmakers, the state passed a Cinema Law in 1993 that dedicated money to support filmmaking and a cinema council, CONACINE, composed of five filmmakers and five government officials. The council approves and supports film productions with a fund from which filmmakers may borrow money. CONACINE is also authorized to award permissions for any film or video shoots as well as assist in arranging international coproductions. While several film projects have been produced through CONACINE, the video makers from CEFREC and CAIB told me that they have not found the council supportive for their projects.

5. This story was recounted to me by Amalia Cordova from the Film and Video Center of the National Museum of the American Indian (New York).
6. Amazonian Indian political tactics and movements are saturated with the self-conscious deployment of images of both savage and noble "Indianness" (see, e.g., Conklin 1997; Oakdale 2004; Ramos 1994; and Turner 1991).

Bibliography

Abercrombie, Nicholas, Scott Lash, and Brian Longhurst. 1992. "Popular Representation: Recasting Realism." In *Modernity and Identity*, ed. S. Lash and J. Friedman, 115–40. Oxford: Blackwell.

Abercrombie, Thomas A. 1991. "To Be Indian, to Be Bolivian: 'Ethnic' and 'National' Discourses of Identity." In *Nation States and Indians in Latin America*, ed. J. Sherzer and G. Urban, 95–130. Austin: University of Texas Press.

———. 1996. "Q'aqchas and La Plebe in 'Rebellion': Carnival vs. Lent in Eighteenth-Century Potosí. *Journal of Latin American Anthropology* 2, no. 1: 62–111.

———. 1998. *Pathways of Memory and Power: Ethnography and History among an Andean People.* Madison: University of Wisconsin Press.

———. 2003. "Mothers and Mistresses of the Urban Bolivian Public Sphere: Postcolonial Predicament and National Imaginary in Oruro's Carnival." In *After Spanish Rule*, ed. M. Thurner and A. Guerrero, 176–220. Durham, N.C.: Duke University Press.

Abu-Lughod, Lila. 2005. *Dramas of Nationhood: The Politics of Television in Egypt.* Chicago: University of Chicago Press.

Acland, Charles R. 2003. *Screen Traffic: Movies, Multiplexes, and Global Culture.* Durham, N.C.: Duke University Press.

Ahmad, Aijaz. 1987. "Jameson's Rhetoric of Otherness and the 'National Allegory.'" *Social Text* 17 (Autumn): 3–25.

Albó, Javier. 1987. "From MNRistas to Kataristas to Katari." In *Resistance, Rebellion, and Consciousness in the Andean Peasant World, Eighteenth to Twentieth Centuries*, ed. S. J. Stern, 379–419. Madison: University of Wisconsin Press.

———. 1991a. "Bolivia: La Paz/Chukiyawu: Las Dos Caras de Una Ciudad." *América Indígena* 51, no. 4: 107–58.

———. 1991b. "El retorno del indio." *Revista Andina* 2: 299–345.

Albó, Xavier, and Matías Preiswerk. 1986. *Los Señores del Gran Poder.* La Paz: Centro de Teología Popular.

Albro, Robert. 1997. "Virtual Patriliny: Image Mutability and Populist Politics in Quillacolla, Bolivia." *Political and Legal Anthropology Review* 20, no. 1: 73–92.

———. 1998a. "A New Time and Space for Bolivian Popular Politics." Introduction to theme issue. *Ethnology* 37, no. 2: 99–115.

———. 1998. "Neoliberal Ritualists of Urkupiña: Bedeviling Patrimonial Identity in a Bolivian Patronal Fiesta." *Ethnology* 37, no. 2: 133–64.

———. 2000. "The Populist Chola: Cultural Mediation and the Political Imagination in Quillacollo, Bolivia." *Journal of Latin American Anthropology* 5, no. 2: 30–88.

———. 2005. "The Indigenous in the Plural in Bolivian Oppositional Politics." *Bulletin of Latin American Research* 24, no. 4: 433–53.

Albro, Robert, and Jeff Himpele. n.d. "Popularizing the Public, Publicizing the Popular." Manuscript.

Allon, Joan. 1980. "The Film Viewer as Consumer." *Quarterly Review of Film Studies* 5, no. 4: 481–99.

Alvarez, Sonia, Evelina Dagnino, and Arturo Escobar, eds. 1998. *Cultures of Politics, Politics of Cultures: Re-Visioning Latin American Social Movements.* Boulder, Colo.: Westview Press.

Anderson, Benedict. 1983. *Imagined Communities: The Origin and Spread of Nationalism.* London: Verso.

———. 1998. "'Nationalism, Identity and the World-in-Motion: On the Logics of Seriality.'" In

Cosmopolitics: Thinking and Feeling beyond the Nation, ed. P. Cheah and B. Robbins, 117–33. Minneapolis: University of Minnesota Press.

Ang, Ien. 1991. *Desperately Seeking the Audience*. London: Routledge.

———. 1996. *Living Room Wars: Rethinking Media Audiences for a Postmodern World*. London: Routledge.

Appadurai, Arjun. 1986. "Introduction: Commodities and the Politics of Value." *The Social Life of Things*, 3–63. Cambridge: Cambridge University Press.

———. 1996a. "Disjuncture and Difference in the Global Cultural Economy." *Modernity at Large: Cultural Dimensions of Globalization*, 27–47. Minneapolis: University of Minnesota Press.

———. 1996b. "The Production of Locality." *Modernity at Large: Cultural Dimensions of Globalization*, 178–99. Minneapolis: University of Minnesota Press.

———. 2000. "Grassroots Globalization and the Research Imagination." *Public Culture* 12, no. 1: 1–19.

———. 2006. "The Thing Itself." *Public Culture* 18, no. 1: 15–22.

Archondo, Rafael. 1991. *Compadres al Micrófono: La Resurrección Metropolitana del Ayllu*. La Paz: Hisbol.

Arellano-López, Sonia, and James Petras. 1994. "Non-Governmental Organizations and Poverty Alleviation in Bolivia." *Development and Change* 25: 555–68.

Aretxaga, Begona. 2000. "A Fictional Reality: Paramilitary Death Squads and the Construction of State Terror in Spain." In *Death Squad: The Anthropology of State Terror*, ed. J. A. Sluka, 46–69. Philadelphia: University of Pennsylvania Press.

Armbrust, Walter. 1998. "When the Lights Go Down In Cairo: Cinema as Secular Ritual." *Visual Anthropology* 10, no. 2–4: 413–12.

Armes, Roy. 1987. *Third World Film Making and the West*. Berkeley: University of California Press.

Askew, Kelly M. 2002. *Performing the Nation: Swahili Music and Cultural Politics in Tanzania*. Chicago: University of Chicago Press.

Askew, Kelly, and Richard Wilk, eds. 2002. *The Anthropology of Media: A Reader*. London: Blackwell.

Auyero, Javier. 1999. "'From the Client's Point(s) of View': How Poor People Perceive and Evaluate Political Clientelism." *Theory and Society* 28: 297–334.

Ayo Saucedo, Diego. 1999. *Desafíos de la Participacíon Popular*. La Paz: CEBEM.

Bakhtin, M. M. 1981. "Discourse in the Novel. " In *The Dialogic Imagination*, ed. M. Holquist, 259–422. Austin: University of Texas Press.

Barragán, Rossana. 1990. *Espacio Urbano y Dinamica Etnica: La Paz en el Siglo XIX*. La Paz: HISBOL.

———. 1992. "Identidades indias y mestizas: Una intervención al debate." *Autodeterminación* 10: 17–44.

———. 1993. "Entre polleras, lliqllas y ñañacas: Los mestizos y la emergencia de la tercera republica." In *Etnicidad, Economia, y Simbolismo en los Andes*, ed. S. Arce, R. Barragán, L. Escobari, and X. Medinacelli, 85–128. La Paz: HISBOL.

Bartra, Roger. 1992. *The Imaginary Networks of Political Power*. New Brunswick, N.J.: Rutgers University Press.

Battaglia, Debora. 1997. "Ambiguating Agency: The Case of Malinowski's Ghost." *American Anthropologist* 99, no. 3: 505–10.

Bauman, Richard, and Charles L. Briggs. 1990. "Poetics and Performance as Critical Perspectives on Language and Social Life." *Annual Review of Anthropology* 19: 59–88.

Bazín, Andre. 1967. *What Is Cinema?* Berkeley: University of California Press.

Beck, Ulrich, Anthony Giddens, and Scott Lash. 1994. *Reflexive Modernization: Politics, Tradition and Aesthetics in the Modern Social Order*. Stanford, Calif.: Stanford University Press.

Beidelman, T. O. 1989. "Agonistic Exchange: Homeric Reciprocity and the Heritage of Simmel and Mauss." *Cultural Anthropology* 4, no. 3: 227–59.

Beller, Jonathan. 2006. *The Cinematic Mode of Production: Attention Economy and the Society of the Spectacle*. Hanover, N.H.: Dartmouth College Press: University Press of New England.

Beltran, Luis Ramiro. 1993. "The Quest for Democracy in Communication: Outstanding Latin American Experiences." *Development* 3: 45–47.

Bennett, Jane. 2004. "The Force of Things: Steps toward an Ecology of Matter." *Political Theory* 32, no. 3: 347–72.

———. 2005. "The Agency of Assemblages and the North American Blackout." *Public Culture* 17, no. 3: 445.

Bennett, Tony. 1994. "The Exhibitionary Complex." In *Culture/Power/History: A Reader in Contemporary Social Theory*, ed. N. B. Dirks, G. Eley, and S. B. Ortner, 123–54. Princeton, N.J.: Princeton University Press.

Bhabha, Homi. 1984. "Of Mimicry and Man: The Ambivalence of Colonial Discourse." *October* 28 (Spring): 125–33.

———. 1990. "DissemiNation: Time, Narrative, and the Margins of the Modern Nation." In *Nation and Narration*, ed. H. K. Bhabha, 291–322. London: Routledge.

Bird, S. Elizabeth. 1992. "Travels in Nowhere Land: Ethnography and the 'Impossible' Audience." *Critical Studies in Mass Communication* 9: 250–60.

Birri, Fernando. 1985. "For a Nationalist, Realist, Critical and Popular Cinema." *Screen* 26, nos. 3–4: 89–91.

Bouysse-Cassagne, Thérese, and Thierry Saignes. 1993. "El cholo: Actor olvidado de la historia." In *Etnicidad, Economia, y Simbolismo en los Andes*, ed. S. Arce, R. Barragán, L. Escobari, and X. Medinacelli. 129–44. La Paz: HISBOL.

Boyd-Barrett, Oliver. 1977. "Media Imperialism: Towards an International Framework for the Analysis of Media Systems." In *Mass Communication and Society*, ed. J. Curran, M. Guretvitch, and J. Woollacott, 116–35. New York: Edward Arnold.

———. 1982. "Cultural Dependency and the Mass Media." In *Culture, Society, and the Media, ed.* M. Gurevitch, T. Bennett, J. Curran, and J. Woollacott, 174–95. London: Routledge.

Branigan, Edward. 1992. *Narrative Comprehension and Film*. London: Routledge.

Bruner, Jerome. 1991. "The Narrative Construction of Reality." *Critical Inquiry* 18, no. 1: 1–21.

Brysk, Alison. 2000. *From Tribal Village to Global Village*. Stanford, Calif.: Stanford University Press.

Buck-Morss, Susan. 1994. "The Cinema Screen as Prosthesis of Perception: A Historical Account." In *The Senses Still: Perception and Memory as Material Culture in Modernity*, ed. C. N. Seremetakis, 45–62. Boulder, Colo.: Westview Press.

Buechler, Hans, and Judith-Maria Buechler. 1996. *The World of Sofia Velasquez: The Autobiography of a Bolivian Market Women*. New York: Columbia University Press.

Buechler, Judith-Maria. 1978. "The Dynamics of the Market in La Paz, Bolivia." *Urban Anthropology* 7, no. 4: 343–59.

———. 1997. "The Visible and Vocal Politics of Female Traders and Small-Scale Producers in La Paz, Bolivia." In *Women and Economic Changes: Andean Perspectives*, ed. A. Miles and H. Buechler, 75–88. Washington, D.C.: Society for Latin American Anthropology.

Burton, Julianne. 1991. *Cine y Cambio Social en America Latina*. Colonia del Valle, Mexico: Editorial Diana.

———. 1997. "Film Artisans and Film Industries in Latin America, 1956–1980: Theoretical and Critical Implications of Variations in Modes of Filmic Production and Consumption." In *New Latin American Cinema: Theory, Practices, and Transcontinental Articulations*, ed. M. T. Martin, 157–84. Detroit: Wayne State University Press.

Cabellero Hoyos, J. Ramiro, Freddy Carranza, and Sandra Cárdenas Barragán. 1991. *La difusión cinematográfica en La Paz y El Alto*. Propuesta de un programa cognitivo de investigación: Cinemateca Boliviana.

Canessa, Andrew, 2006. "'Todos Somos Indígenas': Towards a New Language of National Political Identity." *Bulletin of Latin American Research* 25, no. 2: 241-67.

Carpignano, Paolo, 1999. "The Shape of the Sphere: The Public Sphere and the Materiality of Communication." *Constellations* 6, no. 2: 177–89.

Carpignano, Paolo, Robin Anderson, Stanley Aronowitz, and William DiFazio. 1993. "Chatter in the Age of Electronic Reproduction: Talk Television and the 'Public Mind.'" In *The Phantom Public Sphere*, ed. B. Robbins, 93–120. Minneapolis: University of Minnesota Press.

Chalmers, Douglas A., Scott B. Martin, and Kerianne Piester. 1997. "Associative Networks: New Structures of Representation for the Popular Sectors?" In *The New Politics of Inequality in Latin America: Rethinking Participation and Representation*, ed. D. Chalmers et al., 543–82. Oxford: Oxford University Press.

Chanan, Michael. 1997. "The Economic Conditions of Cinema in Latin America." In *New Latin American Cinema*, Vol. 1: *Theory, Practices, and Transcontinental Articulations*, ed. M. T. Martin, 185–200. Detroit: Wayne State University Press.

Charney, Leo, and Vanessa R. Schwartz, eds. 1995. *Cinema and the Invention of Modern Life*. Berkeley: University of California Press.

Choque, María Eugenia, and Carlos Mamani. 2001. "Reconstitución del ayllu y derechos de los pueblos indígenas: El movimiento indio en los Andes de Bolivia." *Journal of Latin American Anthropology* 6, no. 1: 202–24.

Clark, Gracia, ed. 1988. *Traders versus the State: Anthropological Approaches to Unofficial Economies*. Boulder, Colo.: Westview Press.

Clifford, James. 1997. *Routes: Travel and Translation in the Twentieth Century*. Cambridge, Mass.: Harvard University Press.

Comaroff, Jean, and John L. Comaroff, eds. 2001. *Millennial Capitalism: First Thoughts on a Second Coming*. Durham, N.C.: Duke University Press.

Condori, Carlos Mamami. 1989. "History and Prehistory in Bolivia: What about the Indians?" In *Conflict in the Archaeology of Living Traditions*, ed. R. Layton, 46–59. London: Unwin Hyman.

Conklin, Beth. 1997. "Body Paint, Feathers, and VCRs: Aesthetics and Authenticity in Amazonian Activism." *American Ethnologist* 24, no. 4: 711–37.

Connerton, Paul. 1989. *How Societies Remember*. Cambridge: Cambridge University Press.

Cook, David A. 1990. *A History of Narrative Film*. New York: W. W. Norton.

Coronil, Fernando. 1997. *The Magical State: Nature, Money, and Modernity in Venezuela*. Chicago: University of Chicago Press.

Crandon-Malamud, Libbet. 1991. *From the Fat of Our Souls: Social Change, Political Process, and Medical Pluralism in Bolivia*. Berkeley: University of California Press.

———. 1993. "Blessings of the Virgin in Capitalist Society: The Transformation of a Rural Bolivian Fiesta." *American Anthropologist* 95, no. 3: 574–96.

Crary, Jonathan. 1990. *Techniques of the Observer: On Vision and Modernity in the Nineteenth Century*. Cambridge, Mass.: MIT Press.

Crawford, Peter I., and Sigurjon Baldur Hafsteinson, eds. 1996. *The Construction of the Viewer: Media Ethnography and the Anthropology of Audiences*. Hojbjerg: Intervention Press.

Crawford, Peter Ian. 1992. "Film as Discourse: The Creation of Anthropological Realities." In *Film as Ethnography*, ed. P. I. Crawford and D. Turton, 66–84. Manchester: Manchester University Press.

Crofts, Stephen. 1993. "Reconceptualizing National Cinema/s." *Quarterly Review of Film and Video* 14, no. 3: 49–67.

Csordas, Thomas, ed. 1994. *Embodiment and Experience: The Existential Ground of Culture and Self*. Cambridge: Cambridge University Press.

Curtin, Michael. 2003. "Media Capital: Towards the Study of Spatial Flows." *International Journal of Cultural Studies* 6, no. 2: 202–28.

Dagron, Alfonso Gumucio. 1979. *Cine, Censura, y Exilio en América Latina*. La Paz: Ediciones Film/Historia.

———. 1982. *Historia del Cine en Bolivia*. La Paz: Editorial Los Amigos del Libro.

Dagron, Alfonso Gumucio, and Lupe Cajías. 1989. *Las Radios Mineras de Bolivia*. La Paz: CIMCA-UNESCO.

Dandler, Jorge, and Juan Torrico A. 1987. "From the National Indigenous Congress to the Ayopaya Rebellion: Bolivia 1945–1947." In *Resistance, Rebellion, and Consciousness in the Andean Peasant World, Eighteenth to Twentieth Centuries*, ed. S. J. Stern, 334–78. Madison: University of Wisconsin Press.

de Certeau, Michel. 1984. *The Practice of Everyday Life*. Berkeley: University of California Press.

de la Cadena, Marisol. 2000. *Indigenous Mestizos: The Politics of Race and Culture in Cuzco, 1919–1991*. Durham, N.C.: Duke University Press.

DeLanda, Manuel. 2006. *A New Philosophy of Society: Assemblage Theory and Social Complexity*. New York: Continuum.

Deleuze, Gilles. 1989. *Cinema 2: The Time-Image*. Minneapolis: University of Minnesota Press.

Deleuze, Gilles, and Félix Guattari. 1983 [1977]. *Anti-Oedipus: Capitalism and Schizophrenia*. Minneapolis: University of Minnesota Press.

Delgado-P., Guillermo. 1994. "Ethnic Politics and the Popular Movement." In *Latin America Faces the Twenty-First Century: Reconstructing a Social Justice Agenda*, ed. S. Jones and E. J. McCaughn, 77–88. Boulder, Colo.: Westview Press.

del Granado, Javier. 1989. *The Devil Is Dead: Democracy in Bolivia*. La Paz: Los Amigos del Libro.

Demelas, Marie-Daniele. 1981. "Darwinismo a la Criolla: El Darwinismo Social en Bolivia, 1880–1910." *Historia Boliviana* 1–2: 55–82.

Dickey, Sara. 1993. *Cinema and the Urban Poor in South India*. Cambridge: Cambridge University Press.

———. 1997. "Anthropology and Its Contributions to Studies of Mass Media." *International Social Science Journal* 49: 413–27.

Dirks, Nicholas B. 1990. "History as a Sign of the Modern." *Public Culture* 2, no. 2: 25–32.

Donaghue, Susanne Mary. 1987. *American Film Distribution: The Changing Marketplace*. Ann Arbor, Mich.: UMI Research Press.

Dornfeld, Barry. 1998. *Producing Public Television, Producing Public Culture*. Princeton, N.J.: Princeton University Press.

Dowell, Kristin L. 2006. "Honoring Stories: Aboriginal Media, Art, and Activism in Vancouver." Ph.D. dissertation, Department of Anthropology, New York University.

Edelman, M. 2001. "Social Movements: Changing Paradigms and Forms of Politics." *Annual Review of Anthropology* 30, no. 1: 285–317.

Eiss, Paul K. 2002. "Hunting for the Virgin: Meat, Money, and Memory in Tetiz, Yucatan." *Cultural Anthropology* 17, no. 3: 291–330.

Eitzen, Dirk. 1995. "When Is a Documentary? Documentary as a Mode of Reception." *Cinema Journal* 35, no. 1: 81–102.

Eley, Geoff. 1994. "Nations, Publics, and Political Cultures: Placing Habermas in the Nineteenth Century." In *Culture/Power/History: A Reader in Contemporary Social Theory*, ed. N. B. Dirks, G. Eley, and S. B. Ortner, 297–335. Princeton, N.J.: Princeton University Press.

Emirbayer, Mustafa, and Mimi Sheller. 1999. "Publics in History." *Theory and Society* 28: 145–97.

Espinal, Luis. 1982. *Historia del Cine*. Vol. 1. La Paz: Editorial Don Bosco.

Fabian, Johannes. 1983. *Time and the Other: How Anthropology Makes Its Object*. New York: Columbia University Press.

Faris, James C. 1992. "Anthropological Transparency: Film, Representation and Politics." In *Film as Ethnography*, ed. P. I. Crawford and D. Turton, 171–82. Manchester: Manchester University Press.

Feldman, Allen. 1993. "From Desert Storm to Rodney King via ex-Yugoslavia: On Cultural Anesthesia." In *The Senses Still: Perception and Memory as Material Culture in Modernity*, ed. C. N. Seremetakis, 87–107. Boulder, Colo.: Westview Press.

Ferguson, James. 1999. *Expectations of Modernity: Myths and Meanings of Urban Life on the Zambian Copperbelt*. Berkeley: University of California Press.

Fischer, Michael M. J. 2003. *Emergent Forms of Life and the Anthropological Voice*. Durham, N.C.: Duke University Press.

Flaxman, Gregor, ed. 2000. *The Brain Is the Screen*. Minneapolis: University of Minnesota Press.

Foster, Robert J. 1998. "Your Money, Our Money, the Government's Money: Finance and Fetishism in Melanesia." In *Border Fetishisms: Material Objects in Unstable Spaces*, ed. P. Spyer, 60–90. New York: Routledge.

Fox, Aaron A. 2004. *Real Country: Music and Language in Working-Class Culture*. Durham, N.C.: Duke University Press.

Fraser, Nancy. 1993. "Rethinking the Public Sphere: Toward a Critique of Actually Existing Democracy." In *The Phantom Public Sphere*, ed. B. Robbins, 1–32. Minneapolis: University of Minnesota Press.

Friedberg, Anne. 1993. *Window Shopping: Cinema and the Postmodern*. Berkeley: University of California Press.

Gaines, Jane. 1999. "Political Mimesis." In *Collecting Visible Evidence*, ed. J. Gaines and M. Renov, 84–102. Minneapolis: University of Minnesota Press.

Gaines, Jane, and Michael Renov, eds. 1999. *Collecting Visible Evidence*. Minneapolis: University of Minnesota Press.

Gal, Susan. 1995. "Language and the 'Arts of Resistance'." *Cultural Anthropology* 10, no. 3: 407–24.

Ganti, Tejaswini. 2002. "'And Yet My Heart Is Still Indian'; The Bombay Film Industry and the (H)Indianization of Hollywood." In *Media Worlds*, ed. F. D. Ginsburg, L. Abu-Lughod, and B. Larkin, 281–300. Berkeley: University of California Press.

Gaonkar, Dilip Parameshwar. 2002. "Toward New Imaginaries: An Introduction." *Public Culture* 14, no. 1: 1–19.

Gaonkar, Dilip Parameshwar, and Elizabeth A. Povinelli. 2003. "Technologies of Public Forms: Circulation, Transfiguration, Recognition." *Public Culture* 15, no. 3: 383–97.

García Canclini, Néstor. 1995. *Hybrid Cultures: Strategies for Entering and Leaving Modernity*. Minneapolis: University of Minnesota Press.

———. 2001. *Consumers and Citizens: Globalization and Multicultural Conflicts*. Minneapolis: University of Minnesota Press.

Gill, Lesley. 1994. *Precarious Dependencies: Gender, Class, and Domestic Service in Bolivia*. New York: Columbia University Press.

———. 1997. "Power Lines: The Political Context of Nongovernmental Organizations (NGO) Activity in El Alto, Bolivia." *Journal of Latin American Anthropology* 2, no. 2: 144–69.

———. 2000. *Teetering on the Rim: Global Restructuring, Daily Life, and the Armed Retreat of the Bolivian State*. New York: Columbia University Press.

Ginsburg, Faye. 1993. "Aboriginal Media and the Australian Imaginary." *Public Culture* 5, no. 3: 557–58.

———. 1994. "Culture/Media: A Mild Polemic." *Anthropology Today* 10, no. 2: 5–14.

———. 1995. "Production Values: Indigenous Media and the Rhetoric of Self-Determination." In *Rhetorics of Self-Making*, ed. D. Battaglia, 121–38. Berkeley: University of California Press.

———. 1997. "'From Little Things, Big Things Grow': Indigenous Media and Cultural Activism." In *Between Resistance and Revolution: Cultural Politics and Social Protest*, ed. R. G. Fox and O. Starn, 118–44. New Brunswick, N.J.: Rutgers University Press.

———. 1998. "Institutionalizing the Unruly: Charting a Future for Visual Anthropology." *Ethnos* 63, no. 2: 173–201.

———. 2002. "Screen Memories: Resignifying the Traditional in Indigenous Media." In *Media*

Worlds, ed. F. D. Ginsburg, L. Abu-Lughod, and B. Larkin, 39–57. Berkeley: University of California Press.

———. 2003. "Atanarjuat Off-Screen: From 'Media Reservations' to the World Stage." *American Anthropologist* 105, no. 4: 827–31.

Ginsburg, Faye D., Lila Abu-Lughod, and Brian Larkin. 2002a. Introduction to *Media Worlds: Anthropology on New Terrain*, ed. F. D. Ginsburg, L. Abu-Lughod, and B. Larkin, 1–36. Berkeley: University of California Press.

———, eds. 2002b. *Media Worlds: Anthropology on New Terrain*. Berkeley: University of California Press.

Goldstein, Daniel M. 2004. *The Spectacular City: Violence and Performance in Urban Bolivia*. Durham, N.C.: Duke University Press.

Graeber, David. 2001. *Toward an Anthropological Theory of Value: The False Coin of Our Own Dreams*. New York: Palgrave.

Grant, Bruce. 2001. "New Moscow Monuments, or States of Innocence." *American Ethnologist* 28, no. 2: 332–62.

Greishaber, Erwin P. 1985. "Fluctuaciones en la definición del Indio: Comparacion de los censos de 1900 y 1950." *Historia Boliviana* 1–2: 45–55.

Gugelberger, George M., ed. 1996. *The Real Thing: Testimonial Discourse and Latin America*. Durham, N.C.: Duke University Press.

Gunning, Tom. 1986. "The Cinema of Attraction: Early Film, Its Spectator and the Avant-Garde." *Wide Angle* 8, nos. 3–4: 63–70.

Gupta, Akhil. 1995. "Blurred Boundaries: The Discourse of Corruption, the Culture of Politics, and the Imagined State." *American Ethnologist* 22, no. 2: 375–402.

Gupta, Akhil, and James Ferguson, eds. 1997. *Anthropological Locations: Boundaries and Grounds of a Field Science*. Berkeley: University of California Press.

Guss, David. 2000. *The Festive State: Race, Ethnicity, and Nationalism as Cultural Performance*. Berkeley: University of California Press.

Hahn, Elizabeth. 1994. "The Tongan Tradition of Going to the Movies." *Visual Anthropology Review* 10, no. 1: 103–11.

Hale, R. Charles. 1997. "Cultural Politics of Identity in Latin America." *Annual Reviews in Anthropology* 26: 567–90.

———. 2005. "Neoliberal Multiculturalism: The Remaking of Cultural Rights and Racial Discourse in Central America." *PoLAR* 28, no. 1: 10–28.

Hall, Stuart. 1993 [1980]. Encoding and Decoding. In *The Cultural Studies Reader*, ed. S. During, 90–103. London: Routledge.

Hamilton, Annette. 1993. "Video Crackdown, or The Sacrificial Pirate: Censorship and Cultural Consequences in Thailand." *Public Culture* 5, no. 3: 515–31.

———. 2002. "The National Picture: Thai Media and Cultural Identity." In *Media Worlds*, ed. F. D. Ginsburg, L. Abu-Lughod, and B. Larkin, 152–70. Berkeley: University of California Press.

Hansen, Miriam. 1991. *Babel and Babylon: Spectatorship in America Silent Film*. Cambridge, Mass.: Harvard University Press.

Hardman, Martha James. 1988. "Jaqi Aru: La lengua humana." In *Raíces de América: El mundo Aymara*, ed. X. Albó, 155–205. Madrid: UNESCO.

Hardt, Michael. 1998. "The Withering of Civil Society." In *Deleuze and Guattari: New Mappings in Politics, Philosophy, and Culture*, ed. E. Kaufman and K. J. Heller, 23–39. Minneapolis: University of Minnesota Press.

Harris, Olivia. 1989. "The Earth and State: The Sources and Meanings of Money in Northern Potosí, Bolivia." In *Money and the Morality of Exchange*, ed. J. Parry and M. Bloch, 232–68. Cambridge: Cambridge University Press.

———. 1995. "Ethnicity and Market Relations: Indians and Mestizos in the Andes." In *Ethnicity, Markets, and Migration in the Andes*, ed. B. Larson and O. Harris, 352–90. Durham, N.C.: Duke University Press.

Harvey, David. 1985. "Money, Time, Space, and the City." *The Urban Experience*, 165–99. Oxford: Oxford University Press.

———. 1989. *The Condition of Postmodernity: An Enquiry into the Origins of Cultural Change*. Cambridge, Mass.: Blackwell.

Heath, Stephen. 1981. *Questions of Cinema*. Bloomington: Indiana University Press.

Herzfeld, Michael. 1992. *The Social Production of Indifference: Exploring the Symbolic Roots of Western Bureaucracy*. Chicago: University of Chicago Press.

Higson, Andrew. 1989. "The Concept of National Cinema." *Screen* 30, no. 4: 36–46.

Himpele, Jeff. 1996a. "Distributing Difference: The Distribution and Displacement of Media, Spectacle, and Identity in La Paz, Bolivia." Ph.D. dissertation, Princeton University.

———. 1996b. "Film Distribution as Media: Mapping Difference in the Bolivian Cinemascape." *Visual Anthropology Review* 12, no. 1: 47-66.

———. 2002. "Arrival Scenes: Complicity and Media Ethnography in the Bolivian Public Sphere." In *Media Worlds*, ed. F. Ginsburg, L. Abu-Lughod, and B. Larkin, 301–16. Berkeley: University of California Press.

———. 2003. "The Gran Poder Parade and the Social Movement of the Aymara Middle Class: A Video Essay." *Visual Anthropology* 16, nos. 2–3: 207–43.

———. 2004. "Packaging Indigenous Media: An Interview with Ivan Sanjínes and Jesús Tapia." *American Anthropologist* 106, no. 2: 354–63.

Himpele, Jeff, and Quetzil Castañeda. 1997. *Incidents of Travel in Chichén Itzá*: Watertown: Documentary Educational Resources.

Hjort, Mette. 2005. *Small Nation, Global Cinema*. Minneapolis: University of Minnesota Press.

Hjort, Mette, and Scott MacKenzie, eds. 2000. *Cinema and Nation*. New York: Routledge.

Hodgson, Dorothy L. 2002. "Introduction: Comparative Perspectives on the Indigenous Rights Movement in Africa and the Americas." *American Anthropologist* 104, no. 4: 1037–49.

Houston, Beverly. 1984. "Viewing Television: The Metapsychology of Endless Consumption." *Quarterly Review of Film Studies* 9, no. 3: 183–94.

Huesca, Robert. 1995. "Subject-Authored Theories of Media Practice: The Case of Bolivian Tin Miners' Radio." *Communication Studies* 46 (Fall-Winter): 149–68.

Hughes, Alex, and Suzanne Reimer, eds. 2004. *Geographies of Commodity Chains*. London: Routledge.

Hylton, Forrest, and Sinclair Thompson. 2005. "The Chequered Rainbow." *New Left Review* 35 (September–October): 2–26.

Jackson, Jean. 1994. "Chronic Pain and the Tension between Body as Subject and as Object." In *Embodiment and Experience: The Existential Ground of Culture and Self*, ed. T. Csordas, 201–28. Cambridge: Cambridge University Press.

Jameson, Fredric. 1984. "Postmodernism, or the Cultural Logic of Late Capitalism." *New Left Review* 144: 53–92.

———. 1986. "Third-World Literature in the Era of Multinational Capitalism." *Social Text* 15 (Fall): 65–88.

Johnson, Randal. 1987. *The Film Industry in Brazil: Culture and the State*. Pittsburgh: University of Pittsburgh Press.

———. 1993. "In the Belly of the Ogre: Cinema and the State in Latin America." In *Mediating Two Worlds: Cinematic Encounters in the Americas*, ed. J. King, A. M. López, and M. Alvarado, 204–13. London: British Film Institute.

Jonnes, Jill. 2004. *Empires of Light: Edison, Tesla, Westinghouse, and the Race to Electrify the World*. New York: Random House.

Katz, Elihu. 1977. "Can Authentic Cultures Survive New Media?" *Journal of Communication* (Spring): 113–21.

Kavlin, Marcos. 1958. "Historia del cine y su desarrollo nacional." *Khana* 2, nos. 31–32: 192–205.

Keane, Webb. 1997. *Signs of Recognition: Powers and Hazards of Representation in an Indonesian Society*. Berkeley: University of California Press.

———. 2003. "Semiotics and the Social Analysis of Material Things." *Language and Communication* 23, no. 3–4: 409–25.

Kelly, John D. 1992. "Fiji Indians and 'Commoditization of Labor.'" *American Ethnologist* 19, no. 1: 97–120.

Kelly, John D., and Martha Kaplan. 2001. *Represented Communities: Fiji and World Decolonization*. Chicago: University of Chicago Press.

King, John. 1990. *Magical Reels: A History of Cinema in Latin America*. London: Verso.

Kittler, Friedrich A. 1999. *Gramophone, Film, Typewriter*. Stanford, Calif.: Stanford University Press.

Klein, Herbert S. 1992. *Bolivia: The Evolution of a Multi-Ethnic Society*. New York: Oxford University Press.

Kleinman, Arthur, and Joan Kleinman. 1997. "The Appeal of Experience, the Dismay of Images: Cultural Appropriation of Suffering in Our Times." In *Social Suffering*, ed. A. Kleinman, V. Das, and M. Lock, 1–23. Berkeley: University of California Press.

Kopytoff, Igor. 1986. "The Cultural Biography of Things: Commoditization as Process." In *The Social Life of Things: Commodities in Cultural Perspective*, ed. A. Appadurai, 64–95. Cambridge: Cambridge University Press.

Laclau, Ernesto and Chantal Mouffe. 1985. *Hegemony and Socialist Strategy*. London: Routledge.

Lagos, Maria L. 1993. "'We Have to Learn to Ask:' Hegemony, Diverse Experiences, and Antagonistic Meanings in Bolivia." *American Ethnologist* 20, no. 1: 52–71.

Larkin, Brian. 1998–99. "Theaters of the Profane: Cinema and Colonial Urbanism." *Visual Anthropology Review* 14, no. 2: 46–62.

———. 2002. "The Materiality of Cinema Theaters in Northern Nigeria." In *Media Worlds*, ed. F. D. Ginsburg, L. Abu-Lughod, and B. Larkin, 319–36. Berkeley: University of California Press.

———. 2004. "Degraded Images: Nigerian Video and the Infrastructure of Piracy." *Public Culture* 16, no. 2: 289–314.

Larson, Neil. 1995. *Reading North by South: On Latin American Literature, Culture, and Politics.* Minneapolis: University of Minnesota Press.

Latour, Bruno. 1993. *We Have Never Been Modern.* Cambridge, Mass.: Harvard University Press.

Lazarte, Jorge. 1993. *Bolivia: Certezas e incertidumbres de la democracia: Problemas de Representación y Reforma Política.* La Paz: ILDIS and Los Amigos del Libro.

Lee, Benjamin. 1993. "Going Public." *Public Culture* 5, no. 2: 165–78.

Lee, Benjamin, and Edward LiPuma. 2002. "Cultures of Circulation: The Imaginations of Modernity." *Public Culture* 14, no. 1: 191–213.

Lefebvre, Henri. 1991. *The Production of Space.* Trans. D. Nicholson-Smith. Oxford: Blackwell.

Liechty, Mark. 1996. "Kathmandu as Translocality: Multiple Places in a Nepali Space." In *The Geography of Identity*, ed. P. Yaeger, 98–130. Ann Arbor: University of Michigan Press.

———. 2002. *Suitably Modern: Making Middle-Class Culture in a New Consumer Society.* Princeton: Princeton University Press.

LiPuma, Edward, and Thomas Koelble. 2005. "Cultures of Circulation and the Urban Imaginary: Miami as Example and Exemplar." *Public Culture* 17, no. 1: 153–79.

Lomnitz, Claudio. 2002. *Deep Mexico, Silent Mexico: An Anthropology of Nationalism.* Minneapolis: University of Minnesota Press.

López, Ana M. 2000a. "Early Cinema and Modernity in Latin America." *Cinema Journal* 40, no. 1: 48–78.

———. 2000b. "Crossing Nations and Genres: Traveling Filmmakers." In *Visible Nations: Latin American Cinema and Video*, ed. C. A. Noriega, 33–50. Minneapolis: University of Minnesota Press.

Lowe, Lisa, and David Lloyd. 1997. *The Politics of Culture in the Shadow of Capital.* Durham, N.C.: Duke University Press.

MacDougall, David. 1998. *Transcultural Cinema.* Princeton, N.J.: Princeton University Press.

Mallon, Florencia E. 1983. *The Defense of Community in Peru's Central Highlands: Peasant Struggle and Capitalist Transition, 1860–1940.* Princeton, N.J.: Princeton University Press.

Mankekar, Purnima. 1999. *Screening Culture, Viewing Politics: An Ethnography of Television, Womanhood, and Nation in Postcolonial India.* Durham, N.C.: Duke University Press.

Mannheim, Bruce, and Dennis Tedlock. 1995. Introduction. *The Dialogic Emergence of Culture*, ed. D. Tedlock and B. Mannheim, 1–32. Urbana: University of Illinois Press.

Marcus, George. 1994. "The Modernist Sensibility in Recent Ethnographic Writing and the Cinematic Metaphor of Montage." In *Visualizing Theory: Selected Essays from V.A.R., 1990–1994*, ed. L. Taylor, 37–52. New York: Routledge.

———. 1998. "The Uses of Complicity and Changing Mise-en-Scène of Anthropological Fieldwork." In *Ethnography through Thick and Thin*, 105–31. Princeton, N.J.: Princeton University Press.

Marcus, George E., ed. 1992. *Rereading Cultural Anthropology.* Durham, N.C.: Duke University Press.

Marcus, George E., and Fred R. Myers, eds. 1995. *The Traffic in Culture: Refiguring Art and Anthropology.* Berkeley: University of California Press.

Marks, Laura. 2000. *The Skin of the Film: Intercultural Cinema, Embodiment, and the Senses.* Durham, N.C.: Duke University Press.

Martín-Barbero, Jesús. 1988. "Communication from Culture: The Crisis of the National and the Emergence of the Popular." *Media, Culture and Society* 10: 447–65.

———. 1993. *Communication, Culture and Hegemony: From the Media to Mediations.* Trans. R. A. White. London: Sage Publications.

———. 2000. "Transformations in the Map." *Latin American Perspectives* 27, no. 4: 27–48.

Marx, Karl. 1978. *The Marx-Engels Reader*, ed. R. C. Tucker. New York: W. W. Norton.

Masiello, Francine. 2001. *The Art of Transition: Latin American Culture and Neoliberal Crisis.* Durham, N.C.: Duke University Press.

Mattelart, Armand. 1994. *Mapping World Communication: War, Progress, Culture.* Minneapolis: University of Minnesota Press.

Mattingly, Cheryl. 1998. *Healing Dramas and Clinical Plots: The Narrative Structure of Experience.* Cambridge: Cambridge University Press.

Mayorga, René Antonio. 1995. *Antipolítica y Neopopulismo.* La Paz: CEBEM.

McDermott, R. P., and Henry Tylbor. 1995. "On the Necessity of Collusion in Conversation." In *The Dialogic Emergence of Culture*, ed. B. Mannheim and D. Tedlock, A218–36. Urbana: University of Illinois Press.

Medina, Javier. 1992. *Repensar Bolivia: Cicatrices de un Viaje a Sí Mismo, 1972–1992.* La Paz: HISBOL.

Melucci, Alberto. 1988. "Social Movements and the Democratization of Everyday Life." In *Civil Society and the State*, ed. J. Keane, 245–60. London: Verso.

Mesa Gisbert, Carlos d. 1985. *La Aventura del Cine Boliviano*. La Paz: Editorial Gisbert.

——, ed. 1979. *Cine Boliviano: Del Realizador al Critico*. La Paz: Editorial Gisbert.

Michaels, Eric. 1994. *Bad Aboriginal Art: Tradition, Media, and Technological Horizons*. Minneapolis: University of Minnesota Press.

Miller, Daniel. 1992. "The Young and the Restless in Trinidad: A Case of the Local and the Global in Mass Consumption." In *Consuming Technologies: Media and Information in Domestic Spaces*, ed. R. Silverstone and E. Hirsch, 163–82. London: Routledge.

——, ed. 1998. *Material Cultures: Why Some Things Matter*. Chicago: University of Chicago Press.

Miller, Toby, Nitin Govil, John McMurria, Richard Maxwell, and Ting Wang. 2005. *Global Hollywood 2*. London: British Film Institute.

Mitchell, Timothy. 1991. "The Limits of the State: Beyond Statist Approaches and Their Critics." *American Political Science Review* 85, no. 1: 77–96.

Montenegro, Carlos. 1944. *Nacionalismo y Coloniaje*. La Paz: Editorial Juventud.

Moreiras, Alberto. 2001. *The Exhaustion of Difference: The Politics of Latin American Studies*. Durham, N.C.: Duke University Press.

Morley, David, 1993. "Active Audience Theory: Pendulums and Pitfalls." *Journal of Communication* 43, no. 4: 13–19.

Morris, David B. 1997. "About Suffering: Voice, Genre, and Moral Community." In *Social Suffering*, ed. A. Kleinman, V. Das, and M. Lock, 25–45. Berkeley: University of California Press.

Morris, Meaghan. 1990. "Banality in Cultural Studies." In *Logics of Television: Essays in Cultural Criticism*, ed. P. Mellencamp, 14–43. Bloomington: Indiana University Press.

Myers, Fred R. 2001a. "Introduction: The Empire of Things." *The Empire of Things: Regimes of Value and Material Culture*. Santa Fe, N.M.: School of American Research Press.

——, ed. 2001b. *The Empire of Things: Regimes of Value and Material Culture*. Santa Fe, N.M.: School of American Research Press.

——. 2002. *Painting Culture: The Making of an Aboriginal High Art*. Durham, N.C.: Duke University Press.

——. 2004. "Ontologies of the Image and Economies of Exchange." *American Ethnologist* 31, no. 1: 5–20.

Naficy, Hamid. 1993. *The Making of Exile Cultures: Iranian Television in Los Angeles*. Minneapolis: University of Minnesota Press.

——. 2001. *An Accented Cinema: Exilic and Diasporic Filmmaking*. Princeton, N.J.: Princeton University Press.

Nash, June, 1979. *We Eat the Mines and the Mines Eat Us: Dependency and Exploitation in Bolivian Tin Mines*. New York: Columbia University Press.

——. 1992. "Interpreting Social Movements: Bolivian Resistance to Economic Conditions Imposed by the International Monetary Fund." *American Ethnologist* 19, no. 2: 275–93.

Navaro-Yashin, Yael. 2002. *Faces of the State: Secularism and Public Life in Turkey*. Princeton, N.J.: Princeton University Press.

Nichols, Bill. 1991. *Representing Reality*. Bloomington: Indiana University Press.

——. 1994. *Blurred Boundaries: Questions of Meaning in Contemporary Culture*. Bloomington: Indiana University Press.

Noriega, Chon, ed. 2000. *Visible Nations: Latin American Cinema and Video*. Minneapolis: University of Minnesota Press.

Oakdale, Suzanne. 2004. "The Culture-Conscious Brazilian Indian: Representing and Reworking Indianness in Kayabi Political Discourse." *American Ethnologist* 31, no. 1: 60–75.

Ong, Aihwa, and Stephen J. Collier. 2005. "Global Assemblages, Anthropological Problems." In *Global Assemblages: Technology, Politics, and Ethics as Anthropological Problems*, ed. A. Ong and S. J. Collier, 3–21. Malden, Mass.: Blackwell.

Orta, Andrew. 2001. "Remembering the Ayllu, Remaking the Nation: Indigenous Scholarship and Activism in the Bolivian Andes." *Journal of Latin American Anthropology* 6, no. 1: 198–201.

Pacheco Balanza, Diego. 1992. "Politica Aymara Contemporanea." *Textos Antropologicos* 4: 51–73.

Page, Joanna. 2005. "The Nation as the Mise-en-Scène of Film-Making in Argentina." *Journal of Latin American Cultural Studies* 14, no. 3: 306–24.

Palus, Matthew M. 2005. "Building an Architecture of Power: Electricity in Annapolis, Maryland in the Nineteenth and Twentieth Centuries." In *Archaeologies of Materiality*, ed. L. Meskell, 162–89. Malden, Mass.: Blackwell .

Peters, John Durham. 1997. "Seeing Bifocally: Media, Place, Culture." In *Culture, Power, Place: Explorations in Critical Anthropology*, ed. A. Gupta and J. Ferguson, 75–92. Durham, N.C.: Duke University Press.

Peterson, Mark Allen. 2003. *Anthropology and Mass Communication*. New York: Berghan.

Philips, Lynne, ed. 1998. *The Third Wave of Modernization in Latin America*. Wilmington, Del.: Scholarly Resources.

Pick, Zuzana. 1993. *The New Latin American Cinema: A Continental Project*. Austin: University of Texas Press.

Pike, Robert, and Dwayne Winseck. 2004. "The Politics of Global Media Reform, 1907–23." *Media, Culture and Society* 26, no. 5: 643–75.

Platinga, Carl. 1991. "The Mirror Framed: A Case for Expression in Documentary." *Wide Angle* 13, no. 2: 40–53.

Platt, Tristan. 1982. *Estado Boliviano y Ayllu Andino: Tierra y Tributo en El Norte de Potosí*. Lima: Instituto de Estudios Peruanos.

———. 1987. "The Andean Experience of Bolivian Liberalism." In *Resistance, Rebellion, and Consciousness in the Andean Peasant World, 18th to 20th Centuries*, ed. S. J. Stern, 280–323. Madison, University of Wisconsin Press.

———. 1993. "Simón Bolivar, the Sun of Justice, and the Amerindian Virgin: Andean Conceptions of the 'Patria' in Nineteenth-Century Potosí." *Journal of Latin American Studies* 25: 159–85.

Polanyi, Karl. 1944. *The Great Transformation: The Political and Economic Origins of Our Time*. Boston: Beacon Press.

Ponce Sanginés, Carlos. 1981 [1972]. *Tiwanaku: Espacio, Tiempo, y Cultura*. 4th ed. La Paz: Los Amigos del Libro.

Poole, Deborah. 1997. *Vision, Race and Modernity*. Princeton, N.J.: Princeton University Press.

Postero, Nancy. 2005. "Indigenous Responses to Neoliberalism: A Look at the Bolivian Uprising of 2003." *PoLAR: Political and Legal Anthropology Review* 28, no. 1: 73–92.

Prins, Harald E. L. 2002. "Visual Media and the Primitivist Perplex: Colonial Fantasies, Indigenous Imagination, and Advocacy in North America." In *Media Worlds*, ed. F. D. Ginsburg, L. Abu-Lughod, and B. Larkin, 58–74. Berkeley: University of California Press.

Radcliffe, Sarah, and Sallie Westwood. 1996. *Remaking the Nation: Place, Identity, and Politics in Latin America*. London: Routledge.

Radway, Janice. 1988. "Reception Study: Ethnography and the Problems of Dispersed Audiences and Nomadic Subjects." *Cultural Studies* 2, no. 3: 359–76.

Rama, Angel. 1996. *The Lettered City*. Durham, N.C.: Duke University Press.

Ramos, Alcida. R. 1994. "The Hyperreal Indian." *Critique of Anthropology* 14, no. 2: 153–71.

Rasnake, Roger. 1988. *Domination and Cultural Resistance: Authority and Power among an Andean People*. Durham, N.C.: Duke University Press.

Richards, Keith John. 2005. "Bolivian Oblivion: National Allegory and Teleology in Sci-Fi and Futurism from the High Andes, Mauricio Calderon's *El Triangulo Del Lago* (1999) and Spedding's *De Cuando en Cuando Saturnina* (2004)." *Journal of Latin American Cultural Studies* 14, no. 2: 195–209.

Rivandeneira Prada, Raúl. 1988. "Bolivian Television: When Reality Surpasses Fiction." In *Media and Politics in Latin America: The Struggle for Democracy*, ed. E. Fox, 164–70. London: Sage.

———. 1991. *Diagnóstico de la Incomunicación en Bolivia*. La Paz: Signa.

Rivadeneira Prada, Raúl, and Nazario Tirado Cuenca. 1986. *La Televisión en Bolivia*. La Paz: Editorial Quipus.

Rivera Cusicanqui, Silvia. 1990. "Ayllu Democracy and Liberal Democracy in Bolivia: The Case of Northern Potosí." *Journal of Development Studies* 26, no. 4: 97–121.

———. 1993. "La Raiz: Colonizadores y Colonizados." In *Violencias Encubiertas en Bolivia*, ed. X. Albó and R. Barrios, 27–141. La Paz: Ediciones Aruwiyiri.

Rivero Pinto, Wigberto, and Ives Encinas Cueto. 1991. "La presencia Aimara en la Ciudad de La Paz, Chuquiyawu Marka: Entre la participación y la sobrevivencia." *América Indígena* 51, nos. 2–3: 272–92.

Robbins, Bruce, ed. 1993. *The Phantom Public Sphere*. Minneapolis: University of Minnesota Press.

Rogers, Mark, ed. 1998. "Performance, Identity and Historical Consciousness in the Andes." Special issue of the *Journal of Latin American Anthropology* 3, no. 2.

Rowe, William, and Vivian Schelling. 1991. *Memory and Modernity: Popular Culture in Latin America*. London: Verso.

Ruoff, Jeffrey, ed. 2006. *Virtual Voyages: Cinema and Travel*. Durham, N.C.: Duke University Press.

Sahlins, Marshall. 1994. "Cosmologies of Capitalism: The Transpacific Sector of 'The World System.'" In *Culture/Power/History: A Reader in Contemporary Social Theory*, ed. N. B. Dirks, G. Eley, and S. B. Ortner, 412–55. Princeton, N.J.: Princeton University Press.

Sanchez-H., Jose. 1999. *The Art and Politics of Bolivian Cinema*. Lanham, Md.: Scarecrow Press.

Sanjinés, Javier. 1992. "Crisis de Motivación Socio-cultural: Introducción al Tema." In *Diversidad Etnica y Cultural*, ed. C. F. T. Roca, 75–89. La Paz: ILDIS.

———. 1996. "Beyond Testimonial Discourse." In *The Real Thing: Testimonial Discourse and Latin America*, ed. G. M. Gugelberger, 245–65. Durham, N.C.: Duke University Press.

———. 2004. *Mestizaje Upside-Down: Aesthetic Politics in Modern Bolivia*. Pittsburgh: University of Pittsburgh Press.

Sanjinés, Jorge. 1979. *Teoría y Práctica de un Cine Junto al Pueblo*. Mexico City: Siglo Ventiuno Editores.

———. 1986. "Revolutionary Cinema: The Bolivian Experience." In *Cinema and Social Change in Latin America*, ed. J. Burton, 35–47. Austin: University of Texas Press.

Scarry, Elayne. 1985. *The Body in Pain: The Making and Unmaking of the World*. New York: Oxford University Press.

Schein, Louisa. 2002. "Mapping Hmong Media in Diasporic Space." In *Media Worlds*, ed. F. D. Ginsburg, L. Abu-Lughod, and B. Larkin, 229–44. Berkeley: University of California Press.

Schelling, Vivian. 2000. "Introduction: Reflections on the Experience of Modernity in Latin America." In *Through the Kaleidoscope: The Experience of Modernity in Latin America*, ed. V. Schelling, 1–33. London: Verso.

Schivelbush, Wolfgang. 1986. *The Railway Journey: The Industrialization of Time and Space in the Nineteenth Century*. Berkeley: University of California Press.

Scott, James. 1976. *The Moral Economy of the Peasant: Rebellion and Resistance in Southeast Asia*. New Haven, Conn.: Yale University Press.

———. 1990. *Domination and the Arts of Resistance: Hidden Transcripts*. New Haven, Conn.: Yale University Press.

Seligmann, Linda J. 1993. "To Be in Between: The Cholas as Market Women." In *Constructing Culture and Power in Latin America*, ed. D. H. Levine, 267–310. Ann Arbor: University of Michigan Press.

———. 2004. *Peruvian Street Lives: Culture, Power, and Economy among Market Women of Cuzco*. Champaign-Urbana: University of Illinois Press.

Seltzer, Mark. 1997. "Wound Culture: Trauma in the Pathological Public Sphere." *October* 80: 3–26.

Shattuc, Jane M. 1997. *The Talking Cure: TV Talk Shows and Women*. London: Routledge.

Simis, Anita. 2002. "Movies and Moviemakers under Vargas." *Latin American Perspectives* 29, no. 1: 106–14.

Simmel, Georg. 1990. [1900]. *The Philosophy of Money*. London: Routledge.

Sinclair, John. 1996. "Mexico, Brazil, and the Latin World." In *New Patterns in Global Television*, ed. J. Sinclair, E. Jacka, and S. Cunningham, 33–66. Oxford: Oxford University Press.

Singer, Beverly. 2001. *Wiping the War Paint off the Lens: Native American Film and Video*. Minneapolis: University of Minnesota Press.

Smith, Neil. 2004. *American Empire: Roosevelt's Geographer and the Prelude to Globalization*. Berkeley: University of California Press.

Sommer, Doris. 1990. "Irresistible Romance: The Foundational Fictions of Latin America." In *Nation and Narration*, ed. H. K. Bhabha, 71–98. New York: Routledge.

Spitulnik, Debra. 1993. "Anthropology and Mass Media." *Annual Reviews of Anthropology* 22: 293–315.

———. 2002. "Mobile Machines and Fluid Audiences: Rethinking Reception through Zambian Radio Culture." In *Media Worlds*, ed. F. Ginsburg, L. Abu-Lughod, and B. Larkin, 337–54. Berkeley: University of California Press.

Spyer, Patricia. 1998. *Border Fetishisms: Material Objects in Unstable Spaces*. New York: Routledge.

Sreberny-Mohammadi, Annabelle, and Ali Mohammadi. 1994. *Small Media, Big Revolution: Communication, Culture, and the Iranian Revolution*. Minneapolis: University of Minnesota Press.

Stead, Peter. 1989. *Film and the Working Class: The Feature Film in British and American Society*. London: Routledge.

Stephenson, Marcia. 2002. "Forging an Indigenous Counterpublic Sphere: The Taller de Historia Oral Andina in Bolivia." *Latin American Research Review* 37, no. 2: 99–118.

Stern, Steve J., ed. 1987. *Resistance, Rebellion, and Consciousness in the Andean Peasant World, 18th to 20th Centuries*. Madison: University of Wisconsin Press.

Susz, Pedro. 1985. *La Pantalla Ajena: El Cine que Vimos, 1975–1984*. La Paz: Editorial Gisbert.

———. 1990. *La Campaña del Chaco: El Ocaso del Cine Silente Boliviano*. La Paz: Universidad Mayor de San Andres and ILDIS.

Taussig, Michael. 1987. *The Devil and Commodity Fetishism in South America*. Chapel Hill: University of North Carolina Press.

Taylor, Charles. 2002. "Modern Social Imaginaries." *Public Culture* 14, no. 1: 91–124.

Taylor, Lucien. 1996. "Iconophobia: How Anthropology Lost It at the Movies." *Transitions* 6, no. 69: 64–88.

Thomas, Nicholas. 1991. *Entangled Objects: Exchange, Material Culture, and Colonialism in the Pacific*. Cambridge, Mass.: Harvard University Press.

Thompson, E. P. 1966 [1963]. *The Making of the English Working Class*. New York: Vintage.

Thompson, Sinclair. 2002. *We Alone Will Rule: Native Andean Politics in the Age of Insurgency*. Madison: University of Wisconsin Press.

Tomlinson, John. 1991. *Cultural Imperialism*. London: Routledge.

Trouillot, Michel-Rolph. 2000. "The Anthropology of the State in the Age of Globalization." *Current Anthropology* 42, no. 1: 125–38.

Tsing, Anna. 2000. "The Global Situation." *Cultural Anthropology* 15, no. 3: 327–60.

———. 2005. *Friction: An Ethnography of Global Connection*. Princeton, N.J.: Princeton University Press.

Turner, Terence. 1991. "Representing, Resisting, Rethinking: Historical Transformations of Kayapo Culture and Consciousness." In *Colonial Situations: Essays on the Contextualization of Ethnographic Knowledge*, ed. G. W. Stocking Jr., 285–313. Madison: University of Wisconsin Press.

———. 1992. "Defiant Images: The Kayapo Appropriation of Video." *Anthropology Today* 8, no. 6: 5–16.

———. 1993. "Anthropology and Multiculturalism: What Is Anthropology That Multiculturalists Should Be Mindful of It?" *Cultural Anthropology* 8, no. 4: 411–29.

———. 2002a. "Representation, Politics, and Cultural Imagination in Indigenous Video: General Points and Kayapo Examples." In *Media Worlds*, ed. F. D. Ginsburg, L. Abu-Lughod, and B. Larkin, 75–89. Berkeley: University of California Press.

———. 2002b. "Representation, Polyphony, and the Construction of Power in a Kayapo Video." In *Indigenous Movements, Self-Representation, and the State in Latin America*, ed. K. B. Warren and J. Jackson, 229–50. Austin: University of Texas Press.

———. n.d. "Indigenous and Culturalist Movements in the Contemporary Global Conjuncture." Unpublished manuscript.

Urban, Greg. 2001. *Metaculture: How Culture Moves through the World*. Minneapolis: University of Minnesota Press.

Urla, Jacqueline. 1997. "Outlaw Language: Creating Alternative Public Spheres in Basque Free Radio." In *The Politics of Culture in the Shadow of Capital*, ed. L. Lowe and D. Lloyd, 280–300. Durham, N.C.: Duke University Press.

Usabel, Suzanne. 1982. *The High Noon of American Films in Latin America*. Ann Arbor, Mich.: UMI Research Press.

Valdivia, José Antonio. 1998. *Testigo de la Realidad: Jorge Ruiz: Memorias del Cine Documental Boliviano*. La Paz: Cinemateca Boliviana and CONACINE.

Van Cott, Dorothy Lee, ed. 1994. *Indigenous Peoples and Democracy in Latin America*. New York: St. Martin's Press.

Wachtel, Nathan. 1994. *Gods and Vampires: Return to Chipaya*. Trans. C. Volk. Chicago: University of Chicago Press.

Wang, Shujen. 2003. "Recontextualizing Copyright: Piracy, Hollywood, the State, and Globalization." *Cinema Journal* 43, no. 1: 25–43.

Warner, Michael. 2002. "Public and Counterpublics." *Public Culture* 14, no. 1: 49–90.

Warren, Kay B. 1998. *Indigenous Movements and their Critics: Pan-Maya Activism in Guatemala*. Princeton, N.J.: Princeton University Press.

Warren, Kay, and Jean Jackson, eds. 2002. *Indigenous Movements, Self-Representation and the State in Latin America*. Austin: University of Texas Press.

Weatherford, Elizabeth. 1990. "Native Visions: The Growth of Indigenous Media." *Aperture* 119: 58–61.

Weiner, Annette B. 1992. *Inalienable Possessions: The Paradox of Keeping-While-Giving*. Berkeley: University of California Press.

Weiner, James F. 1997. "Televisualist Anthropology: Representation, Aesthetics, Politics." *Current Anthropology* 38, no. 2: 197–235.

Weismantel, Mary. 2001. *Cholas and Pishtacos: Stories of Race and Sex in the Andes*. Chicago: University of Chicago Press.

Wilk, Richard R. 2002. "Television, Time, and the National Imaginary in Belize." In *Media Worlds*, ed. F. D. Ginsburg, L. Abu-Lughod, and B. Larkin, 171–88. Berkeley: University of California Press.

Willeman, Paul. 1995. "The National." In *Fields of Vision: Essays in Film Studies, Visual Anthropology, and Photography*, ed. L. Devereaux and R. Hillman, 21–34. Berkeley: University of California Press.

Williams, Brackett F. 1989. "A Class Act: Anthropology and the Race to Nation across Ethnic Terrain." *Annual Reviews in Anthropology* 18: 401–44.

Williams, Garth. 2002. *The Other Side of the Popular: Neoliberalism and Subalternity in Latin America*. Durham, N.C.: Duke University Press.

Williams, Mark. 1999. "History in a Flash." In *Collecting Visible Evidence*, ed. J. M. Gaines and M. Renov, 292–312. Minneapolis: University of Minnesota Press.

Wilson, Clint C., and Félix Gutiérrez. 1985. *Minorities and the Media: Diversity and the End of Mass Communication*. Beverly Hills: Sage Publications.

Winston, Brian. 1996. *Technologies of Seeing: Photography, Cinematography and Television.* London: British Film Institute.

Wittel, Andreas. 2001. "Toward a Network Sociality." *Theory, Culture and Society* 18, no. 6: 51–76.

Wortham, Erica Cusi. 2002. "Narratives of Location: Televisual Media and the Production of Indigenous Identities in Mexico." Ph.D. Dissertation, Department of Anthropology, New York University, New York.

———. 2004. "Between the State and Indigenous Autonomy: Unpacking Video Indigena in Mexico." *American Anthropologist* 106, no. 2: 363–68.

Xavier, Ismael, 1997. *Allegories of Underdevelopment: Aesthetics and Politics in Modern Brazilian Cinema.* Minneapolis: University of Minnesota Press.

Yaeger, Patricia. 1996. "Introduction: Narrating Space." In *The Geography of Identity,* ed. P. Yaeger, 1–38. Ann Arbor: University of Michigan Press.

Yang, Mayfair Mai-hui. 1997. "Mass Media and Transnational Subjectivity in Shanghai: Notes on (Re)Cosmopolitanism in a Chinese Metropolis." In *Ungrounded Empires: The Cultural Politics of Modern Chinese Transnationalism,* ed. A. Ong and D. M. Nonini, 287–319. New York: Routledge.

Yashar, Deborah. 1999. "Democracy, Indigenous Movements, and the Postliberal Challenge in Latin America." *World Politics* 52: 76–104.

———. 2005. *Contesting Citizenship in Latin America: The Rise of Indigenous Movements and the Postliberal Challenge in Latin America.* Cambridge: Cambridge University Press.

Young, Allan. 1993. "A Description of How Ideology Shapes Knowledge of a Mental Disorder (Posttraumatic Stress Disorder)." In *Knowledge, Power, and Practice,* ed. S. Lindendbaum and M. Lock, 108–28. Berkeley: University of California Press.

Yúdice, George. 1996. "Testimonio and Postmodernism." In *The Real Thing: Testimonial Discourse and Latin America,* ed. G. M. Gugelberger, 42–57. Durham, N.C.: Duke University Press.

Yúdice, George, Jean Franco, and Juan Flores, eds. 1992. *On Edge: The Crisis of Contemporary Latin American Culture.* Minneapolis: University of Minnesota Press.

Žižek, Slavoj. 1997. *The Plague of Fantasies.* London: Verso.

Index

Coronil, Fernando, 219n3
Courage of the People, The (Sanjinés, 1971), 128–31, 193
Crandon-Malamud, Libbet, 159
Crawford, Peter, 169
Crofts, Stephen, 217n1
CSCB (Bolivian Settlers Syndicate Confederation), 200
CSUTCB (Bolivian Rural Workers Sole Syndicate), 200
cultural alienation, 59
cultural media, Bolivian, xvii
cultural strategies, 158–60
culture: films spatializing, 122–23; mobility of, 14; representation and, xvi, 12
culture of circulation: dynamics of, 24; interface in, 25; as mediation, 13–14; performance of, 15; significance of, xx–xxii; social imaginary in, 23–25; study of, 14–16; as urban imaginary, 48–49, 215n1
Cursed Gold (2002), 199

Dagron, Alfonso Gumucio, 18, 99–100, 109
dance fraternities, 1
de Certeau, Michel, 48–49, 51
Decree 21060, 138
Defense Committees *(Open Tribunal)*, 142, 221n8
Deleuze, Gilles, 95, 209–10, 218n8; and Félix Guattari, 215n3
Democratic and Popular Unity (Unidad Democrática y Popular, UDP), 138–39, 221n1
de pollera, 34
devil, Andean, 213n1
Diablada (devil's dance), 2, 6–8
Diario, El (newspaper), 101, 105
Dirks, Nick, 107
Dogma 95 (Danish film movement), 62
Dornfeld, Barry, 13, 32, 152
double bind of certainty and advocacy, 184–85
Dracula (Coppola, 1993): distribution in La Paz, 41–46, 57–58; pirated copies of, 42
Dracula (Fisher, 1958), 113, 115–16
drug war, U.S., 138, 194–95, 198

economic metaphors, 208, 223n3
economic reforms, 138, 194–95
Eguino, Antonio, 214n5
Eiss, Paul K., 213n4
Eley, Geoff, 162
Environmental Film Festival, 186, 212
Ernst, Raul, 100
ethnic movements: emergence of, xv
ethnography of media: anthropology and, 152; convergence with media producers, 32–33; knowledge available in films, 169–70; materialities in, 170–71, 223n4; matrix of, 28–33
event: audience as, 25, 35, 63–64, 71–72, 221n3; cinema as, 71, 88, 90, 95; cities as, 216n8; exchange as, 215n5; film festivals as, 201; linguistic communication as, 154; narratives and, 51; *Open Tribunal* cases as, 181; television and, 167, 176; theaters as, 51; viewing film as, 130. *See also* assemblage

exchange: of agency, 155; at box office, 25, 215n5; circulation and, 213n4; as event, 215n5; mediated, 31; money and, 218n15; as ritual on *Open Tribunal*, 156, 158, 161, 177, 185, 194; of surplus wealth, 208; social networks and, xx, 25, 76, 208
exhibitionary complex, 63
Eye of the Condor video tour. *See* Ojo de Condor video tour

fantasy. *See* modernity fantasies
fat: cultural significance of, 208
Fernandez, Max, 141
fictive kinship *(compadrazgo)*, xxi, 34–35, 158–59
film distribution: as active medium, 47; block booking, 73; in Bolivia, 21; circularity in, 51–52, 215n5; city as film festival, 61–64; consolidation of, 216n6; distributors as intermediaries, 47; *Dracula*, 41–46; economics of, 53; genres and publics for, 59–61; Hollywood films, 59–60, 70, 73–74; itineraries of, 46–47, 50–51, 89, 90; "Llama de Plata" award for, 63; as media, 22–23, 46–52; mobility of films, 48–49; narrative paths of, 24, 48–51, 62; post–World War I, 70; post–World War II, 73–74; publics of circulation and, 24–25, 50; social imagination and, 52–56; social stratification of audiences, 47–48, 52–54, 56–58; spatial practices in, 48–49; subtitles and, 60–61; synchronous film debuts, 88–90; trajectories of, 23, 81, 83–84
film exhibition, 66, 98
film festivals: city as, 61–64; as events, 201; First Nations/First Features Festival, 37, 197, 201; Indigenous Peoples' Film and Video Festivals, 201; "Llama de Plata," 63; Native American Film and Video Festivals, 37, 201; Taos Talking Picture Film Festival, 190
filmmaking: as circulation, 8, 21–22; definition, 213n3; early history in Bolivia, 98–99; episodic nature in Brazil, 7; pre–World War I costs of, 99; resources for, 21–22; transnational networks in, 8; unevenness in Brazil, 8. *See also* indigenous video
film production, 22, 213n3
film viewing: as event, 130
First Nations/First Features Festival, 37, 197, 201
folklore: indigenous culture as, 108, 123; in media and spectacles, 7; national heritage and, 123, 192–93; traditional characters in, 1
folklore festivals and parades: cultural identity and, 7–8, 75–76, 208; displacement of cinema by, 25–26; elite criticism of, 71; impacts on cinema, 73; indigeneity and, 105; in La Paz, xix–xx, 1–2, 6–7, 123; as mass media, 7; as mobile vehicles of indigenization, 8; popular culture and, 9, 191; theaters' appropriation of, 80
Fortress, The (film), 89
Foster, Robert, 219n3
Fox, Aaron, 12
Fraser, Nancy, 35–36
Fusilamiento de Juaregui, El (Castillo, 1927), 101

194–95; social transformation of 1980s, 137–38; U.S. influence on, 124–25

multiculturalism, neoliberal, 36, 195

Museum of Art, Smithsonian Institution, 186

Museum of Modern Art (New York), 201

Myers, Fred, 12, 215n5

Nación, La (newspaper), 105

Nación Clandestina, La (Sanjinés, 1989), 131, 193

Naficy, Hamid, 18, 31

narrative: coherence by Palenque, 147–49, 171, 180–82; film distribution as, 23, 51; film-making as, 21–22; movement through space as, 49–50

national allegory: cinema as, 95

national cinema, 93–97, 105. *See also* Bolivian cinema

National Indigenous Congress (1945), 222n18

National Museum of the American Indian (NMAI), 186, 190, 201, 210

Nationalist Revolutionary Movement. *See* Movimiento Nationalista Revolucionario (MNR)

Native American Film and Video Festivals, 37, 201

negotiations: binary vs. mediated exchanges, 31

neoliberal discourse, 151

neoliberal fantasies, 137–38, 194

neoliberal multiculturalism, 36, 195

New Economic Plan (NEP), 138, 193–94

newspapers: revolution of 1952 and, 97

Nichols, Bill, 138, 222n2

nongovernmental organizations (NGOs), 196

objectification, 215n5; of agency, 155, 161; of culture, 11; of national cinema, 94; of the popular, 161; of voice, 181–82, 223n8

Ocurrió Así (TV program), 148–49

oil reserves: Chaco War and, 108–9

Ojo de Condor video tour, 186–91; Bolivian expatriate reaction to, 188–89; films shown on, 199; indigenous identity representations in, 211–12; itinerary of, 190–91; opposing static view of culture, 188–89; participants and sponsors of, 186; receiving Taos Mountain Achievement Award, 190, 210; video sales during, 209

Ong, Aihwa, 95

Open Tribunal of the People, The (TV program), 10–11; agency play in, 155–56; assembling cases for, 171–72, 180–81; authority of program, 155; background music, 183; bodily presence of interlocutors, 167; co-hosts for, 144; connecting discourse with urban social spaces, 144; criticism of, 162–63; demands for sympathy from viewers, 164–66; discursive exchange in, 181; double bind of certainty and advocacy, 184–85; editing of, 178, 180–81; fragmentation of testimony, 171–74; framing the popular, 144–51; government closure of, 142; Himpele's appearance on, 28–33; indexical realism of, 166–67; indigenization and, xviii–xix, 28, 143–44; intimacy of, 141; location footage in, 176–78; loss of legitimacy, 143; materiality of, 167, 181; media agency and,

154–62; as mediating window onto world, 148; neoliberal fantasies of, 194; Palenque's narrative control of, 144–46, 148, 173–76, 180; political and social power of, 141–42; producing new popular publics, 33, 35, 140, 143–44, 221n8; production of, 174–81; reformatting of, 148; ritual exchange on, 156, 158, 161, 177, 185, 194; self-representation in public sphere, 162–63, 194–95, 198; set of, 150; social discourse of, 154; social mission of, 176–77, 178, 180; as stage for Condepa, 29, 144; support for *mestizaje*, 147; sustaining vs. solving social problems, 160–61; terms of address as cultural strategy, 158–60; testimonial realism of, 140–41, 144–48; three-camera live direction of, 174–76; traumatic texture and immediacy of, 164–66; turning *testimonio* into spectacle, 153. *See also* Palenque, Carlos

Pachamama (Mother Earth), xxi

Paco, Adolfo, 29, 144, 150, 155, 221n14

Page, Joanna, 94

pain: shattering language, 168

Palenque, Carlos: agency play of, 155–57; charisma of, 184; death of, 33, 142–43, 184; as diagnostician of social conditions, 167; double bind of, 184–85; as exploiter of social problems, 151; framing discourses of, 144–46, 154; as host of *Open Tribunal*, 29–30, 32, 141–42, 145, 175–76; indexical function of framing discourses, 180–81; narrative treatment of social problems, 146–47; as presidential candidate, 142, 221n6; social authority of, 31, 145–46, 154–55, 172–73; voice of, 181–84

parades. *See* folklore festivals and parades

Para recibir el canto de los pájaros (Sanjinés, 1995), 132

Paseo de Prado (La Paz, Bolivia), xix–xx, 1–2, 6–7, 41–42

Passion of the Christ, The (film), 89

Pathé Brothers (film company), 67

Patria, La (newspaper), 101

patron-client relationships, xxi, 158–59, 222nn16–18

Paz Zamora, Jaime, xiv

Peñarada, Juan, 110–11

photography, 6–7

Pick, Suzanna, 129–30

pirated videos, 217nn10–12; *Dracula*, 42; economic impact on film industry, 86; itineraries of, 87–88; poor quality of, 74, 87–88; proliferation of, 22, 58

Plains of Green (film, 1933), 109

Platt, Tristan, 158–59, 222n17

political mimesis, 130, 185

political protests of 2003, 196–98

politics, indigenization of, 196–99

Ponce Sangines, Carlos, 218n11

Poole, Deborah, 18–19, 66

popular, the, 9, 150; objectification of, 161

popular culture: folklore and, 9, 191; in Latin America, 217n7; massification of, 6

Popular Participation, Law of, 36, 139, 194–95

Tedlock, Dennis, 161
Telecine (film company), 119, 123, 220n6
Telepolicial (TV program), 148, 222n15
Telesur (satellite TV network), 210
television: broadcast, incompatibility with indigenous experience, 187; enlargement of social field, 223n7; as event, 167, 176, 181; history in Bolivia, 139–40, 221n2; immediacy of, 150; impact on movie attendance, 79; indexical realism of, 166–67, 222n1; neoliberal fantasies of, 137–38; production, defined, 213n3; programming in Bolivia, 79; stations in Bolivia, 217n6; talk show audiences and viewers as performers, 152; wound culture and, 168. See also indigenous video
terms of address: as cultural strategy, 162
testimonio discourse, 153
theaters: appropriation of local spectacles, 80; architecture of, 71–72, 78; as chronotopes, 50–51, 215n3–4; as containers, 48, 71–72; as events, 50–51, 215n3; expansion in La Paz, 69–70; multiplexes, 84, 90; publics of circulation and, 24–25, 63–64, 71–72, 215n5; showing new films, 21; as sites for immigrant assimilation, 77; social asymmetries of, 77–79, 84, 216n2
THOA (Andean Oral History Workshop), 195
Thomas, Nicholas, 215n5
Thompson, E. P., 221n3
ticket prices: regulation of, 70–71
tin mines, 75
tin prices, 138
Tiwanaku (archaeological site), xiii–xiv, 107, 198, 218n10–11, 221n5
Transcultural Cinema (MacDougall), 169
Troy (film), 89
Tsing, Anna, 14, 61–64, 85–86
Turner, Terence, xvi–xvii, 11, 203, 212
Tylbor, Henry, 161

UCS Party, 141
UDP. *See* Unidad Democrática y Popular (Democratic and Popular Unity, UDP)
Ukamau (Sanjinés, 1966), 127
Ukamau Group, 17, 193
Unidad Democrática y Popular (Democratic and Popular Unity; UDP), 138–39, 221n1
Unión Cívica Solidaridad, 149
United Nations: Decade for Indigenous People, 196; Permanent Forum on Indigenous Issues, xvi
United States: Agency for International Development (USAID), 125, 220n7, 220n9; Coordinator of Inter-American Affairs (CIAA), 217n5; war

on drugs, 138, 194–95, 198. *See also* Hollywood films
University Folklore Parade (La Paz), 1
Urban, Greg, 14, 61–62
urban imaginary, 48–49, 215n1
Urla, Jacqueline, 152
USAID (U. S. Agency for International Development), 125, 220n7, 220n9

Valdivia, José Antonio, 18
Van Dyke, Willard, 119
Venezuela: as "the festive state," 7
Vertiente, La (Ruiz, 1958), 125–26
Vest Made of Money (Qulqi Chaliku) (Luna, 1998), 205, 207–10
videos. *See* indigenous video; pirated videos
Villamil, Antonio Diez, 102
Villarroel López, Gualberto, 222n18
Virgin of Urkupiña, xix
visual economy, 19
Vitascope projector, 66
Voces de la Tierra, Las (Voices of the Earth) (Ruiz, 1954), 123, 192–93, 211
Voice of the Quena, The (Villamil), 102
voices, 181–83, 223n8
Vuelve Sebastiana (Come Back Sebastiana) (Ruiz, 1953), 120–23, 220n4

Wara Wara (Maidana, 1930), 101–4, 192
Warner, Michael, 23–24, 52
war on drugs (U.S.), 138, 194–95, 198
Warren, Kay, 37
Wasson, Kenneth, 119
Water War (Cochabama, 2002), 196–97
Whispers of Death (2002), 199
White, Hayden, 215n2
Wiener, Annette, 213n4
Wilk, Richard, 58
Willi, Z., 56, 59–60
Williams, Gareth, 219n3
Wilson, Clint, 216n7
Winston, Brian, 216n1
wound culture, 167–68

Xavier, Ismael, 95

Yaeger, Patricia, 215n2
Yasimientso Petroliferos Fiscales de Bolivia (YFPB), 114
Yúdice, George, 153

Žižek, Slavoj, 117–18
ZW Films (distributor), 53

Series page continued from ii.

JEFF D. HIMPELE is associate director for the McGraw Center for Teaching and Learning at Princeton University. He is an anthropologist and documentary filmmaker; his films include the award-winning *Incidents of Travel in Chichen Itza* and *Taypi Kala: Six Visions of Tiwanaku.*